Naukar, Rajp

The ethnohistory of the military labour market in Hindustan, 1450–1850

DIRK H. A. KOLFF
University of Leiden

The right of the University of Cambridge to print and sell all manner of books was granted by Henry VIII in 1534. The University has printed and published continuously since 1584.

CAMBRIDGE UNIVERSITY PRESS
CAMBRIDGE
NEW YORK PORT CHESTER
MELBOURNE SYDNEY

University of Cambridge Oriental Publications
published for the Faculty of Oriental Studies

PUBLISHED BY THE PRESS SYNDICATE OF THE UNIVERSITY OF CAMBRIDGE
The Pitt Building, Trumpington Street, Cambridge, United Kingdom

CAMBRIDGE UNIVERSITY PRESS
The Edinburgh Building, Cambridge CB2 2RU, UK
40 West 20th Street, New York NY 10011–4211, USA
477 Williamstown Road, Port Melbourne, VIC 3207, Australia
Ruiz de Alarcón 13, 28014 Madrid, Spain
Dock House, The Waterfront, Cape Town 8001, South Africa

http://www.cambridge.org

First published 1990
First paperback edition 2002

A catalogue record for this book is available from the British Library

Library of Congress Cataloguing in Publication data
Kolff, Dirk H. A.
Naukar, Rajput and Sepoy: the ethnohistory of the military labour market in
Hindustan, 1450–1850 / Dirk H. A. Kolff.
p. cm. – (University of Cambridge oriental publications: no. 43).
Originally presented as the author's thesis (Ph. D. – Leiden University, 1983)
under title: An armed peasantry and its allies
Rajput tradition and state formation, 1450–1850.
Bibliography.
Includes Index.
ISBN 0 521 38132 0
1. Manpower – India – History. 2. Soldiers – India – History.
3. India – Armed Forces – Recruiting, enlistment, etc. – History.
4. Labor supply – India – History. I. Title. II. Series.
UA17.5.14K65 1990
355.2′2′0954–dc20 89–34310 CIP

ISBN 0 521 38132 0 hardback
ISBN 0 521 52305 2 paperback

University of Cambridge Oriental Publications No. 43

Naukar, Rajput and Sepoy

Saiṁyāṁ aḍaba tūṁ kavana mahinavā meṁ.
Apane ta jāi piyā nokari uṭhavale,
Hamarā ke chāṛale mahaliyā meṁ.
Dui cāri dina saiṁyāṁ chuṭi le aïle,
Hota bhinasaravā bidā bhaïle.

My lord, in what month wilt thou return?
My beloved has gone away, and entered into service,
Leaving me alone in the house.
He took two or four days leave and came,
And went away at dawn.

Bhojpuri song (Grierson, *Some Bihari Folk-Songs*, 237)

CONTENTS

PREFACE

In the medieval islamic world, India was not so much unique because of its largely non-muslim population but because of its numerous peasantry. As a result, it is first and foremost the demographic factor that set Indian state formation apart from the politics in the sultanates further west. This study aims to do justice to the manpower factor in late medieval North India. It tries to reconstruct the cultural and social evolution of the labour market for armed peasants from Lodi to British times. It is, therefore, not so much about the 'intermediate' levels of Indian society, which nowadays get so much attention from historians, but largely about the peasantry itself. In other words, it is an attempt to analyse – that is to understand and describe in a coherent narrative – the 'subaltern' dynamics of agrarian society in the medieval period as they impinged upon politics, the formation of rural elites, on popular religion, and even on the world of sect and caste.[1]

The book grew out of work on two themes: the history of Bundelkhand in the late nineteenth century and editorial work on the Dutch chronicle of Mughal history written by Francisco Pelsaert in 1626. Though widely different areas of enquiry, both suggested questions about the traditions of Rajput service to muslim and colonial rulers and, more generally, about the importance of military earnings in the survival strategies of the North Indian peasantry. The military labour market of Hindustan began to emerge as both a central phenomenon in Indian history and a useful research concept. It then became necessary to trace the many historical features it inspired to as early a period as the printed English, Portuguese, Hindi and Persian sources allowed. In

[1] An earlier version, entitled 'An Armed Peasantry and its Allies: Rajput Tradition and State Formation, 1450–1850', was passed as a PhD in Leiden University, The Netherlands, in 1983.

the process, I have attempted to do justice to both the 'folk' and political implications of the enquiry. I realise, however, that I have by no means analysed all aspects of the manpower theme in medieval North India. I only hope that its wide-ranging importance is shown in this work.

Much of Indian society as it is understood today is too rich, too pluriform and too dynamic and fluid to be approached with the concepts of an older tradition of Indian anthropology still grounded in British census report classifications. Some of these worn-out terms, such as 'ethnic' and even 'peasantry', will still be found in this study but they are used in a loose, non-essentialist sense, 'peasantry' referring to agrarian society as a whole and often including the notion of a 'dominant caste' as well as a *kāmin* category of artisans and agricultural labourers. Certainly Indian terms often provide firmer ground to base one's analysis on. I have singled out the notion of *naukarī* in its medieval sense as giving substance to the theoretical concept of the Indian military labour market.

I am grateful to M. Athar Ali, R. J. Barendse, Christopher A. Bayly, Satish Chandra, J. C. Heesterman, Iqtidar Alam Khan, G. H. Schokker, Peter T. van der Veer, S. Inayat Ali Zaidi, and Sunita Budhwar Zaidi for their comments on earlier versions of part of the manuscript and after those seminars of mine which they attended. I thank the Committee on Southern Asian Studies of the University of Chicago – and especially Bernard S. Cohn, Lloyd I. Rudolph and Susanne Hoeber Rudolph – for making it possible for me to spend a term in Chicago. From all of them I learned a lot.

Leiden, June 1989

ABBREVIATIONS

AR	*The Asiatic Review*
ARA	National Archives (*Algemeen Rijksarchief*), The Hague
BTLV	*Bijdragen tot de Taal-, Land- en Volkenkunde*
CIS	*Contributions to Indian Sociology*
CSSH	*Comparative Studies in Society and History*
HA	*History in Africa*
IA	*The Indian Antiquary*
IESHR	*The Indian Economic and Social History Review*
IHR	*The Indian Historical Review*
JAOS	*Journal of the American Oriental Society*
JAS	*Journal of Asian Studies*
JASB	*Journal of the Asiatic Society of Bengal*
JASL	*Journal of the Asiatic Society, Letters*
JBRS	*The Journal of the Bihar Research Society*
JIH	*Journal of Indian History*
JIntH	*The Journal of Interdisciplinary History*
JRAS	*The Journal of the Royal Asiatic Society*
MAS	*Modern Asian Studies*
MI	*Man in India*
MIQ	*Medieval India Quarterly*
SA	*South Asia*
SH	*Studies in History*
ZDMG	*Zeitschrift der Deutschen Morgenländischen Gesellschaft*

GLOSSARY

Note

Ar. = Arabic
H. = Hindustani, Hindi
P. = Persian
Port. = Portuguese
S. = Sanskrit

Sanskrit and Hindi words in this list have, on the whole, been written with full diacritical marks. In the case of Arabic and Persian words, only long vowels have been indicated.

akhāṛā (H.): wrestling ground, band of sadhus, dancing floor.
alfândega (Port.): customs house.
amīr (Ar.): lord, nobleman. Plural: *umarā*.
ashrafī (Ar.): gold coin, gold mohur.
Avadhi: pertaining to Awadh, especially the variety of Hindi spoken in Awadh.
avatar (Sanskrit: avatāra): an incarnation on earth of a divine being.
Awadh: the country of Ayodhyā, now part of Uttar Pradesh; the old spelling is Oudh.
bādshāh (H.): king; also *pādshāh* (P.). Adjective is *bādshāhī*.
baniyā (= banian, banyan) (H.): a hindu trader.
begum (from Persian *begam*): a muslim lady of rank.
bhūmiyāvat (H.): the activity of fighting for one's landed inheritance; a campaign for land.
brahman (from Sanskrit *brāhmaṇa*): a member of one of the many brahman castes.
caste *sabhā*: an association of some members of a certain caste.
cabūtra: dais, platform.
crore (Hindi: *karoṛ*): a hundred lakhs (1,00,00,000).

dārogā (P.): superintendent of a police, customs or excise station.
desāī (Marathi): petty chief, *zamīndār* in Western India.
dharma (S.): moral duty, custom, role in life.
dharmaśāstra (S.): book of laws or duties.
dīwān: chief financial officer of a state or of an *amīr*.
fatwā (Ar.): opinion of a muslim law-officer (*muftī*) on any point of law.
faujdār (P.): military governor.
firman (Persian: *farmān*): a written order.
gaddī (H.): royal cushion, throne.
ghātwāl (H.): superintendent of mountainous paths.
grihastha (S.): householder.
hazārī (P.): commander of a thousand men.
jāgīr (P.): assignment on the public revenues of a given tract of land.
jāgīrdār (P.): holder of a *jāgīr*.
jama'dār (P.): the head of any body of men, jemadar, sepoy officer.
jauhar (H.): the last ascetic sacrifice of Rajputs, when they kill their wives and children, and then sell their lives dearly on the field of battle.
jawān (H.): a youth, especially a young soldier.
jemadar (P. *jama'dār*): captain of mercenary soldiers; later: rank in the British East India Company's sepoy army.
kāfir (Ar.): infidel.
khilat (Ar., H.): a ceremonial present presented by a superior to an inferior, especially a dress of honour.
kotwāl (P.): city magistrate, superintendent of police.
kror: see crore.
kṣatriyadharma: the dharma of the *kṣatriya*s, i.e. the *varna* ('caste') of the rulers, protectors and warriors.
lākh (H.): a hundred thousand (100,000).
mahmūdī: silver coin current in Gujarat; it was worth about half a rupiya.
majlis (Ar.): assembly.
mālguzār (P.): person who pays the revenue assessed on an estate; *mālguzārī* is the revenue paid.
mālik (Ar.): possessor, ruler, lord.
man: a weight of forty kilograms or *ser*.
mansab (Ar.): station, dignity, post, office.
mansabdār (P.): holder of an office.

naukar (P.): retainer; *naukarī* is the service of a *naukar*.
nawāb (Ar.): an Arabic plural word applied in a singular sense to officials of very high rank, viceroy.
nāyak (H.): chief, sepoy officer.
nazar (Ar.): a ceremonial present from an inferior to a superior.
nazrāna (P.): same as *nazar*, also fee paid to government as acknowledgement for a grant of land or office.
pālkī (H.): covered litter, palanquin.
pān (H.): betel leaf.
pargana (P.): fiscal barony, subdivision of a *sarkar*.
pāyak (H.): foot-soldier.
peon, peão (Port.): foot-soldier, orderly.
peshkash (P.): tributary gift, especially from an appointee on the occasion of his investiture.
phūl katāra: a kind of short sword.
qānūngo (P.): district revenue registrar.
qasba (P.): township.
qāzī (P.): judge, magistrate, muslim notary public.
rānā (H.): title of a prince or raja, especially of the Sisodiya Rajput prince of Mewar (Udaipur).
rānī (H.): queen, princess.
rishi (S.): an inspired poet or sage (*ṛṣi*).
ryot (from Arabic *raʿīyat*): peasant, subject, tenant of the soil, but in the sixteenth century apparently also: village head.
sādhu (H.): pious man, devotee, ascetic.
sagāī (H.): betrothal, marriage, relationship, alliance.
sanad (Ar.): royal deed or grant.
sarkār (P.): government, district comprehending several *parganas*.
sayyid (Ar.): any descendant of Muhammad, especially a descendant of Husain.
seer: (Hindi: *ser*), a weight of about a kilogram.
serai (P.): *sara*, inn, caravanserai.
Shudra (S.): *śūdra*, a member of the fourth *varna* ('caste'), that of the menial classes.
sūbah (P.): province of the Mughal empire.
sūbahdār (P.): governor of a *sūbah*.
subedar (Anglo-Indian): derived from the preceding, the chief Indian officer of a company of sepoys in the East India Company's Army.
suwār (P.): trooper, cavalier.

tahsīl (Ar.): a revenue district, collection.
tanka (S.): a kind of copper, silver, or gold coin.
thānadār (H.): the chief of a police station (*thāna*).
ulema: from *'ulamā* (Ar. plural of *'ālim*), the learned, doctors of law and religion.
umma (Ar.): the people of the same religion.
watan (Ar.): native country, home land.
wazīr (Ar.): a minister.
yuva rāja: young raja, crown prince.
zamīndār (P.): an occupant of a tract of land, landlord. The adjective is *zamīndārī*.

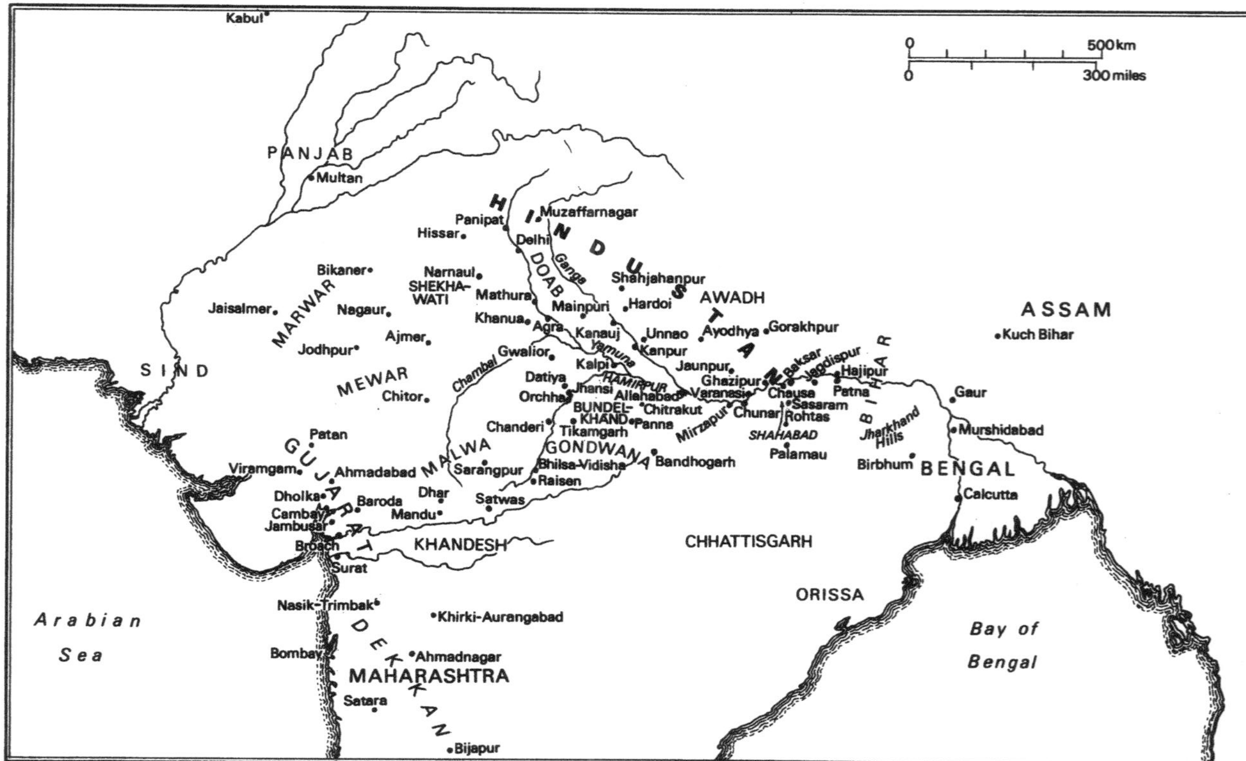

Map of Northern India

1
The polity and the peasantry

The emperor Jahangir remarked about the most powerful *zamīndārs* of Gujarat, that what mattered in politics were 'territory and forces', in other words, agrarian revenue and manpower.[1] In the present century, and increasingly since the last world war, much has been added to what is known about the medieval Indian economy. Production, taxation, prices and, in particular, agrarian relations and the system of land revenue have received a relatively large proportion of historians' attention.[2] The aim of this book is to investigate some of the aspects of the other source of power: manpower, which, as a factor contributing to the formation and upholding of the state deserves attention in itself. Moreover, the ways in which a large portion of the income of the state was distributed to what one could call the military workforce of India must be held to be an important subject of analysis if one is to understand the nature of the medieval economy. At the very least it seems natural to ask how numerous the recipients of the state's distributive system were. And, as the most important distributive institutions of the states we are dealing with were their armies, one is eager to know the number of military dependants of the various North Indian states as well as the kinds of men recruited for the armies of the sultanates, the rajadoms and, lastly, the Mughal empire. It is also crucial to know what proportion of the state's income was dispensed to entirely professional soldiers, perhaps of foreign origin, who had no agrarian interest whatever and, on the other hand, what part was surrendered to peasant-soldiers, recruited perhaps from the same landed communities who had

[1] Jahangir, *Tūzuk*, II, 19.

[2] See in particular Raychaudhuri and Habib (eds.), The *Cambridge Economic History of India I*; Moreland, *Agrarian System*; I. Habib, *Agrarian System*; Siddiqi, *Land Revenue Administration*.

helped, by yielding a share of their harvest as land revenue, to fill the coffers from which they were paid their salaries.

I would suggest that any analysis of the mechanisms and scope of the distribution of the resources of medieval Indian political centres presupposes an understanding of the workings of the Indian military labour market. In this chapter I shall try to show the importance of this concept for the study of North Indian history. In other words, my contention is that an enquiry into the nature of the military labour market is called for if we are to acquire a better understanding of the North Indian distributive system, the social history of much of its peasantry and the processes of state formation in *ancien régime* South Asia.[3]

I will restrict myself mainly to the Mughal period. The difficulties, even then, appear insurmountable. We do not even know the size of the Mughal army in its heyday, the seventeenth century. Long ago, Irvine listed a few of the estimates, made by contemporaries, as to the numbers of cavalry and infantrymen who served the emperor, but the result was confusing. For Aurangzeb's reign (1658–1707), for instance, Bernier gave 240,000 cavalry and only 15,000 infantry, whereas Catrou thought the correct numbers were 300,000 cavalry and 600,000 infantry.[4] The discrepancy in the number of footsoldiers should at least be explained. Since Irvine not much has been added to our knowledge of the Mughal army, though there have been great advances in other fields of Mughal history. There is, it seems, a good reason for this. I would suggest that the idea of the Mughal army as a distinct institution, to be described and analysed, is a false one. The Mughal army can never be made into a neat category of research outside the context of North Indian society: as such, it defies definition. It can only be described in terms of the dilemma in which the Mughal empire itself seems to have been caught, to wit, the dilemma between, on the one hand, the territorial state where the writ of the emperor was unopposed, and, on the other hand, the state as the largest and most honourable employer of the country whose huge army was the fundamental expression of its achievement.

3 On the latter aspect, see my 'The End of an Ancien Regime: Colonial War in India, 1798–1818' in J. A. de Moor and H. L. Wesseling (eds), *Imperialism and War: Essays on Colonial Wars in Asia and Africa (Comparative Studies in Overseas History, 8)*, Leiden 1989, 22–49.

4 Irvine, *Army*, 61

Let us leave the state to its own devices for a moment. No investigation of state activity, however complete, can hope to encompass the whole of the history of North Indian soldiering. A large proportion of the military labour force of India, i.e. the total number of fighting men, remained, either permanently or temporarily, beyond the purview of the state. As I shall try to show, the states of medieval India not only had to leave the recruitment of troopers largely to middlemen, but also, notwithstanding the impressive size of their army camps, they could never come anywhere near to engaging, whether directly or indirectly, all those in North India who had taken up arms for a living, let alone all those who were skilled in the use of arms. Therefore, any enquiry into the sociology of the North Indian soldier which limited itself to the employment of armed men by any state or state-like structure, would find that much information as to their origin, recruitment and careers remained beyond its range. The military labour market has to be studied as a phenomenon in itself.

The challenge of an armed peasantry

An idea of the almost limitless proportions of the military profession in medieval India is conveyed by Abul Fazl's *Ā'īn* which gives, for the twelve *sūbahs* of the empire in the 1590s, a number of 342,696 horsemen and no fewer than 4,039,097 footsoldiers.[5] From these figures no conclusion whatever can be drawn as to the size of the Mughal army. They apparently include all those men who were considered on occasion to be acceptable reinforcements of the state at any of its many executive levels. This is, in other words, not an army list, but an inventory, a census of the military labour market. The fact that the census was taken indicates not only a desire to know where troops could be had. The state could never employ all these men. The count also appears to betray an uneasy awareness of the problem of how to control millions of men who were essentially as free to become rebels as they were to turn auxiliaries. Abul Fazl's census of the military labour force of Northern India lists the retainers who could be produced by the innumerable unruly *zamīndārs* of the empire. They cannot have represented less than 10 per cent of the active male population, and if Valentijn, who wrote that the empire in 1707 yielded more than four million

[5] Abu-l Faẓl, *Ā'īn*, II, 141–367.

soldiers, is right, then this proportion did not decrease much during the seventeenth century.[6]

The numbers involved are staggering. There is indeed no doubt that most of these men never served the Mughal state during their lifetime. Irvine rightly remarked that the figures of the *Āʿīn* include 'all the militia levies and zamindar's retainers throughout the provinces'.[7] However, probably even Abul Fazl's enumeration did not exhaust the North Indian reservoir of armed men. There were more potential soldiers than those employed by the emperor, his officials or the innumerable *zamīndārs* of the country. Let us take an example.

Peter Mundy, travelling between Surat, Agra and Patna in 1632–3, at one time hired a convoy of 25 soldiers, at another 22 footmen and 3 horsemen, in the towns on his route. His caravan also employed some 440 Jats, Baluchis, carters, and cameleers, who had fire-arms and swords. They were an unruly lot. At one stage, as Mundy explained, the Baluchis and camel-drivers, who were muslims, clashed with the Jats and carters, who were hindus. One Baluchi died. Mundy concluded it was dangerous to take both carters and cameleers and both Jats and Baluchis in one caravan.[8] On another occasion even Jats and carters fought with each other. But such men were nonetheless indispensable. In the records of the Dutch East India Company one finds frequent mention of troops hired to protect caravans on the Agra to Surat road. Thus, in 1637, to accompany 22 carts, 37 soldiers were hired, most of them armed with bows and arrows, some with muskets. They received Rs 3½ a month, except their leader Ibrahim, who was engaged for Rs 4. Similarly, in 1644, to escort bullion to the value of Rs 300,000, 190 soldiers were employed.[9] Two lists are preserved giving the names of 77 and 65 peons who were sent from Agra to the coast in 1638 and 1639 respectively. The first distinguishes again between Jats, most of whom were musketeers (*roerdragers*) and Baluchis, almost all of whom were archers. They and their two leaders were paid the same wages as those engaged in 1637. Their leaders were styled

[6] Valentijn, *Oud en Nieuw Oost-Indiën*, IV, 2, 276–9. Valentijn, oddly enough, supposed there were exactly as many cavalrymen as foot-soldiers. The population of what is now Bangladesh, India, and Pakistan has been estimated at 130 million in 1600 AD, 160 million in 1700 AD, McEvedy and Jones, *Atlas*, 185.

[7] Irvine, *Army*, 61

[8] Mundy, *Travels*, II, 256–7, 261, 287, 294–6.

[9] ARA The Hague, Coll. Geleynssen no. 102, W. Geleynssen to C. Jansen Silvius, Agra 25. xi. 1637; ARA The Hague, VOC 1157 f. 408 v°, C. Weijlandt to A. van Diemen, Surat 5.vii. 1644.

muqaddam or *mirdah* and travelled with their men.[10] Such men did not only conduct caravans. Any journey seems to have been inconceivable without a certain number of them. William Hawkins, who was in India from 1608 to 1613, found that 'almost a man cannot stirre out of dores throughout all his [i.e. Jahangir's] dominions without great forces, for they are all become rebels'. Tavernier said that, in about 1660, to travel with honour in India, one hired 20 to 30 armed men, some with bows and arrows and others with muskets. They cost Rs 4 a month. The profession must have been rather well organised, because in the towns where the men were hired, they had a headman who answered for their honesty 'and when you employ them, each one gives him a rupee'.[11]

They appear often to have been based in the *qasbas* or district towns of some importance along the road. There in the end they may well have lost all connection with the villages they probably originated from. In the process, their behaviour and reputation could change almost beyond recognition. Thus Nicholas Withington, who lived in India from 1612 to 1616, found that the Baluchis of Baluchistan were bloodyminded villains; 'yet there are manye verye honeste men of that caste dwellinge about Guyseratt, but moste of them aboute Agra'.[12]

At the Gujarati end of the great caravan routes worked by the Baluchis, these people would undergo quite a transformation over time, their activities widening again into quite a 'portfolio' of possible sources of income. This was the case in the towns of Dholka, Viramgam and Ahmadabad, where muslim soldiers of Rajput, Baluchi and Pathan origin, a 'powerful and warlike body' significantly known as Qasbatis, flourished for several generations. The *Mirāt-i-Ahmadī* described their sphere of action as follows: 'They became source of resistance against the Kolis in this very region in thorny places and ravines. They attacked villages, drove away cattle, escorted Nazims, took responsibility of collecting peshkash from zamindars on a small salary, they got enlisted as recruits in the army for a few days, served the faujdars and the thanadars. They, thus, maintained themselves. Most of them lived on fodder and grains of their fields.' They could afford to refuse

10 ARA The Hague, Coll. Geleynssen no. 113, 'Notitie der naamen van 77 pijons . . .' and 'Notitie der naemen van 65 pijons . . .'

11 Foster, *Early Travels*, 113, 114; Tavernier, *Travels*, I, 38.

12 Foster, *Early Travels*, 220.

service in the Mughal armies fighting the Marathas on the Dekkan and did not even accept service outside Gujarat. Only later on some of them, finding themselves in reduced circumstances, tried their luck in other *sūbahs* and 'made bravery their profession'.[13] To sum up, this group of military settlers acquired a stake in agricultural pursuits and in the military administration as centred on provincial towns. In this way they were largely successful in avoiding direct service in the emperor's camp. Ultimately, such men certainly came within the range of Abul Fazl's census of North India's military labour force. It is difficult to say at which point a family of Baluchi camel-drivers, who turned to escorting caravans and mercenary soldiering and then to a combination of agrarian pursuits and military duties as organised by government officials in the *qasbas*, became sufficiently useful or dangerous to be taken cognisance of by the imperialist administration. But it is important to notice the social mobility that was a corollary of the dynamics of North India's military labour market. The military entrepreneurship of the Baluchis-turned-Qasbatis provides a striking example of this.

If carting and camel-driving were unthinkable without skill in the use of arms, this applied with equal force to the most widespread economic activity in India, agriculture. The Dutch East India Company servant Simon Diodati, whose caravan was stopped in 1717 in Malwa by 2,000 people armed with muskets and 3,000 others, described his attackers as peasants (*boeren*).[14] In 1632, Peter Mundy actually saw, in the present-day Kanpur district, 'labourers with their guns, swords, and bucklers lyeing by them whilest they ploughed the ground, being att varience with a little towne ½ a mile out of the way', where 'rebels' lived.[15] And Irfan Habib cites a manuscript where it is said about the Bhadauriya Rajputs in the Agra area around 1650: 'They are a numerous industrious and brave race. Every village has a small fort. They never pay revenue to the *hakim* (= *jāgīrdār*) without a fight. The peasants (*ri'aya*) who drive the plough keep a musket (*banduq*)

13 *Ibid.*, see also 314; Robertson, *Glossary*, 59. Ali Muhammad Khan, *Mirāt*, 580; this work contains numerous references to the Qasbatis of the eighteenth century. See also Nightingale, *Trade and Empire*, 227.

14 ARA The Hague, VOC 1913 'Kort dagverhaal van de Agrase residenten . . .', 97–100 ('Souratta'). See also Das Gupta, *Indian Merchants*, 143, and, for specific mention of plundering villagers, Mundy, *Travels*, II, 110, 111; Manucci, *Storia*, I, 307.

15 Mundy, *Travels*, II, 90. Irfan Habib quotes from the same passage, see next note.

slung over the neck, and a powder-pouch at the waist. The relief-loan (*taqavi*) they get from the *hakim* is in the form of lead (and) gunpowder.' Similarly, Manucci described how in Akbar's days the villagers of the Mathura region defended themselves against Mughal revenue collecting officers: 'The women stood behind their husbands with spears and arrows. When the husband had shot off his matchlock, his wife handed him the lance, while she reloaded the matchlock.' Habib assumes that those who had matchlocks or even only swords belonged to the higher strata of the peasantry. Yet, it is clear that Indian agrarian society was to a large extent an armed society, skilled in the use of arms, and that very few men would have been without at least a spear or bow and arrows. Moreover, the countryside was studded with little forts like those of the Bhadauriyas. As late as the end of the eighteenth century, Dubois could still write that 'it frequently happened that a wretched little fortified town, surrounded by nothing but mud walls and defended by a few hundred peasants ('*campagnards*') armed with a few wornout matchlocks, was able to hold out for months against the attacks of a host of assailants'. The phenomenon of such occasional armed resistance against the revenue collecting activities of Indian officials is too well-known to demand further elaboration. Rightly Gautam Bhadra speaks of 'the general tradition of rebellion and agrarian resistance' in Mughal India.[16]

In such a society, no government, however powerful, could even begin to think of achieving a monopoly on the use of arms. In some respects, the millions of armed men, cultivators and otherwise, that government was supposed to rule over, were its rivals rather than its subjects. Indeed, the peasant's arms frequently proved of use for other than defensive purposes. Whenever the risks seemed worth taking, they resisted and fell upon intruding mercenaries, whether the latter were collecting revenue or not. Significantly, historical sources often refer to peasants and townspeople assaulting soldiers and not only in the hills and inaccessible places far from the well-subdued plains, sometimes described as the peaceful core of the empire. Thus, the great Rana Sanga's camp was once looted by villagers in the Agra area, whereas the townsmen of Dhar in Malwa participated in the plunder of Silhadi's

[16] I. Habib, 'Forms of Class Struggle'; Manucci, *Storia*, I, 134; Dubois, *Hindu Manners*, 680; Dubois, *Moeurs*, II, 492. Gautam Bhadra, 'Two Frontier Uprisings', 59. According to the commissioners of the Bombay Government reporting on Malabar in 1792, 'even the labourers in the fields were armed', Nightingale, *Trade and Empire*, 76.

camp in 1531–2. A few years later, peasants attacked, plundered and seized the horses of parties of Afghan troopers retreating before Humayun's army from Chitor in the direction of Malwa. In 1540, villagers (*gūwārān*) of the central Doab closed the market for Humayun's men and attacked them; then, they collected nearly 3,000 horse and foot many of whom were subsequently killed by the Mughal's troops. Another report says that, on this occasion, 'needy men' intercepted the Mughals, some taking away the horses' saddle cloths, others striking them down with *lāṭhī*-blows from behind; it was said that in this way 20,000 horsemen forming Humayun's escort were killed and their horses stolen.[17] Other instances of such attacks are reported during Jahangir's reign. The inhabitants of the village of Bharwal in Assam once exterminated an imperial contingent of 200 matchlockmen. And after Sultan Khusru had been defeated in the Panjab in 1606, peasants (*landslieden*) killed most of the fugitive soldiers they could lay their hands on and captured all the prince's horses, camels and other animals. Similarly, after Abdullah Khan's defeat of 1623 near Ahmadabad, large numbers of his men were killed by the peasantry (*boeren*). Peter Mundy tells of the people of the *qasba* of Bhadohi in the present-day Mirzapur district, who in 1632 attacked the soldiers of a Mughal governor killing 200 of them. The governor had arrested seven Banyas who, he thought, had stolen goods from a serai. The Bhadohi men made an attempt to liberate them and besieged the local castle which contained some 2,000 horsemen. Mundy noticed that the Mughal nobleman was compelled to entertain extra parties of foot and horse to re-establish his authority. In 1658, the peasants (*paysans*) to the east of Agra robbed many of the followers of Sulaiman Shikoh after the latter's defeat on the field of battle and killed some of them.

This was a well-known pattern. For the period down to 1818, when British arms to a great extent succeeded in demilitarising large-scale politics in India, such incidents were commonplace as a few examples dating from the end of the period illustrate. When, after the battle of Panipat in 1761, nearly 3,000 exhausted Maratha horsemen entered the city of Delhi, they were plundered by the 'local vagabonds' of the capital. This contributed to the flight of

[17] Niamatullah, *History*, 177; Nizamuddin, *Tabaqāt*, III, 357; Digby, *Dreams*, 68; Abu-l Fazl, *Akbarnāma*, I, 354, 355; Roy, 'Some interesting anecdotes', 223. See also Al-Badaoni, *Muntakhab*, II, 10, about villagers getting hold of Hemu's gold in 1555.

these defeated men, large numbers of whom soon fled across the Chambal towards Gwalior. Some of them lost their way and sought refuge in distant and nearby villages and towns. 'Cultivators killed many of them', a contemporary observer reported. Many had to give up their garments and were made to drink salt water on suspicion of having swallowed *ashrafīs* and jewels. Those on whom such things were found, were killed. In 1804, Arthur Wellesley told Lord Lake that if you moved after your enemy with 'celerity' and sufficiently distressed him, armed peasants could help you a great deal. 'Whenever the largest and most formidable bodies of [the freebooters] are hard pressed by our troops, the village people attack them upon their rear and flanks, cut off stragglers, and will not allow a man to enter their villages.' Something very much like that happened in 1818, when many of the retreating Pindari freebooters in Central India were cut up by 'the villagers, who now regarded their destruction as certain and no longer hesitated to retaliate on them the cruelties they had so often suffered at their hands'. But the same peasantry could turn quite as easily against the Company's troops. When, in 1804, Colonel Burn's battalion retreated before Holkar, peasants rose in his rear and seized the baggage he had to leave behind.[18] I suggest, in conclusion, that not only the rebellious *zamīndārs* of the countryside or the hill rajas with their pernicious war-bands were jealous rivals of central government in North India. More fundamental to the state was the problem of how to deal with the peasantry at large, how to subject to some manner of control and collect revenue from these almost ungovernable tens of millions of people protected by mud forts, jungles and ravines all over the plains of Hindustan and above all by the weapons they were so familiar with. It is clear that the Indian process of state formation and the Indian state itself cannot adequately be described with the help of models inspired by the phenomenon of the early modern European state if these presuppose the achievement of a central monopoly, or something nearly approaching it, on the use of arms.

What solutions to this challenge did the Mughal emperor and his

[18] Mirza Nathan, *Bahāristān-i-Ghaybī*, I, 301; Pelsaert, *Geschriften*, 126, 179; Mundy, *Travels*, II, 109, 110, 118, 119; Bernier, *Travels*, 60; Bernier, *Voyages*, I, 85; Ali Muhammad Khan, *Mirāt*, 917; Brett-James, *Wellington*, 103; Prinsep, *History*, II, 116; G.R.C. Williams, 'The Sikhs in Upper Doab', *Calcutta Review 1875*, cited in Madanjit Kaur, 'Some Reflections on the Socio-economic Conditions of the Jamuna-Gangetic Doab in the 19th Century: A Contemporary Account', Indian History Congress 1984, Annamalai, 9.

amīrs have at their disposal, faced as they were with a constant threat to their authority? The most radical measures that were taken amounted to a virtual uprooting of peasant society as such. There is irrefutable evidence for the enslavement and deportation of thousands and thousands of peasants by the Mughal aristocracy.[19] Many of these were sold to countries to the west of India. The trade had flourished before 1400, when Multan was a considerable slave-market,[20] but it was continued after that, with Kabul as the main entrepôt. Babur, in his description of Kabul in 1504, mentions slaves as the first of the articles brought up from Hindustan to that city. It was also often deemed expedient to kill many of them straight away. It was said that when, in the cold season of 1528–9, the Mandahar of the area north of Delhi plundered villages and then defeated Babur's forces to the number of 3,000 men, a force consisting of 4,000 cavalry and several elephants was sent against them; their settlement was razed to the ground. Babur kept twenty of the women, the remainder being distributed amongst his companions. According to Ahmad Yadgar, 'The male Mandahars were half buried in the ground and were shot to death with arrows.' Abul Fazl quoted, as a point 'about which both sound jurists and innovators are agreed', the opinion that 'the binding, killing or striking [of] the haughty and the chastising [of] the stiff-necked are part of the struggle for empire'. The fortress of Chitor, for instance, besieged by Akbar from October 1567 to February 1568, was not only defended, Abul Fazl says, by 8,000 Rajput warriors, but also by some 40,000 peasants who had shown 'great zeal and activity'. This widespread participation in the resistance against his imperialist conquest had made the emperor decide to have nearly 30,000 of the defenders killed on the day the fortress fell. It seems that public opinion at the time compared these drastic measures with the procedures of Sultan Alauddin Khilji, who it was recalled, had left the peasantry alone when he conquered Chitor in 1303. But Abul Fazl justifies Mughal ruthlessness by pointing out that, on the earlier occasion, the peasantry had not engaged in the fighting, an

[19] See for the making of slaves and captives by Mughals and others, e.g. Mirza Nathan, Bahāristān-i-Ghaybī, I, 11, 125, 130, 231, 273, 369, 395, 412, 419, and II, 477, 495, 501, 635, 668; Jahangir, *Memoirs*, 22.

[20] The Ghaznavids continually replenished their Indian slave (*ghulam*) army from their expeditions there; 'thus 53,000 captives were brought back' from the Kanauj campaign of 1018 AD, Bosworth, *Ghaznavids*, 102. See, for many other examples of slave raids in pre-1400 North India, Irfan Habib's paragraph on 'Slavery' in Raychaudhuri and Habib, *Cambridge Economic History of India I*, 84, 85, 89–93.

assertion that must then have been, as it is now, impossible to disprove or support on the basis of fact.

Of the remainder of the defenders of Chitor in 1568, a large number were taken prisoner. The sight of groups of newly enslaved people must have been a common one at the time. This is illustrated by a story preserved by Abul Fazl, about some thousand musketeers from Kalpi, many of them muslims it seems, who had shown great skill in defending Chitor in the service of the Rana. 'When the victorious army', the *Akbarnāma* recalls, 'was hotly engaged in plundering and capturing, these musketeers . . . bound their wives and children as if they were prisoners and set off with them. The truth remained concealed from the searchers, and they thought that they were royal troops carrying off their prisoners.' Naturally, Akbar's conquests must have fed the slave trade towards the northwest. According to Monserrate, who travelled from Lahore to Kabul in 1581, the Ghakkars of the Panjab exchanged men for horses and a saying 'Slaves from India, horses from Parthia' was current among them. They supplemented their supply of the former commodity by getting hold of free travellers whom they shaved and transported to Persia to be sold there. If the trade in slaves was as brisk as the horse trade, then many thousands of people must have left India each year. In these deportations, Jahangir also had a share. William Finch, who was in India between 1608 and 1611, tells how the emperor hunted around Agra, usually from November to the end of March. Finch wrote, 'He causeth with choise men, a certain wood or desart place to be incircled, so contracting themselves to a neerer compasse till they meet againe; and whatsoever is taken in this inclosure is called the Kings sikar [Hind. *shikār*] or game, whether men or beasts; and whosoever lets ought escape without the Kings mercy must loose his life. The beasts taken, if mans meat, are sold and the money give to the poore; if men, they remain the King's slaves, which he yearly sends to Cabul to barter for horse and dogs; these being poore, miserable, theevish people that live in woods and desarts, little differing from beasts.'[21] The emperor Shahjahan also used to have offenders against the state trans-

21 Bābur, *Bābur-Nāma*, 202; Hussain Khan, *Sher Shah Sur*, 167, 168; Abu-l Fazl, *Akbarnāma*, II, 246, 247, 475, 476; Monserrate, *Commentary*, 112, 117; Foster, *Early Travels*, 154. In the early 1830s in Central Asia, a common subject of conversation among Turkmens, then the main slave takers, was 'slaves and horses', Burnes, *Travels*, II, 61

ported beyond the river Indus to be 'exchanged for Pathān dogs'.[22]

According to Abul Fazl, in 1562 Akbar forbade the practice, then current among his troops, of keeping or selling the wives, children, and other relatives of the rebellious people they killed or captured. But such a prohibition must have been almost impossible to enforce, particularly as it was not the emperor himself but the Mughal nobility who must have undertaken the lion's share of the state's enslavement, deportation, and even extermination policies. During the 1620s and 1630s, an especially prominent part in this respect was played by Abdullah Khan Firuz Jang, an Uzbeg immigrant *amīr*. It is reported that in 1619–20 Abdullah Khan defeated all the hitherto un-subdued Chauhan rajas and 'rebels' of the Kalpi-Kanauj area he had been given to rule: he then had the principal men beheaded, while the peasants' women, daughters and children, to the number of 200,000, were at his instance transported to Iran and sold there.[23] Mundy, who travelled from Agra to Patna in 1632, saw, during the four days of his passage through this area, 200 minars or pillars on which a total of about 7,000 heads were fixed with mortar. This, he added, was the exploit of Abdullah Khan and a force of 12,000 horse and 20,000 foot, 'whoe destroyed all their townes, tooke all their goods, their wives and children for slaves, and the chiefest of their men, causeing their heads to be cutt off and to be immortered'. On his way back, four months later, he noticed that meanwhile another 60 minars with between 2,100 and 2,400 heads had been added and that the erection of new ones had not yet stopped.[24] For Abdullah Khan this was regular practice. Already in about 1627 he had said to a visitor who had, very politely, asked him how many infidels' heads he had caused to be cut off: 'There would be 200,000 heads so that there might be two rows of minarets of heads from Agra to Patna.' His guest had then suggested that there would certainly have been an innocent muslim among these men, but Abdullah's angry answer had been: 'I made prisoners of five lacs of women and men and sold

[22] Manucci, *Storia*, I, 204. See also, for Persian and central Asian dogs in North India, Bute, *Private Journal*, I, 234–5, and Burnes, *Travels*, I, 24.

[23] Abu-l Faẓl, *Akbarnāma*, II, 246, 247 (see also Beveridge's note about the expeditions of Husain Khan Tukria in Akbar's reign); Pelsaert, *Geschriften*, 148; Pelsaert, who arrived in Agra in April 1621, says that '2 lack' women and children were carried off to Iran yoked together or in rows ('met coppelen ofte rijen'). See, on the practice of yoking prisoners-of-war together, Jahangir, *Memoirs*, 165.

[24] Mundy, *Travels*, II, 90, 185, 186; see for the Chauhans of the Kalpi and Kanauj sarkars during Akbar's reign, Abu-l Faẓl, *Akbarnāma*, II, 195, 196.

them. They all became Muhammadans. From their progeny there will be krors by the judgement day.'[25]

Forced migrations were part of a deliberate policy in this area. Great numbers passed the Indus both ways. Whereas Rajputs in Western Hindustan were exterminated and deported as slaves beyond the Indus, Afghans were deported towards the east and settled in areas notorious for Rajput turbulence. The Dilzak Afghans, for instance, completely disappeared from their native land as a result of intensive military enrolment in India, but also because Jahangir deported a large number of them and 'distributed them all over Hindustan and the Deccan'. Afghans seem to have been especially in demand to deal with Rajputs and they played a crucial role in what may be called the partially successful Mughal attempt at the de-Rajputisation of Western Hindustan. During Shahjahan's reign, Bahadur Khan Rohilla, then Abdullah Khan's successor as *jāgīrdār* of Kalpi and Kanauj, brought a caravan of 9,000 Afghans to populate all the '52 *mohallas*' of the newly founded city of Shahjahanpur. His brother Diler Khan laid the foundation of several Afghan colonies between Shahjahanpur and Hardoi. Similarly, Aurangzeb invited Afridi Afghans to settle in Muzaffarnagar and control the rebellious Rajputs there.[26]

Admittedly, Abdullah Khan was noted for his tyranny and cruelty and no doubt more given to these methods of pacification than most of his contemporaries. But many peasant communities left their rulers with no choice but to consider an attack upon them. In January 1624, Jahangir wrote in his memoirs that he was compelled to send a force against 'the villagers and cultivators' (*ganwārān u muzariʿān*) of the Doab on the other side of the river Jumna. The Jats of the Agra region on both sides of the Jumna were, on several occasions, treated in a manner similar to Abdullah Khan's subjects; in 1634 10,000 of their men were killed and their women and children 'beyond computation' were seized.[27] The most eloquent witness, again, is Jahangir himself. Towards the end of 1619, he sent Abdullah Khan to quell the insurgency in the Kanauj area of which we have already made mention. There was some hard fighting before the enemy's fort was carried, 30,000 of the rebels being killed. The 'cap, or tiara', of the chief, containing jewels

25 Samsām-ud-daula, *Maāthir*, I, 105. As late as the 1830s, in Central Asia, slave taking was justified in exactly these terms, Burnes, *Travels*, I, 190.

26 Rita Joshi, *Afghan Nobility*, 15, 16, 105, 110, 128–9, 167.

27 Jahangir, *Tūzuk*, II, 285; I. Habib, *Agrarian System*, 339.

worth twenty lakhs of rupees, and 10,000 of the heads of the rebels, fixed on spears, were brought to the emperor's presence. The tragic character of all this was not lost on Jahangir and he wrote philosophically: 'And here I am compelled to observe, with whatever regret, that notwithstanding the frequent and sanguinary executions which have been dealt among the people of Hindustan, the number of the turbulent and disaffected never seems to diminish; for what with the examples made during the reign of my father, and subsequently of my own, there is scarcely a province in the empire [there were about 14 *sūbahs* at the time] in which, either in battle or by the sword of the executioner, five and six hundred thousand human beings have not, at various periods fallen victims to this fatal disposition to discontent and turbulence. Ever and anon, in one quarter or another, will some accursed miscreant spring up to unfurl the standard of rebellion; so that in Hindustaun never has there existed a period of complete repose.'[28]

This description probably remained valid for much of the seventeenth century. The export of slaves also went on for some time more. Aurangzeb, in the beginning of his reign, deprived the Persian ambassador of all the Indian slaves he was taking with him on his return to Persia. The reason was not that the emperor was against the slave trade in principle, but that he had an account to settle with the ambassador. It may be true, however, that by this time the practice was criticised more generally than before. Bernier, for one, comments on the incident as follows: 'It is certain that the number of these slaves was most unreasonable; he had purchased them extremely cheap on account of the famine, and it is also said that his servants had stolen a great many children.' Anyway, it is clear that, in the 1660s, Indian supply of and Persian demand for slaves was still considerable.[29]

As far as the demand side is concerned, it is probable that many of these Indian slaves were employed as peasants and artisans in Central Asia, as were the 120 slaves – tillers of grain, diggers of canals for irrigation, bronze and metal workers, a potter, a cook, a tinker, and a bowl maker; 'fathers, sons and grandsons', 'all

[28] Jahangir, *Memoirs*, 225, 226. This version of Jahangir's memoirs has been called 'garbled', but in my view they contain much that must have been written by Jahangir himself, whereas the official *Tūzuk* was thoroughly edited and enlarged by the imperial chancery's clerks; see Rieu, *Catalogue*, I, 253–54.

[29] Bernier, *Travels*, 151.

Hindustanis' – employed on an estate near Bukhara towards the end of the fifteenth century.[30]

The matter of the export of slaves – particularly, it seems, of women and children – deserves attention because of the light it sheds on the measure of violence that went with the aristocratic government of peasant society in Mughal as well as pre-Mughal times. Yet, as the passage quoted from Finch's account seems to indicate, a fair number of its victims may not have been agriculturalists, but pastoralists, semi-nomadic people who in this period still made up a large proportion of the population of North India. Also, violent repression and de-Rajputisation on this scale cannot have been applicable as an administrative method for any length of time nor does it seem to have been generally successful when resorted to. Even the drastic measures adopted, as we saw, against the Jats of the Agra region did not stop their 'huge plundering movement' and could not prevent them from greatly extending the area of Jat *zamīndāri*, particularly in the middle Doab.[31] A recent study of agrarian revolts in the Agra, Delhi and Ajmer *sūbahs* during the 1675–1730 period has shown that peasant support of such long sustained revolts was often extensive and crucial.[32] Clearly, an important reason for the limited achievement of Mughal state formation in the 'early modern' European sense was that the state was faced not with individual *zamīndārs* or rebels, but with parties of armed peasants who represented the backbone of society and who could not be destroyed without dire consequences to the agrarian productivity on which the regime depended for its survival.

Of course, any government in these circumstances would have liked to be in a position to separate soldiers from ryots, then to

30 Chekhovich, *Samarkandskie Dokumenti*, 232, 233; for Persian text, see 172. See also Foster, *Early Travels*, 271, for a muslim from the Panjab who spent some time as a slave in the Mediterranean. Alexander Burnes reported in the 1830s that three-quarters of the population of Bukhara was of slave extraction; by then, however, Iran – not India – was the main supplier of slaves, Burnes, *Travels*, I, 276.

31 I. Habib, *Agrarian System*, 341; as to the Chauhans, who were, as we saw, so ruthlessly visited by Abdullah Khan in about 1620, in 1865 they were still very numerous in the Etawah district though perhaps not much can be concluded from this, as the name Chauhan was generally adopted by a variety of 'spurious' Rajputs in this region; see Elliot, *Memoirs*, I, 171, 286, and Rowe, 'New Cauhans'.

32 Rana, 'Agrarian Revolts', 318–22. See also Smith, 'Lower-class Uprisings', and the rebellions of *zamīndārs*, tribal and village leaders listed in Naqvi, *Urbanisation*, 175–86.

employ the former and to recast the latter in the image of peaceful agricultural producers. The celebrated Mir Jumla may have attempted to do something like this, when he sent back to tillage 12,000 unemployed miners, who otherwise might well have turned to adventurous soldiering. But as a general policy, it would have required the actual disarming of the peasantry and that was even more impractical than their extermination. Weapons were as indispensable as ploughs in peasant society and to take them away would have seriously reduced the cultivators' chances of survival. Thus, when, about the year 1700, attempts were made to confiscate horses and arms in Maharashtra, the result was the opposite of what was envisaged, the peasants taking their weapons and horses with them and joining the Maratha war-bands.[33] Only the British Company would, in the 1798 to 1818 period, achieve something approaching a demilitarisation of India. Let us, therefore, examine another course that was perhaps, as already suggested, open to the Mughal state, namely that of employing as soldiers those men it could not otherwise control.

Clearly, there were insurmountable restrictions of a financial nature on this policy, the employment of Abul Fazl's four and a half million men being out of the question. Moreover, the wholesale engagement of auxiliary *zamīndārs* and their retainers must have been open to serious objection, as such alliances with war-bands, unless supported by marriages, were generally unreliable and of uncertain duration. More attractive seemed the direct recruitment of foreigners and of well-chosen peasant-soldiers. In countries where the occupational and spatial mobility of peasants was limited, this might have proved difficult, but in Northern India, at least as far as a large section of the rural population was concerned, there were no restrictions of this kind. Often, men were not only familiar with the use of arms, but served as part-time rebels and seasonal soldiers. According to a Dutch observer writing in August 1636, plundering ceased on the roads of Gujarat soon after the onset of the monsoon that year. This was partly because the rains made the peasants devote their time to agriculture again.[34] Similarly, the weavers of the town of Baroda in the 1620s, usually at home during the rainy season, went to serve in the army

[33] Tavernier, *Travels*, I, 230; Bhimsen, *Tarikh-i-Dilkasha*, 231.
[34] ARA The Hague, VOC 1119, p. 1936, A. Barentse to B. Pietersen, Baroda 30. viii. 1636.

in the dry months of the year.[35] Occasional income from soldiering or looting may have enabled quite a number of people in town and countryside to survive the slack season. In times of dearth or famine, this mobility of labour must have saved many lives. Thus, during the 1630 famine in Gujarat, a large party of weavers went to the Dekkan wars and did not return for quite a while.[36] Particularly in the countryside, this kind of mobility of labour must have been the rule rather than the exception. Since a careful dosage of violence or a measured threat of arms was a necessary part of *zamīndāri* management, armed gangs were an inseparable part of the country scene. If the food or pay offered were good, then, for a man used to such martial duties, an occasional try at service with an officially maintained road *caukī* (checkpoint) or with a local *faujdār* was not too radical a step. But what use did the Mughals, their predecessors, and successors make of this readiness to serve? In what way did the survival strategies of the empire and the peasantry meet and suit each other?

Participation in empire

Did the state in India actively 'pull' peasants into their armies and make them participants in empire or was their army basically in the hands of non-peasant troopers of largely foreign origin such as Afghans, Iranis and Turanis? What choice, in other words, did the Mughal government make from amongst the enormous potential of human resources which seemed to be at its disposal? Obviously, cheapness must have been an important consideration in this, as the following case to some extent shows. A provincial Mughal force, active against rebels in Gujarat in 1684, consisted of 3,000 cavalry, 1,500 infantry and, in addition, 'a numberless multitude of men of the country [i.e. Gujarat], consisting of Grasiyas and Kolis, who are tillers of the soil but follow the army by command in exchange for freedom of tribute; as they receive nothing but food, they keep themselves going mostly by theft'.[37] Cheap such men certainly

35 Geleynssen, *Remonstrantie*, 28. Geleynssen does not say whether these men went to the army to fight or to weave, but the former occupation seems probable. Anyway, the distinction between the army and its bazaar lacks just as much precision as that between the military and the civilian in medieval Indian society.

36 ARA The Hague, Coll. Geleynssen no. 30, W. Geleynssen to J. van de Graaf, Broach 23.viii.1630.

37 ARA The Hague, VOC 1409, 'Verhaal van't overweldigen . . .', 6.xi.1685, f. 1693 v°.

were, though in the long run of course such cheapness, which was dependent on opportunities for looting, was self-defeating. But the case of the Grasiyas and Kolis, here converted into a kind of military bondsmen, is significant in another respect; they partook of the quality that 'marginal peoples' generally have from a military point of view: peasant-robbers from the hills and forests make excellent skirmishers against their own kind and may well become a main element in established armies.[38] Such men had always been enlisted by Indian states and, to a certain extent, the Afghans and Rajputs, who for long were so numerous in North Indian armies, also belong to this category.

As another example of such soldiers of marginal peasant origin, the Barha Sayyids, a celebrated troop of soldiers under the Mughals, deserve attention. They were said to be the descendants of families who had, at an uncertain date, moved from their homes in the Panjab to a sandy and infertile tract of what is now the eastern part of the Muzaffarnagar district. During Akbar's reign, they were as yet men of rustic habits and their claim to be true Sayyids was not generally admitted. Jahangir wrote of them that 'some people make remarks about their lineage, but their bravery is a convincing proof of their being Saiyids'. Though by definition 'Sayyid' was an identity that could be had by birth only, in actual practice it could be acquired by effort or even by luck. The case of the Sayyids or Barha brings to mind the well-known proverb, which, in the nineteenth century, was found in various forms in Northern India: 'Last year I was a Jolaha; now I am a Shekh; next year if prices rise, I shall become a Saiyad.'[39] The Barha Sayyids achieved even more. Gradually, they rose to great power and about 1720 they were supreme in the imperial capital for a while. In 1737, however, the power of their most conspicuous lineage was crushed by the Delhi *wazīr* and they never regained their former position as recruiters and occupants of great imperial offices, though they held out for much longer as landlords and *jāgīrdārs* of the villages they had acquired through military service.[40] Their association with

[38] See for the concept of marginal area soldiers, Pipes, *Slave Soldiers*, 75–86.

[39] Jahangir, *Tūzuk*, II, 269; *Census Bengal 1901*, VI, pt.I, 441; Risley, *People*, 121–2. Similar proverbs seem to have been current all over India. See Shulman, 'South Indian Bandits', 288 (on a Tamil proverb about Kallar slowly turning into Velalar) and O'Hanlon, 'Maratha History as Polemic', 10 (on a Marathi proverb 'when a Kunbi prospers he becomes a Maratha').

[40] See on the Barha Sayyids especially: Abu-l Faẓl, *Ā'īn*, I, 425–32; *Muzaffarnagar Gazetteer*, 159–74.

empire must have wrought great changes in the community. What must have begun as a sociologically open category of families and men became a closed group whose members, in the nineteenth century, had 'private marks of recognition, which they say have been very successful in excluding imposters from the tribe'.[41]

The example of the Barha Sayyids shows that 'marginal' peasant-soldiers, valued for their cheapness and fighting qualities, could, as in other parts of the world, be successfully incorporated into the armies of an Indian state. It also indicates that, like all recruits of humble origins, they could, within a few generations, become powerful landed gentries and even the rivals of the elites ruling the empire. But this was not the only problem that came up when the recruitment of peasants was involved. Could the court employ whomever they chose? Why, if so many warlike men were pulled into Mughal service and thus made, at least temporarily, harmless, did the empire not succeed in employing the Maratha Bargis of Maharashtra who later on would be instrumental in seriously weakening its existence?

The solution to this problem lies beyond the scope of this book, but posing the question and the context in which it should, in my view, be approached, does not. I suggest that the Mughal polity was held together by a political economy that was constantly fed by flows of honours, gifts, and intelligence which gave it substance by causing Indian alliance politics to revolve around the Timurid throne. As a result, the imperial reciprocities with a plethora of Indian and immigrant elites did not allow the court to become the foundation of a unilateral 'law and order' imposed on the peasant strata of society. Political and military energies at that level of society could not possibly be frozen into any kind of 'early modern' repose. Yet, if they could not be 'ruled', they could be let into the empire in a rationed manner. To large sections of the urban and agrarian population, the significance of the Mughal enterprise and its widely scattered subcontractors was that, with its proliferating redistributive apparatus – the so-called *mansabdāri* 'apparatus of empire', to borrow M. Athar Ali's phrase – they were drawn into all kinds of mediated relationships. In the last quarter of the sixteenth century, the system acquired its full momentum, and – to a far greater extent than its Khilji, Tughluq, or Lodi predecessors had done – overflowed into parts of North Indian agrarian society.

That this was not an altogether new experience in India is shown

41 Elliot, *Memoirs*, I, 12.

in the origin of two concepts that would play an important role in sustaining the newly booming activity of the military labour market of agrarian North India: both these terms were brought to India by conquerors from the northwest who preceded Babur and his barons. They are *namak* – salt, the marketable pay of the soldier, hence salary, employment – and *naukarī* – honourable service in the warband, the retainership of the lord's companion, hence employment. As Mughal successes spread the idiom of *naukarī* to the mud forts of Hindustan, the details of Mughal political grammar were continuously being undone and rearticulated, accommodating concepts that were new to it and proposing dialects adapted to regional use. Later on, we shall have something to say about one of these dialects, the one that sealed the Rajput–Mughal alliance.

It should be clear, however, that an accommodation was not always reached. The question as to the causes of the Mughal failure to employ and thus incorporate a significant number of the Marathas in their polity is significant in this respect. There was no lack of precedents after all. The Nizamshahis of Ahmadnagar had depended heavily on Maratha soldiers and Ibrahim Adil Shah of Bijapur (1534–58) is said to have disbanded most of his foreign troops and to have entertained 30,000 Dekkani horsemen, introducing the practice of enlisting Bargirs or men who are supplied with a horse by their employer.[42] For a long time, the Mughals also appeared rather eager to employ Maratha help. About 1620 they welcomed Jadhav Rao, one of the principal Maratha chiefs who had quit Malik Ambar's service, and, in 1624, Shahjahan borrowed 10,000 Bargis (i.e. Marathas) under the command of an Abyssinian lord from Malik Ambar.[43] Both Shahjahan and Aurangzeb were off and on served by members of Jadhav Rao's lineage including the latter's grandson Shivaji who, in 1665, assisted the Mughal army at the head of 2,000 horsemen and 7,000 footsoldiers.[44]

Looking for reasons why the Mughal emperors did not acquire a permanent grip on the Maratha military labour force, one might feel that, in spite of the recruitment of Barha Sayyids and others of rustic origins, the imperial tradition was on the whole so geared to the enlistment of foreign cavaliers as to be unable to admit into

[42] Grant Duff, *History*, I, 36.
[43] *Ibid.*, I, 47, 58; Pelsaert, *Geschriften*, 155, 182, 195.
[44] J.N. Sarkar, *Military Despatches*, 102, 103.

their armies more than a limited number of peasant-soldiers, however 'marginal' and fierce they might be.

Indeed, this is an oft-repeated view and it should be considered carefully because it implicitly denies the historical role of India's armed peasantries. Irvine, the author of the classic study on the subject, concluded that the Mughal army was essentially an army of horsemen, the Indian footsoldier being 'little more than a night-watchman, and guardian over baggage'.[45] Now in the context of the gentleman-immigrant versus peasant-soldier issue, the question of the relative numbers of horsemen and footsoldiers assumes an added importance, if one assumes – as I do – that most footsoldiers were likely to be of peasant origin. It is true that Rajputs – often on horseback – and the bands of Maratha light cavalry were largely of peasant extraction. Inversely, some foreigners could make elite infantrymen. To give an example, it is reported that the Abyssinians of Western India in the 1680s had 20,000 footmen and only 400 horsemen, one of their infantry being equal in battle to two or three horsemen.[46] Yet, throughout Indian history, the vast majority of Indian infantrymen must, I think, have belonged to categories of martial peasants as their sheer numbers indicate. A few examples should suffice to illustrate the point.

The army which, at the beginning of the eighth century, defended Sind against its Arab conquerors, consisted of 20,000 or 30,000 foot and a number of horse amounting to only a third or even a fourth of this.[47] About 1250, a powerful hindu chief of Malwa had 5,000 cavalry and 200,000 infantry and in the next century the sultan of Bengal put into the field 10,000 horse and 200,000 foot.[48] Though these figures should not be accepted uncritically, and granted that the numbers given for footsoldiers must have included many servants, orderlies and camp-followers, the proportion of horse to foot is significant. About 1518 it was said of 'the heathen' of the Dekkan states, who were 'black and well-built' and who ate no beef and burned their dead, that 'the more part of them fight on foot, but some on horseback, yet these are few. The footsoldiers carry swords and daggers, bows and arrows. They are right good archers, and their bows are long like those of England. They go bare from the waste up, but are clad below.' Raja Ramdeo of Jodhpur's army

45 Irvine, *Army*, 57. 46 Syed, *Aurangzeb*, 373.

47 Kalichbeg, *Chachnamah*, 134.

48 Digby, *War-Horse*, 49; Minhaj-ud-Din, *Tabakāt*, 690, 691; Raverty points out, however, that according to another source this Malwa chief had 60,000 horse and 200,000 foot.

in 1543 was said to consist of 50,000 horse and 300,000 foot.[49] The raja of Vijayanagar had, reportedly, 30,000 cavalry and 300,000 infantry[50] and Mirza Nathan thought that, about 1610, the army of the Oriya raja consisted of 10,000 horse and 300–400,000 foot.[51] In 1656, Aurangzeb was attacked by 12,000 'musketeer-footmen' under one Musa Khan who then served Qutb al-Mulk, and, later during the same campaign, he rode against 8,000 horsemen and 20,000 Karnataki musketeers.[52] About 1687, the *zamīndār* of Munshtiwal in the South kept 30–40,000 infantry and, apparently, no cavalry.[53] Grant Duff thought there was exaggeration in the account of the Bijapur king's army in 1626 which gave 80,000 horse 'with upwards of 200,000 infantry in pay, including his garrisons'.[54] But, in 1666, an Adilshahi army counted 25,000 horse and 50,000 foot, while in 1684–5 the Bijapuri force consisted of 40–50,000 cavalry and about 200,000 'famous Karnataki foot-soldiers'. In the army of the *sūbahdār* of Hyderabad in 1724 there were 30,000 matchlockmen of the Dekkan known as *kālā piyādah*, i.e. black-foot soldiers, who were, according to Irvine, if not identical with, very similar to the Karnatakis and who, as their name seems to indicate, were peasants rather than gentlemen.[55]

A closer look at North India, however, suggests a somewhat less uniform picture. In the Delhi sultanate especially, things may have been different. As Digby has suggested, it is highly probable that the superiority of the Delhi armies to those of any hindu power is at least partly to be explained by differential access to military supplies, especially horses. Sultan Balban must have been right for the thirteenth century, when he remarked that 6–7,000 horse could overcome 100,000 footsoldiers of the hindu princes whom the geographical position of his sultanate of Delhi deprived of access to the western supplies of war-horses. By 1398 the resources of Delhi had greatly diminished, its cavalry having dwindled from 80–90,000 to a mere 10,000.[56] But it seems that the Lodi Afghans to a certain

49 Neamet Ullah, *History*, I, 138; Dames, *Duarte Barbosa*, 181.

50 Bhimsen, *Tarikh-i-Dilkasha*, 219.

51 Mirza Nathan, *Bahāristān-i-Ghaybī*, I, 36; on Orissa see also Digby, *War-Horse*, 49.

52 Syed, *Aurangzeb*, 64, 65.

53 Bhimsen, *Tarikh-i-Dilkasha*, 203; see also *ibid.*, 246. Similarly, the South Indian Poligars of the eighteenth century would rarely have any cavalry, Dubois, *Manners*, 677.

54 Grant Duff, *History*, I, 49.

55 Syed, *Aurangzeb*, 231, 333; Irvine, *Army*, 171.

56 Digby, *War-Horse*, 20, 21, 49, 82.

extent restored the old superiority of the Delhi sultanate in this respect. What is true of the supply of war-horses, holds good to some degree in respect of the immigration of warriors from the northwest. The sultanate of Delhi was the most obvious and principal employer of the numerous adventurers who migrated from Iran, Afghanistan and Central Asia into the subcontinent in search of a living and, perhaps, a fortune, though – like the Afghans in Bengal and in the southern sultanate of Bijapur – they found their way to other regions as well. Other foreigners, such as the Abyssinians and Arabs, came to India by quite different, maritime, routes and served primarily in Western India. So Delhi never had a monopoly of foreign elite troops.

The Mughal state, which succeeded to the Afghan sultanate of Delhi, became the heir to the strategic advantages of the northwest with regard to employment. In the composition of its armed forces, it presents a relatively distinct case. The Mughals, moreover, added a military resource with which India may have been relatively unfamiliar, at least since Timur's Turko-Mongol invasion of the Panjab in 1398–9. As recently pointed out by Streusand, the initial Mughal conquests were probably largely due to the superiority of their mounted archers. 'The Turk and Mongol nomads of Central Asia learned to ride and use the bow in early childhood', he writes and he quotes Bernier who, commenting on the battle of Samugarh in 1658, had observed – quite possibly referring to these horsemen of Central Asian origin – that 'the cavalry of this country manoeuver with much ease and discharge their arrows with astonishing quickness, a horseman shooting six times before a musketeer can fire twice'. No doubt Central Asian troopers were superior thanks to their tradition of martial sports. But the difference may have been one of degree, Hindustani cavalry generally receiving as much as 80 per cent of the pay of Turanis and Iranis. Moreover, such highly expert gentlemen troopers were scarce. The records preserved at Hyderabad about some 1750 troopers of Shahjahan's reign show 14 per cent Iranis and Turanis, 15 per cent Afghans, 23 per cent of indistinct ethnicity, and 47 per cent Hindustanis. In Iran, as witnessed by a report of a parade and muster in 1476 AD, the percentage of – no doubt highly trained – gentlemen-archers could be as high as fifty, the other cavalry being supportive and armed with swords and shields. In the central Mughal army that permanently surrounded the emperor in the imperial camp, the proportion of mounted archers may well have reached this level.[57]

In any case, the central imperial army consisted overwhelmingly of cavalry. It is true that Akbar had as many as 12,000 matchlock-men who were footsoldiers, but the number of regular infantry in the immediate pay of the emperor did not greatly increase during the seventeenth century. Bernier's observations about the imperial camp cannot but be accepted as truthful. He remarked that he did not know how to account 'for the prodigious amount of infantry with which some people swell the armies of the *Great Mogol*, otherwise than by supposing that with the fighting men, they confound servants, sutlers, tradesmen and all those individuals belonging to *bazārs*, or markets, who accompany the troops'. He thought that the infantry at the imperial headquarters was inconsiderable and did not exceed 15,000.[58] Irvine, as we saw, agreed with this and thought that it would be fair to take the fighting men, the vast majority of whom were horsemen, at one third or one fourth of the total numbers in a Mughal camp. It would be mistaken, he stressed, to consider the remainder as infantry as we understand the term.[59] They were simply armed camp-followers, though perhaps of peasant background. The majority of cavalrymen, as we have suggested, had no peasant background. Bernier said about them that the emperor's pay was their only means of sustenance. In France, an officer or even a private soldier would have a certain private income. Not so in India, where it was clear that horsemen did not, on the whole, have an income from agriculture or any enterprise but soldiering, though, as we saw, at least some of the Barha Sayyid chiefs must have been an exception to this. Bernier added that it would be difficult to find in the central imperial army 'a soldier who is not married, who has not wife, children, servants, and slaves, all depending upon him for support. I have known many persons lost in amazement while contemplating the number of persons, amounting to millions, who depend for support solely on the King's pay.'[60] Property these men did not have, except for one or two horses and some slaves. Their families

[57] Abu-l Faẓl, *Ā'īn*, I, 261; Streusand, 'Formation', 85, 86; Alavi, *Studies* 23, 62; Minorsky, 'Civil and military review', 165, 167. See Dames, *Duarte Barbosa*, 118, 179–81, for Central Asian or Irani mounted archers in Gujarat and Indian mounted archers on the Dekkan during the 1500–18 period.

[58] Bernier, *Travels*, 219, 220.

[59] Irvine, *Army*, 60.

[60] Bernier, *Travels*, 220, 221.

must have lived in the capitals and *qasba*s of the realm, because only the emperor himself and the chief commanders took their wives with them during campaigns.[61]

However, if it is clear enough that the army immediately about the person of the Mughal emperor does not seem to have had any of the characteristics of a peasant army, this applies less and less as we consider provincial armies which in terms of numbers of men far exceeded the central imperial corps. Further down the hierarchy of the means of violence this tendency increases, the individual *mansabdār*s of various descriptions and, finally, the *zamīndār*s and warrior-entrepreneurs of the countryside employing only indigenous men, whether connected with them through inherited *jajmānī* bonds, or consisting of minor regional bands of strongmen, seasonally migrant peasant servicemen, or tribal hunters. The *zamīndār*s, always negotiating a passage between their complementary roles as the king's rebels and the king's *mansabdār*s, were amongst the foremost dealers in *naukarī*. Abul Fazl avers that the chief of Kuch in North Bengal commanded only 1,000 horse and as many as 100,000 foot, adding figures for the *zamīndār*s of Berar, Gujarat and Sind who all had many more footsoldiers than cavalry.[62] Several of these men are known by name. Thus, Lal Koli, an unruly *zamīndār* of Gujarat, who gave the imperial authorities a lot of trouble until he was defeated and killed about 1615 by Abdullah Khan, had 2–3,000 horse and 10–12,000 foot. The Ujjainiya raja of Bhojpur assisted Shahjahan in 1624 with 5,000 horse and 20,000 foot.[63] In 1665, as we saw, Shivaji served the emperor at the head of 2,000 horsemen and 7,000 footsoldiers.[64] As these figures concern *zamīndār*s only, one might maintain that they do not fundamentally call into question the image of the Mughals as a non-peasant cavalry power. Yet there are several levels of military entrepreneurship and recruitment to be distinguished between the imperial camp proper and the war-bands of the *zamīndār*s. Figures not very different from those of the *zamīndār*s have been quoted above for the force of a Mughal *mansabdār* like Abdullah Khan who had no roots in peasant society himself, but pacified his *jāgīr*s with a force consisting of 12,000 horse and 20,000 foot.[65] One might suppose that these footsoldiers were essentially *zamīndārī*

[61] Irvine, *Army*, 200, 201.

[62] Abu-l Faẓl, *Ā'īn*, II, 130, 237–9, 248, 250, 253–7, 339.

[63] Pelsaert, *Geschriften*, 140, 186. [64] See note 44.

[65] See note 24.

retainers and that their enlistment was restricted to the localities they were used to subdue, but this is not necessarily true. Bhimsen relates that his father, about the year 1660, organised a force in Aurangabad that was made up of footsoldiers recently recruited from Narnal, Bundelkhand, Khandesh and the Dekkan.[66] Here one again catches a glimpse, first, of the great spatial mobility of infantrymen, supposedly of peasant origin – a point we shall revert to in chapter 3 – and, second, of their recruitment into one of the main provincial armies of the empire which have generally been regarded as the special reserve of professional cavalrymen and traditional Rajput allies.

Questions about the relative importance and numbers of such infantry can be answered to a degree, as we saw, even though the Persian chronicles of the period with their preference for the gentleman-warrior and his ethos of chivalry, do not make things easier. But if we are right in assuming that many North Indian soldiers were of peasant origin, there are a number of sociological questions to be asked. For instance, did the recruitment of peasant-soldiers alienate these men from their villages so that the army became the world in which they were at home, or did they maintain social and financial links with the regions they came from? Or inversely, if these men were not, as many *zamīndārs*' retainers may have been, just armed peasants who divided their energies between the complementary fighting and agricultural seasons, but professional infantrymen of peasant origin, did they remain a loose amalgam of mercenaries brought together by fate under the Mughal standards, or did they develop an identity of their own once they composed a body of troops far from home in one of the main imperial armies? In short, what were the dynamics of the relationship between the empire and the peasants in its camps? As these questions will be a main concern of the present work, and as I will only be able to provide an (albeit partial) answer to them after some analysis of North Indian empire building and pastoralist peasant culture, I shall limit myself here to some preliminary remarks.

As indicated above, any enquiry into the history and, particularly, into the social origin and identity of groups of footsoldiers in the seventeenth and eighteenth centuries is impeded by the bias in favour of cavalry that characterises the work of the Mughal and,

66 Bhimsen, *Tarikh-i-Dilkasha*, 34.

one may add, of many modern historians. As to the links maintained by peasant soldiers with their families left behind in the villages, there seems to have been a difference between South India and Hindustan. The Karnatakis of South India who, about 1760, served the British East India Company as sepoys, were followed by their whole family, 'their women carrying the husband's sword and other arms'.[67] The result was that an army of 25–30,000 soldiers often had 300,000 followers of all sorts in its train.[68] It is difficult to imagine how these families, though undoubtedly of peasant origin, could maintain sociological links of any intensity with their home villages. This would remain characteristic of the EIC's Madras army. 'The Madras sepoy', a modern historian writes, 'entered the service very young and his regiment became his permanent home and he had no other ties or views than passing the rest of his life in service; when he got married, his wife, mother and sister all lived with the corps'. Such a regiment of native infantry formed 'a sort of colony' composed of 3,500 or 4,000 people.[69] The Madras regiments were a kind of institution in themselves, alienated from the agrarian society from which its soldiers might originally have been recruited. Even the recruitment of the next generation of soldiers could be restricted to the sepoys' huts. In the 1780s, the commanders of the sepoy battalions of the Madras army trained the young sons of their sepoys as soldiers, clad them in uniforms and drilled them, though naturally arms were not yet given out to them. The eldest or ablest boys were given command over them. Village recruitment under this system must have been rare.[70]

In the North, however, this model did not apply. Maratha armies, as Dubois observed, were less troubled with families in their train and one wonders whether this had anything to do with their peasant background, their families being taken care of in their own villages.[71] As to the Hindustani infantry soldier of North India who would be the mainstay of the EIC's Bengal army, he always looked forward to furlough and to visit his family in the Bhojpur and Awadh countryside.[72] There he was at home as a husband, a peasant, but also as a soldier. In fact, the roots of the martial

[67] La Flotte, *Essais*, 259, 260; Irvine, *Army*, 171.
[68] Dubois, *Hindu Manners*, 679.
[69] M.P. Singh, *Indian Army*, 236.
[70] Best, *Briefe*, 123.
[71] Dubois, *Hindu Manners*, 679.
[72] M.P. Singh, *Indian Army*, 236.

tradition he represented were in the villages and towns of Hindustan rather than in the army camp. As late as the nineteenth century, military sports were very much a part of the daily life of the village. One of these sports was *paṭā hilāna*, a kind of athletic sword fighting. It had come, a citizen of Lucknow would remember early in the present century, from Purab, the eastern part of Hindustan. Anyone who was a master of the art and could properly swing a *paṭā* (a wooden sword), was capable of stopping ten swordsmen from getting near him. It was mostly practised by weavers. Also confined to the lower classes, both hindu and muslim, was *rustam khānī*, a kind of stick fighting. Hundreds of teachers of this art used to be found throughout the villages and towns of Awadh. Other martial arts again were confined to Brahmans, whereas *tīr andāzī*, archery, was the special skill of Pasis and Bhars.[73]

How popular the arts of war were in a city like Agra, which was, admittedly, very much like a huge army camp, is clear from a passage in Jahangir's memoirs. The emperor wished to know the number of the capital's inhabitants and decided that the best way to arrange a count was to direct the *kotwāl* 'to make a tour through the city, and count the individuals assembled in the different maarekahs [*mu'arakah*], or theatres for athletae or pugilists; and his report was, that in none of these places did he find assembled less than two and three thousand persons'.[74] Of course, there are many things one should like to know about these *akhāṛa*s or martial training centres, e.g. what proportion of them was in the hands of sects like the Dadupanthis or Gosains.

But we are dealing with the countryside rather than with the imperial capital. Martial exercises were typical of the way of life of large sections of the North Indian peasantry. Peter Mundy, travelling from Agra to Patna in the 1630s, passed close by an army camp and saw several men whom at first he took for tumblers, but who turned out to be soldiers. They did 'exercises to harden and enure themselves to labour, for they would tugg and wrestle one with another, tumble on the ground, beatinge and thumpinge themselves thereon in a strange manner and posture'. The editor of Mundy's text added – in 1913 – in a note, that this custom was still in use in the native army of his time.[75]

[73] Sharar, *Lucknow*, 109–115.

[74] Jahangir, *Memoirs*, 19. About 1550, Lahore seems to have had a capability for recruitment comparable to that of Agra under Jahangir, Samsām-ud-daula, *Maāthir*, I, 145.

[75] Mundy, *Travels*, II, 110.

The connection between village sports and the regional tradition of soldiering is explicitly shown by Subadar Sita Ram in the memoirs of his life as a sepoy in the service of the EIC. Sita Ram, after he had decided to become a sepoy at the age of seventeen, still had to spend some time in his native village near Ayodhya in Awadh. During this time he 'did very little else than learn to wrestle or play with the sword sticks'. Then, in about 1814, he joined a regiment. The captain of his company was 'a real Saheb', he remembered. 'His name was Burumpeel . . . He was six feet three inches in height, his chest like Hunooman's, and his strength enormous. He used often to wrestle with the sepoys, and when in the *akhāṛā* (wrestling arena) he was the universal admiration of all the men. He had learnt all the *pench*s (throws) and no sepoy could ever overcome him. This officer was always known among ourselves as Pulwan [*pahlwān*: champion, athlete, wrestler] Saheb'.[76] Another instance is shown by the Hindustani sepoys of the EIC's expeditionary force on Java between the years 1811 and 1815. In central Java, sepoy Ripal Singh and some colleagues of his 'delighted' Pakubuwana IV, the Susuhunan of Surakarta, and his court 'by giving them dance performances and gymnastic displays in the private apartments of the kraton'. And while, in the years between 1873 and 1916, the contract labourers recruited in the same Bhojpur and Awadh areas as these sepoys, and in some ways their successors as migrant workers, stayed in the Calcutta depot waiting to be transported to Surinam, favourite pastimes with them were wrestling (*kuśtī*) and fencing with clubs (*gatkā*).[77] One may safely assume that what was shown to the Javanese prince and what kept the emigrants busy in Calcutta, were the military sports of the villages of North India. There can indeed be no doubt that the martial traditions of Hindustani peasants and the fame of regions like Awadh and Bhojpur as recruiting areas mutually reinforced each other and were historically linked.

For the moment, one may conclude that the peasant masses of North India, at least those who in Britain would probably be deemed to belong to the 'yeoman' class, were professionally skilled in the use of all sorts of weapons. In fact, to maintain that skill at a high level was an integral element in the survival strategy of the

[76] Sītā Rām, *From Sepoy to Subadar*, 4, 14, 15.

[77] Cary, 'Sepoy Conspiracy', 301, 303; Budike and Mungra, *Creolen en Hindostanen*, 74. See also on the 'acrobatic avoidance devices' of North Indian swordsmen: Rawson, *The Indian Sword*, 23. For the indological background, see Arion Roşu, 'Les Marman'.

North Indian peasantry. Among the four million infantrymen enumerated in Abul Fazl's census of the military labour force of Northern India, a figure that cannot have represented less than 10 per cent of the active male population, most must have been familiar with the military sports mentioned above. And a much higher percentage than 10, though apparently not judged serviceable from the point of view of the imperial authorities, must have been thoroughly familiar with the use of arms. Villagers formed the majority of the fighting gangs and armies of North India, from *zamīndārī* war-bands to regional armies. Only the Mughal army in the strictest sense, i.e. the camp that accompanied the Mughal dynastic king, was an exception.

In conclusion we may say that the most radical change that could be brought to North India, was the demilitarisation of its politics, its conflict management, and its peasantry. This was partly achieved in 1818, perhaps only in 1858, when the last peasant army of Hindustan, very much, as we hope to show, heir to the soldiering traditions of the North Indian peasant, suffered final defeat. There can be little doubt that, before that year, some segments of North India's peasantry not only suffered under empire, but participated in it. The Mughal empire and the British empire until 1858 were huge employers and tens of thousands of peasants were among the recipients of pay from their main distributive institution, the *mansabdārī* apparatus. As long as they could not be disarmed or uprooted, some of them could become, though never in a direct way, sharers in empire. Later on in this study, I will investigate the most important of these North Indian peasant-soldiering traditions.

As far as the states that presided over this armed society are concerned, the fact that they never achieved a monopoly of the means of force, was largely responsible for their character. To a degree unsuspected by the student of European history, their power had to be based on the control of the channels of information within the empire – the famous system of espionage on which Indian states from ancient times onwards so much depended – on the fame of their treasures and their rulers' credit with merchants that came as a corollary of the reputation of their riches, and, finally, on the extent of their network of relationships that was the essence of the state – the *Personenverbandstaat* to use the German term – and of which an elaborate political economy of honours and gifts centred on the person of the emperor, was an indispensable part.

Let us see what, in the circumstances outlined above, were the possibilities and limitations of state formation in Northern India. They are best shown in an account of an attempt at empire building that pre-dates the establishment of the Mughal system in the 1570s. I am referring to Sher Khan Sur's emergence as a warlord earlier in the sixteenth century. Though Sher Shah, as he came to be known, has become famous, probably rightly so, because Akbar's revenue system was based on his, I will try to explain his rise to power and his decline not in terms of territorial policies but in terms of employment and manpower. I hope to have shown above that, in India, these aspects of rule can only be explained against the background of a uniquely dynamic military labour market. After having thus reconnoitred, through the case study of Sher Khan, the demand side of this labour market, I will return, in chapter 3, to the theme of peasant soldiering, i.e. to the supply side of the phenomenon. Only then shall we be in a position as regards the Mughal polity to approach the problem of the inclusion or exclusion of groups like the Rajputs and Marathas, though I will have something to say about the former category only.

2
A warlord's fresh attempt at empire

Long after they migrated to India in search of land and a soldier's career, the Afghans of Hindustan remained organised as war-bands, ready to migrate with their women, children, tents, and flocks to whatever camp their chiefs would determine upon.[1] In politics they likewise tended to stick to old ways and, when one of their leaders became king of Delhi in 1451, their attitude towards him and his successors remained ambivalent for several generations. The problems of legitimacy were not really solved. Indeed, the Afghan aristocracy of the Lodi period (1451–1526) never quite learnt to live with an indivisible kingship. The experiment of a dual monarchy was tried on more than one occasion; in 1517 it was abolished for the last time only after a good deal of campaigning and intrigues amongst the *amīrs* of the realm.[2] The repeated division of the sultanate of the Lodi family was characteristic of a segmented Afghan society which used the enmities in the royal kin to fight its own and did what it could to fan them. It was a two-way process. The sultans were partners in the feuds of their great nobles and the heads of the aristocratic families were drawn inescapably into conflicts within the ruler's family. The kings were reminded again and again that they had to keep up appearances and share part of the gains of kingship with the high aristocracy. Yet, a trend towards stronger kingship is discernible. The Afghan nobles had no doubt felt at ease with the gregarious ways of Bahlul Lodi (1451–89), who had no throne erected for himself but shared the carpet with his peers.[3] His son Sikandar (1489–1517) had slowly asserted royal authority in the pastoral confederation of tribal lords over which he presided, but he had done so without outraging aristocratic sentiment. Ibrahim, the last sultan of the dynasty (1517–26), however, appears to have followed a policy of outright

[1] Digby, 'Dreams', 58. [2] Hameeduddin, 'Lodis', 148. [3] *Ibid.*, 142.

suppression of his *amīrs*' independent manners. He required them to observe proper court ceremonial and set out to 'purge their minds of any thoughts of equality based on clannish affinity with the king'.[4]

By thus trying to impose new attitudes upon his *amīrs*, Ibrahim threatened the equilibrium and cohesion of the kingdom. He was out to prevent them from periodically reasserting their position through conflicts that involved not only the nobility of the kingdom but also the royal family and thereby kingship itself. But he could never hope to succeed in restraining the chiefs without a corresponding change in the segmentary institutions of Afghan rule in Hindustan. This he failed to do. Nobles who found that the new rules of the game did not allow them to contend for status and profit the way they felt was their birthright, left the arena of the Lodi sultanate, either by declaring themselves independent or by seeking help from outsiders like the Mughal Babur in Kabul.[5] The king could not destroy such great aristocratic rebels against his rule without destroying the legitimacy of Lodi rule itself: too much custom and right were on their side. Understandably, his kingdom had already begun to fall apart before his final defeat at Panipat in 1526.

This, however, would not prove the end of Afghan rule in Hindustan. Within a decade after Panipat, it reasserted itself, this time on a different footing. This chapter addresses itself to the question of whether the power base of Sher Khan Sur, who would be king of Delhi from 1540 to 1545, differed institutionally from that of the Lodis. It will be my contention that, at least initially, his reign presents a new departure in North Indian history. He significantly changed the segmented aristocratic military polity as it had existed in Lodi times. First and foremost this is clear from the way he entered the military labour market and from the alliances his army encompassed.

Abbas Khan's message

Abbas Khan Sarwani who, about 1580, wrote a history of the great Afghan Sher Shah,[6] began his work by tracing the origin of Afghan immigration into Northern India. The movement of poor tribesmen

[4] *Ibid.*, 149. [5] *Ibid.*

[6] The names Farid (proper name), Sher Khan (title conferred about 1526) and Sher Shah (title as sultan of Hindustan from 1540 onwards) are all used in this chapter to denote the same person.

from Afghanistan to the rich plains of India, he contended, had provided the manpower for the armies of the Lodi and Sur dynasties that, with an interruption of only fourteen years, had ruled in Hindustan from 1451 to 1555. Abbas relates how Sultan Bahlul Lodi was at first just one of many petty kings of Northern India who was left at peace so long as he remained stuck within the walls of Delhi, but whose city was besieged by the sultan of Jaunpur as soon as he had left it on an expedition to subdue Multan. Bahlul, however, knew his rivals' weak spot. He told his nobles that none of these kings had a 'national [*qaumdār*] following of their own', whereas, far in the northwest, he had a large number of kinsmen who were valorous and poor and who, if brought to India, would firmly establish his hold over the country. A message was sent to the chiefs of Afghanistan in which Bahlul told them that the preservation of the honour of their kinswomen in Delhi was their affair as well as his. He would share all his possessions with them, he said, as with brothers, keeping only the sovereignty of India for himself. And so they descended to the plains 'like ants and locusts', as the usual cliché has it, to serve Bahlul. The Jaunpur king could not withstand these spirited tribesmen. It is true that he had 'elephants like mountains' and 'innumerable zamindars', but he lacked, Abbas implies, the human resources that Bahlul now commanded: 'dear and near ones ... imbued with the spirit of honour and prestige'. Jaunpur was defeated. The Afghans were richly rewarded with *iqtā*'*s* (fiefs) and more of them began to stream into Hindustan every day.[7]

Here, one feels, Abbas Khan is mainly at pains to preach unity to the Afghans of his own time in which Afghan power had yielded to that of the Mughals. He pleads for a revival of national pride amongst his immigrant countrymen. But as far as historical truth is concerned, one cannot but have one's doubts about Abbas' contention that Bahlul's success was exclusively due to his appeal to ties of kinship and nationhood amongst the Pathans.[8] Certainly, there were ethnic and geographic factors working in his favour. As a Lodi Afghan in control of Delhi and most of the Panjab, he had easy access to the finest recruiting grounds that could be imagined. Perhaps there were also demographic forces pushing men from the hills to the plains of Hindustan. Yet only his success in war enabled

[7] Abbās, *Tārīkh*, 5–9; Persian text (Imamuddin), I, 4.
[8] Here and elsewhere in this study the words Afghan and Pathan are used interchangeably. See on Abbas also: Mukhia, *Historians*, 160–5.

him to turn all this to advantage. Most of his new men must have been simply soldier-adventurers, many of them no doubt experienced fighters, who were drawn by Bahlul's growing fame as a leader rather than by feelings of tribal obligation. Good 'marginal' soldiers were a rare commodity and would remain so for centuries.

But Bahlul's plentiful fortune as a military commander procured for him the wealth the lavish distribution of which allowed him, firstly, to be selective as to whom he permitted to serve in his camp and, secondly, to maintain a certain discipline. This, I suggest, must have been the grain of truth in Abbas' assurance to his readers that, in those early days, there was no factionalism or rivalry amongst the Afghans. On the contrary, 'they looked to the well-being of their nation and never felt jealous of the prosperity of others'. Among Bahlul's *amīrs* the same self-denying spirit prevailed: 'if they knew that their Afghan brethren had better prospects elsewhere, they immediately allowed them to go there with their recommendations, so that they might not be taken to be the ill-wishers to their nation and tribe'.[9] Perhaps this is not just an idyllic myth. In Bahlul's time, the influx of Pathan soldiers into Hindustan very likely grew so intense at one point, that even *amīrs* could pick their men. As long as the supply of men exceeded demand, they were in a position to prevent intertribal and interfactional quarrels from impairing the fighting quality of their hosts. But all this lasted only as long as their coffers and those of their king were full of booty and tribute, that is to say as long as military fortune smiled on them.

Abbas, the Afghan historiographer on whom we shall continue to rely to a great extent in the following pages, was clearly in need of a Golden Age and found it in the reigns of Bahlul and Sikandar Lodi (1451–1517). His demography may contain some truth, as we saw, though, already for at least 200 years before Bahlul, thousands of Afghans had been serving in the Panjab and Hindustan. Abbas, however, was out to make another point, to wit, that the glorious Afghan empire in Hindustan was lost in the 1520s not by the sword, but, as he has Sher Shah say, 'through the feuds that the Afghans had developed among themselves'.[10] In the final paragraph of his work Abbas admitted that these feuds were part of 'the very temper' of the Afghans as a people. But they were not ineradicable. Sher Shah, he said, had completely wiped out 'the contentions, disputes, fights, and feuds which were ingrained in the very temper

[9] Abbās, *Tārīkh*, 12. [10] *Ibid.*, 104, 117, 452.

of the Afghans . . . whether they be in Hind or Roh'.[11] What Sher Shah achieved in the 1530s and 1540s was, according to Abbas, not only a restoration of, but also an improvement of Afghan rule as it had been under Bahlul. It was his greatness to have overcome, for once, the ingrained weakness of the Afghan race.

What then was so particular about this sultan? What exactly did he change? More than any other historian, Abbas answers this question. He points not to the kind of man Sher Shah was, though like Bahlul he must have been a leader of exceptional ability, but to the basis of the relationship between him as an employer and the men on whom he built his kingdom. In this respect Sher Shah apparently could afford to act on new principles to a degree that clearly set him apart from the Lodis.

An important departure from ancient Afghan custom was Sher Shah's rule that the laws of inheritance did not obtain in public affairs. To the Afghan community, the matter must have been fraught with emotion. The tension between the royal prerogative and tribal equality had hardly been problematic during the time of Bahlul Lodi, the founder of the dynasty who, when inviting his kith and kin, had promised to share with them as brothers whatever territories and kingdoms would come into his possession. His son Sikandar, however, decided that, whenever one of his nobles died, his treasures and chattels were to be divided according to the Afghan law of inheritance, whereas his *pargana*s and soldiers would be conferred on the son whom the king considered most able. This principle was revived by Sher Shah who also refused his own relatives a share in the *pargana*s conferred on him by the Lodi king, telling them: 'this land is not the country of Roh that I should make divisions equally among brothers. The country of Hind is completely under the laws of its king and here nobody has any share in it. There is no question of seniority, juniority or fraternity here.'[12] In Hindustan, the sultan's law prevailed over tribal distributive custom and inheritance. Elsewhere, Abbas told an anecdote to remind his audience how proper it was that loyalty to one's family and tribe yield to service to a leader like Sher Shah, because 'the safety of that one man who is powerful and capable leads to the

[11] *Ibid.*, 787. Hind is India and Roh is the home country of the Afghans in Afghanistan.

[12] *Ibid.*, 99. See also the *Tārīkh-i-Daulat-i-Shēr Shāhī* which quotes Sher Khan as saying: 'In the matter of conquest and the business of administration, the ties of kinship are not to be observed', Roy, 'New Light', 57; see also page 60.

well-being of the seven climates'.[13] Throughout his history, Abbas stresses the importance of Sher Shah's empire as the embodiment of Afghan unity,[14] firmly founded on the principles of subordination, discipline, and royal control over the tribal immigrants, however egalitarian the outlook of these freebooters originally may have been. Sher Shah's empire was not a tribal state. On the contrary, tribal custom and closeness of kinship ties is dismissed as belonging to the sphere of personal affairs and is not allowed to impinge on the 'public' interest.

Abbas particularly wanted to stress the discontinuity he saw between the Lodi period and the rule of Sher Shah. After 1526, the old solutions had lost their validity; Bahlul's recipe was no longer applicable. The Lodi dynasty had been based in large measure on a principle opposed to that of discipline; their monarchy had been floating on a loose confederation of aristocratic clan segments. At crucial moments internal feuds proved their undoing, however brave the Pathans might have been individually.[15] The Lodi nobility had lost their kingdom to the Mughals and, in the opinion of Abbas, this failure of theirs disqualified them from future leadership over the Afghans. The point of the insufficiency of genealogy to justify any claim to a share in empire is duly stressed in his history. The aristocratic descendants of the Lodis were judged unfit to serve as advisers under Sher Shah's new dispensation. They had the seal of failure on their foreheads. Providence now favoured another type of leadership.[16] Therefore, Sher Shah was right when he did not join Sultan Mahmud, a son of the last Lodi king who rose against Mughal rule in 1537.[17] The dethronement of the dynasty had exposed the politics of the faction-ridden Afghan elite as hopelessly inadequate in the changed circumstances.

Sher Khan entered the race with a handicap. As late as 1537 aristocratic opinion was that the leadership of a Lodi was necessary to rouse, hold together, and legitimise an attempt at restoration of Afghan authority. The rebellion of Mahmud was an expression of the shared aspirations and the common system of values of the autonomous chiefs of the great Afghan clans. Sher Khan was an outsider to this kind of politics. Abbas himself admits that, if the only hope was for a refurbished confederation of the old type, his hero 'did not command sufficient respectability amongst the

13 Abbās, *Tārīkh*, 271, 272.
14 *Ibid.*, e.g. 255, 265, 269, 375, 383.
15 *Ibid.*, e.g. 382.
16 *Ibid.*, 375, 443, 450.
17 *Ibid.*, 209.

Afghans' to compete with the aristocrats.[18] He was a member of the Sur clan, a minor Afghan group, and his pedigree was singularly unimpressive. In the diplomatic game of tribal politics he was at a natural disadvantage. Yet precisely for this reason, if Sher Khan was to respond at all to the crisis of Afghan unity, he would have to come up with something new. Like Ibrahim Lodi, he would as king make changes in the old etiquette concerning the respect shown by the *amīr*s to their sultan and vice versa. But whereas Ibrahim had the advantage of a certain dynastic legitimacy, Sher Khan first had to build a basis of power for himself that was imposing enough to make his nobles obey him. Though it took him forty years before he was successful, this is what he did achieve.

In a revealing sentence Abbas explained why Sultan Mahmud, the Lodi pretender of 1537, though his respectability for a while won him a large following of allied noblemen, was bound to fail. 'Since Sultan Mahmud', he wrote, 'did not possess the real hold over the country and the treasures, he could not maintain a force of his own.'[19] The prince had no access to the agrarian resources and the hoards of Hindustan and, therefore, could not afford to maintain a sizeable number of soldiers in his pay. Clearly, Abbas is at pains, from the first chapter of his book to his concluding sentence – in which he said that Sher Khan gave peace and tranquillity to peasants and soldiers – to explain how through a long career his hero was successful exactly on the issues where prince Mahmud failed.[20] In Sher Khan's view, he suggests, the crucial ingredients of politics were not the famous lineages of the Afghan nation, but soldiers, treasure, peasants, and the revenue they paid.

Long before he became sultan and probably as early as the second decade of the sixteenth century, Sher Khan, then still only named Farid, began building a base for himself around Sasaram in what are now the Rohtas and Bhojpur districts of western Bihar. Called to the area in about 1511 by his father to administer two *parganas*, he found himself at first without troops of any description. The story goes that he had 200 saddles made and then borrowed horses from the village headmen, which means that these people were capable of war, because in India a horse was a war-horse. Perhaps what Sher Khan tried here was the forced disarming of the local peasantry. Anyway, with these horses he equipped the young Pathans of the district telling them: 'I will provide you with subsistence, allowance and clothings and what-

[18] *Ibid.*, 207. [19] *Ibid.*, 212. [20] *Ibid.*, 788.

ever booty in the shape of cash or kind falls into your hands will be yours. I will never covet them.' The valorous amongst them he would provide with maintenance fiefs.[21] It is clear from these and similar remarks that he did not collect a loose gang of retainers around him: his soldiers received their equipment from their leader and received a basic payment from him, or, to use the Indian idiom, they ate his salt. The *pargana*s he administered and from which he took agrarian taxes, were also his recruiting ground. In fact, the management of land, as practised by Sher Khan, was linked to the recruitment of peasant-soldiers. According to another sixteenth-century chronicle, he put an early stop to the ancient system of forced labour in his *iqtā'* and remitted various kinds of imposts levied by his predecessors, with the result that 1,000 husbandmen, amongst them even Rajputs from Marwar, migrated and came to live under his protection.[22] Later on, we find that Sher Khan, then the virtual ruler of Bihar, returned to his home counties for some months to manage his lands and collect an army.[23] The Sasaram area became Sher Khan's most securely held district virtually by his own efforts. Not surprisingly, once he had become king of Hindustan, of the Panjab, and of Bengal, he had his tomb built in these otherwise obscure southern marches of his realm.

Though we shall have to say something on the subject later, Abbas clearly suggests that Sher Khan's troops were exclusively Afghans.[24] And indeed, he seems to have gone to great lengths to enlist as many men from that nation as he could, first from the Sasaram area and later from elsewhere as well. In the 1530s, when probably already over fifty years old, he at last emerged as the one and only Afghan warlord of North India. He doubtlessly realised that aggressive recruitment methods minimised the possibility of a competing rallying point of Afghan solidarity emerging elsewhere in Hindustan. In building up his strength, he resorted to harsh expedients. 'Those Afghans', Abbas says, 'who had taken to the life of mendicants and indolence on account of their misfortune, were made to give up this life and were enlisted again as soldiers. Those who refused to take to soldiery and continued the life of mendicancy were killed.'[25] Recruiting officers or, if one prefers a less modern expression, press-gangs, were sent to the communities of Pathans which, particularly after their defeat at the hands of the

21 *Ibid.*, 26, 27. 22 Roy, 'New Light', 53, 54.
23 Abbās, *Tārīkh*, 208; see also 757 and Roy, 'New Light', 58.
24 Abbās, *Tārīkh*, 384, 454 and *passim*. 25 *Ibid.*, 249.

Mughals in 1526 and 1527, had spread far and wide, but in the first place to Bihar.[26] One of Sher Khan's men was even reported to have led all the Afghans of Gujarat and Mandu to his army in the North.[27]

Once in camp, military life turned out to involve hard physical labour, most spectacularly the erecting of the earthen entrenchments with which Sher Khan seems invariably to have surrounded his encampments. To a certain degree such hardships were apparently also imposed on Pathan noblemen. For one of these aristocrats, who felt unequal to the exertions required by Sher Shah, this was a reason to try and escape from camp.[28] Others swallowed their pride and became accustomed to this kind of life; perhaps they derived some consolation from the sight of a party of respectable Mughals who, as two fellow-historians of Abbas tell us, were working in camp as common labourers at the circumvallation constructed each day.[29]

In yet another aspect this army astonished Sher Khan's contemporaries. Its soldiers were not only disciplined and used to an idea of soldiering that involved more than just fighting battles, they were also subjected by Sher himself to a certain kind of drill. In 1542, he was in a position to surprise the ex-king of Malwa with a military spectacle that may have been quite new in India at the time. 'When the royal umbrella came in sight', runs a report, 'the cavalry drew their sabres, galloped forwards towards the umbrella, dismounted from their horses, and saluted the king in due form, as was their habit on the day of battle. Each division did this in succession.'[30] Soldiers and king thus solemnly acted out the devotion that bound them to each other in a manner that pronounced the role of the nobility as largely irrelevant. But this demonstration of loyalty also conveys the orderly impression of an exercised manoeuvre. Indeed, Sher Khan is quoted by Abbas as reminding his men on the morning of the battle at Kanauj in 1540 that he had imparted training to all of them. This may certainly be regarded as a striking innovation which, as far as we know, sets apart the army of

26 *Ibid.*, 121; Digby, 'Dreams', 55, 64.

27 Abbās, *Tārīkh*, 447. Some contingents of Afghans, however, remained beyond his control, Digby, 'Dreams', 58.

28 Abbās, *Tārīkh*, 542, 543, 586n, 588n.

29 Elliot and Dowson, *History*, IV, 394n, quoting the *Waqī'at-i-Mushtāqī* and the *Tārīkh-i-Daudī*. See on the Timurids building such ditches and on their *Wagenburg* in fifteenth-century Iran and Turkey, Woods, *Aqquyuulu*, 112, 175. Also Inalcik, 'The Khan', 460.

30 *Ibid.*, 393n, quoting the same sources.

Sher Khan from that of his predecessors as well as from many of the later Indian armies.[31]

Sher Khan's novel methods of recruitment, labour and drill must have made life in his camp hard as compared to conditions under the Lodis. Yet, there were plenty of Afghans who voluntarily joined his standards when they heard that he was, as Abbas says, 'greatly eager to organize them'.[32] After Sultan Bahadur Shah of Gujarat lost control of Malwa in 1535, for instance, the Afghans who had been in his service joined Sher Khan. As with Bahlul Lodi in the fifteenth century, Sher Khan's success in politics and in battle must have made service with him seem attractive. Even the aristocrats gave up their scorn of him when they saw him prosper.[33] But the common soldiers in particular favoured him and they enjoyed his favour. He could not have held his nobles in check if he had not kept his promises to the ranks.

But by what method did Sher Khan achieve this? How did he find the means to keep his promise? Abbas points out that the men in the army were fully equipped, received whatever money they demanded and grew so affluent that their number increased daily.[34] This, of course, was the basis of any warlord's success. Abbas himself, as we shall see, gives Bibi Fateh Malika as an example of a rich *amīr*, whose inherited wealth enabled her to set herself up as a formidable military power.[35] But the information we have is not detailed. What we should like to know is to what extent fixed and regularly paid salaries were a feature of these armies and, most crucially, whether soldiers were paid directly out of Sher Khan's treasury or through the intermediary of *muqta*ʿs (fiefholders) and jobber-commanders. The first question is impossible to answer categorically though Abbas mentions monthly salaries several times in his history, which would lead us to assume that they were the rule at least for a portion of the army.[36] As to the second question, the answer must be that possibly a number of soldiers received pay directly from the treasury, but that the majority, especially those serving away from the capital or the royal camp, was paid by the army officers out of their *iqtā*ʿs. The problem was to make sure that this last category of soldiers received regular pay.

[31] Abbās, *Tārīkh*, 451. However, according to Ahmad Yadgar, in the late 1530s Humayun had men come from Badakhshan to train his troops in up-to-date methods of warfare, Abbās, *Tārīkh*, 302. For a story about Sher testing a man's skill as an archer, see Roy, 'Anecdotes', 260–1.

[32] *Ibid.*, 249. [33] *Ibid.* [34] *Ibid.*, 121, 757. [35] *Ibid.*, 252.

[36] *Ibid.*, 129, 754, 755, 774.

As the inspection, however strict, of his officers' accounts was not a sufficient means to control their spending, Sher Shah introduced the systematic branding of horses, a practice which, according to Abbas, was quite new, though the device seems to have been tried before by Alauddin Khilji in the early fourteenth century.[37] Sher Shah was well aware how, during the reign of Ibrahim Lodi (1517–26), the nobles used to dismiss most of their men as soon as *iqtā*'s came into their possession, and how afterwards, having enriched themselves from their unduly large income as *muqta*'s, they used to forsake their sultan and join another master.[38] His system was designed to avoid a repetition of this. He preferred to have the horses of his men branded in his own presence and, after he had inspected the rolls of soldiers and horses presented to him, he used 'with his own tongue' to announce their monthly pay, while he also personally fixed the monthly emoluments of newly enlisted soldiers. This was done, amongst other reasons, in order 'that there should be no discrimination (*farq*) between the rights of the nobles and the soldiers [and] that the nobles may not be able to deprive the soldiers of their dues . . .'[39] There is no doubt that the sultan in this way made a considerable impact. The Mughals would revive the system.

It is true that Abbas elsewhere draws the attention of his readers to the case of an *amīr* who, when appointed to the charge of the faraway province of Sind, was exempted from branding.[40] But this was clearly an exception. More importantly, Sher Khan's soldiers soon learnt what they were entitled to. They knew they could count on the protection of their master if any noble threatened to deprive them of it. Once the governor of Malwa in conjunction with his aristocratic entourage reserved for himself some of the income meant for distribution to the soldiers. Upon this 'two thousand noted horsemen' decided they would submit the case to the king who, Abbas commented, they knew showed no favour to a man simply because he held a large army or because he was one of the *amīr*s belonging to his own nation. Understanding that Sher Shah would never forgive them if they left their post on the frontier of the realm to resort to his court *en masse*, they sent a *vakīl* and set up a separate camp at a distance from that of the governor. Sher Shah's reporters told him about the affair before the horsemen's *vakīl* or

37 *Ibid.*, 753, 754; Abu-l Fazl, *Akbarnāma*, I, 399.
38 Abbās, *Tārīkh*, 753, 795n.
39 *Ibid.*, 754. 40 *Ibid.*, 533.

spokesman appeared before him. The sultan promptly had a letter written to the Malwa governor reminding him that he had introduced the branding of horses with the intention that the nobles should not encroach on the rights of the soldiers. 'Have you no shame', he asked, 'before the people and fear of God above that you have acted contrary to my laws?' On receipt of this letter, the governor abused his nobles for their bad advice, got on his horse, rode to the camp of the 2,000, offered them his excuses and brought them back to the main camp, 'bestowing on them rewards and favours'. When the *vakīl* of the soldiers returned he was given a horse and a robe of honour while amongst the poor the governor distributed a large sum of money, thus restoring his relationship with God as well as with the common man.[41] For, Abbas seems to imply, the sultanate of Sher Shah was built on those two relationships, and any nobleman had better acknowledge the fact.

Compared to Lodi times, therefore, the distribution of the financial means of the realm was organised on new principles. To sum up, Sher Khan's attempts emphasised subordination and employment by the centre, not horizontal alliances with aristocratic leaders, pastoral tribes and warlords. Sher Khan penetrated the military labour market along a vertical axis with, amongst others, agrarian-based troopers or, as we might perhaps call them, an emerging gentry in his home counties in Bihar and in the *qasbas* situated on the East–West river and land routes that formed the main frame of his realm. This did not, of course, mean he tried to monopolise recruitment – that, in India, is impossible, as we have shown – but it did mean centralisation to the extent that it was feasible. Now what was feasible? Sher Khan's approach presupposes the command of independent means. We need to know, first, what these were and how they were used. Secondly, it is necessary to inquire whether Indian conditions allowed a programme of centralised recruitment and distribution to become a permanent feature of politics and state formation.

Treasure

It is difficult to understand Sher Shah's reign unless we can find an answer to the question of the origin of the resources with which he financed the personal fidelity of his soldiers who alone could keep the Afghan aristocracy in check. For the period after 1540, when he

41 *Ibid.*,772–8.

controlled the great plains of Northern India, the answer is clear. At that time, a careful management of the fiscal resources of the country was feasible enough; regular pay to the army and, therefore, army discipline could be guaranteed. After the battle of Kanauj, Sher Shah devoted himself wholeheartedly to this difficult task. He may have been helped by a continuation of the period of agricultural expansion that had probably characterised the Lodi period. Anyway, though some tribute from the outer regions of the realm still came in, much depended now on his ability in a systematic way to tap into the agricultural resources of Hindustan. On this score, Sher Shah's achievement was reputedly great. Historians, including Abbas, have, probably not without reason, drawn attention to the innovations he introduced in the administration of the land revenue adding that these served as the inspiration for the later agrarian settlements of Todar Mal during Akbar's reign.[42] Thus, after Sher Khan's famous victories at Chausa (1539) and Kanauj (1540) had put the agrarian resources of Hindustan at his disposal, land revenue became the all-important element of his income.

The early years before 1529 do not present much of a problem either. Until that year he was simply a successful commander who divided his time between the ruthless but efficient administration of his father's *parganas* in South Bihar[43] and service with a variety of chiefs mainly in Oudh as well as with Ibrahim Lodi and the Mughal King Babur. Abbas, the historian, did not deny that a good deal of loot fell into the hands of his hero and that, while serving in the camp of the Lodis, he was able to make savings.[44] Yet, however great his success as a revenue assignee and as a soldier of fortune, being a member of the Sur clan and unconnected with any of the powerful clans of the Ghilzai tribe that dominated Afghan politics in Hindustan, there was not much of a future for him either in the Mughal camp or amongst the remnant of the Lodi confederation: politics were on too big a scale there for an as yet comparatively insignificant professional soldier to be much in demand. In 1529, he left the camp of the Mughals and joined the service of the newly

[42] *Ibid.*, 755–7; Spear, *History*, 27, 28.

[43] Abbās, *Tārīkh*, 27–32. See on the controversy about whether Sher settled for the revenue with the village chiefs or with the peasant cultivators, Nurul Hasan, 'Revenue Administration', and Hussain Khan, *Sher Shah Sur*, 55–8. I tend to side with Nurul Hasan who thinks Sher dealt with the chiefs.

[44] *Ibid.*, 27, 47.

established Nuhani (or Lohani) sultanate of South Bihar, a more modest enterprise.

For Sher Khan this field of action had the advantage of being close to his home-base, his recruiting grounds in the Sasaram-Benares area, and of allowing full scope for his personal initiative as a military commander. For the Nuhani sultan, the fact that he was not supported by tribal sentiment and family relationships of any significance meant that he promised to be a stable element of the otherwise baffling scene of Nuhani factionalism. Perhaps that is the reason he was selected for a position of trust: that of guardian (*atālīq*) of the minor prince Jalal Khan. When the sultan died shortly afterwards and his widow ruled for a while on behalf of her son, Sher Khan, the outsider, maintained himself in his position at court. And, when the sultana also died, 'the entire management of the kingdom of Bihar now devolved upon him'.[45] In this way he appears to have won a measure of independence for himself that was far removed from his earlier inferior position as a dispensable mercenary in Lodi or Mughal service. Yet he was still essentially a servant of the Nuhani clan and in times of crisis had to fall back on his military skill and on the income from his own modest home counties around his town of Sasaram. It is doubtful whether he would have been able, faced as he was with the claims of the jealous Nuhani lineage chiefs, to lay his hands on a large part of the sultanate's revenues. We are, therefore, still left with the question as to the origin of the resources on which Sher Khan built his power during the crucial ten years between 1529 and 1539.

Abbas' answer to this is abundantly clear: treasure. Immediately after his account of Sher Khan's emergence as the guardian of the young Jalal Khan, he mentions the subject for the first time. And throughout his account of the decade preceding Sher Khan's overthrow of Humayun, the issue of how his hero came into the possession of wealth accumulated by others remains perhaps the single most important theme of his narrative. Then, as the story reaches the end of the decade, the subject is dropped as abruptly as it was taken up. Abbas is silent about the enormous spoils which must have fallen into the hands of the Afghans immediately after the two decisive battles of 1539 and 1540. Whereas this is perhaps explained by the delicacy of the subject of these Mughal defeats for an author writing during Akbar's reign, he also makes no mention of the acquisition of treasure by Sher Shah during the five years of

45 *Ibid.*, 107, 108.

his kingship. The reason is, no doubt, that the loot of those years was no longer a vital explanatory element in the story he had to tell. During the preceding decade, it had been a different matter. Indeed, there was a wide gulf separating, on the one hand, Sher Khan's modest circumstances before 1529, when he made a living in the pay of several provincial governors, rulers and warlords, and, on the other hand, the state of his affairs in the 1540s when he had seated himself on the throne of Hindustan and could dispose of its entire land revenue. It was treasure, talent and luck alone that enabled him to cover the distance between the two.

The hoarded wealth that fell into Sher Khan's hands between 1529 and 1539 came from the strong-rooms of both *amīrs* and sultans. The exact dates of these acquisitions are difficult to establish. Assuming a rough chronology to be Abbas' intention, we follow the order in which he has placed them. The list starts with Sher Khan's alliance with a certain Makhdum Alam, an *amīr* in the service of the king of Bengal, who was in charge of Hajipur in North Bihar across the Ganges from Patna. When the Bengal sultan sent an army to assert his authority in North Bihar and perhaps wring South Bihar from the hands of the Nuhanis, Sher Khan succeeded in defeating this expedition. 'The huge amount of spoils', Abbas comments, 'in the form of treasures, horses and elephants, etc. which fell into the hands of Sher Khan made him master of the resources'.[46] Now the king of Bengal sent another force to subdue Makhdum Alam who so far had taken no part in the fighting. Sher Khan sent a contingent of troops to his aid receiving as a trust Makhdum Alam's earthly possessions. When the latter was killed in battle, this wealth fell to him as his ally.[47] Thus, to begin with, war booty and wealth confided to him by an ally added to Sher Khan's property.

As a result of his central position in the Nuhani court, Sher Khan appears to have had access, perhaps not to the revenues, but to the treasure of the kingdom of South Bihar. Part of it he seems to have sent as *peshkash* to the Mughals to serve his own diplomatic ends.[48] His growing power and independence and his method of handling the spoils that the Nuhanis regarded as theirs caused a crisis in the little sultanate. He lost the confidence of one Nuhani faction which now left Bihar in search of help, carrying away to Bengal the young sultan Jalal Khan. In the battle that inevitably followed, Sher Khan was again victorious over the Bengalis. 'All the treasures,

[46] *Ibid.*, 109. [47] *Ibid.*, 110. [48] *Ibid.*, 119.

elephants, equipages, and train of artillery fell into the hands of Sher Khan who thus escaped the disgrace of subjection to others and he now became the master of the kingdom of Bihar.'[49] Jalal Khan fled back east. It is not certain whether on this occasion Sher Khan acquired the royal treasure of the Nuhani kingdom of Bihar or whether it was taken to Bengal by Jalal Khan. But we have already noticed that his good use of this treasure had played a role in his rise as a regional political leader in Bihar.

Next in Abbas' account are the resources that three widows yielded to Sher Khan. In medieval India it was not unusual for aristocratic women to assume conspicuous roles. In an elite society torn by rivalry and war at frequent intervals, a woman's brothers and husband often died violent deaths leaving her at the head of family affairs. Also, as girls were married young, there was always a good chance of their surviving their husbands. Thus, noblewomen wielding impressive financial and military power were a common feature of the political scene. As allies they were more eagerly sought after than men, as a measure of control over their resources was a natural corollary of any kind of partnership.

In 1526, the Lodis had been driven from Delhi and Agra by the Mughals and from their Agra treasury Babur had distributed huge gifts to his family, to the tribes of his army, as well as to several recipients in Central Asia.[50] But there was more in the way of Lodi wealth in Hindustan. In the 1530s, a provincial treasure of the defeated dynasty was still kept in the fort of Chunar, not far to the west of Sher Khan's home *parganas*. The fort was held by Lad Malika, the widow of a professional Sarangkhani soldier to whom the Lodis had entrusted it. She was assisted by three Turkoman brothers who were at loggerheads with her stepsons. These partisans of hers, in an effort to strengthen their position, arranged for their mistress' marriage to Sher Khan.[51] On that occasion she presented to Sher Khan '150 precious jewels, 7 maunds of pearls, 150 maunds of gold' as *peshkash*. After this her new husband brought 'all the parganas in the environs of the fort' under his control. Subsequently, he married Guhar Gosain, the – perhaps converted hindu – widow of Nasir Khan Nuhani and took into his

49 *Ibid.*, 129. Cf. Roy, 'New Light', 61.

50 Bābur, *Bābur-Nāma*, 522, 523.

51 Abbās, *Tārīkh*, 201–6, 221n. Abu-l Faẓl, *Akbarnāma*, I, 288. See below for the place of the Sarangkhanis in fifteenth-century North India.

possession sixty *mans* of gold from her. 'His power', Abbas adds, 'came to be fully established'.[52]

Even more important than these marriage alliances was his connection with Bibi Fateh Malika, a lady of unrivalled respectability. She was a Farmuli *sheikhzāda*, i.e. a member of the second most powerful clan of the Lodi sultanate;[53] her father had been a sister's son of Sultan Bahlul Lodi and her husband had been the descendant of a famous sheikh, a religious man of great prestige. She belonged, in short, to the high aristocracy of Hindustan. And she was rich. Her father had possessed some inherited wealth. Being 'a man of prudence', he had, during the prosperous and peaceful years of Lodi rule, taken only few soldiers in his service and had, as a result, made great savings. The whole *sarkār* of Awadh and other *parganas* had been given to him by Bahlul and during more than a generation these *iqtā*'s were never changed. It was said that he never purchased anything but gold and jewels. He had no issue except Bibi Fateh Malika who thus became heiress to the family treasure.[54] Her husband seems to have been more of a fighter than his father-in-law and must have spent some of his riches on soldiers. However he soon died. Bibi Fateh Malika now told her husband's younger brother Bayazid to employ more soldiers 'and that she would give money for it'.[55] This chief subsequently quite successfully opposed the Mughals Babur and Humayun, but his early death and the consolidation of Mughal power in Awadh left the lady to her own devices. She could have taken refuge with the Baghela Rajput raja of Bhata – later known as Rewa – as so many wealthy Afghans did during these critical years. But another possibility now was Sher Khan, a man no doubt of spurious descent, but at least an Afghan and an adroit leader on whom fortune seemed to smile.

Indeed, Sher Khan plotted to bring her 'under his control by adopting a variety of artifices and cunning devices'. To let go such treasure would have been 'a matter of grief to his heart till eternity'. If we are to believe Abbas, he tried to convince her that all the *amīrs* of the Lodi sultans and their sons had exalted him, Sher Khan, by taking shelter with him. Whatever may have been said during the negotiations, she must have known that this was not true. All the same, in the end she did not join the Bhata raja but

52 Abbās, *Tārīkh*, 206. This *man*, or maund, perhaps weighed something like 13 kg. See also Elliot and Dowson, *History*, IV, 343–6 (Abbas Khan).

53 Nizamuddin, *Ṭabaqāt*, I, 356.

54 Abbās, *Tārīkh*, 250.

55 *Ibid.*, 252.

came to Sher Khan's camp. For the latter it was a political breakthrough and financially the advantages were enormous. The wealth of this noblewoman enabled him to take the initiative against Bengal. About 1535 he took 300 *man*s of gold from her leaving her only a small amount of gold and the fief he had conferred upon her so that she might not become dependent on others. Having equipped his army with this money, he set out on his conquering expedition to Bengal. However, in this case a marriage alliance as with Lad Malika and Guhar Gosain was out of the question. The embarrassed Farmulis might have felt compelled to become the Sur leader's allies, but they had not lost their pride and when Sher Khan's son asked Bibi Fateh Malika to marry her daughter to him, she refused and Sher Khan did not judge it politic to press her on the matter.[56]

The next catch was probably the greatest of all. This time it was straightforward loot again. Sher Khan's rise to power in Bihar had been worrying the Afghan nobles in Humayun's service for some time, but the emperor himself had not taken much notice of him. Moreover, Sher Khan had befriended the Mughal governor of Jaunpur by sending him *peshkash*, which in this case amounted to a kind of honourable bribe consisting, according to one source, of some *man*s of gold.[57] He had thus been able for some years to conduct an aggressive war towards the east. In 1537 he again sent an expedition to the east laying siege to the Bengali capital city of Gaur. This at last compelled Humayun to move in his direction. Humayun's Mughal comrades proposed to take Chunar first, Sher Khan's strongest fort, but the Afghan aristocrats in his entourage were now eager to get at their low-born rival with as little delay as possible. There was an added reason for their hurry. 'The counsel of the old', their leader pleaded, 'is that as there is a huge treasure lying in the fort of Gaur, the fort of Gaur should be taken first'; after that, the capture of Chunar would become an easy task. Humayun did not listen to this advice, whereupon the old Afghan could only comment gloomily that as Sher Khan would soon acquire the treasures of Gaur, there was no doubt that he was in the ascendant.[58] So it happened: Gaur fell to the Bihari Afghans in 1538 and, though Sher Khan could only with difficulty find enough

56 *Ibid.*, 250–5.
57 Quoted by Ambashthya from the *Waqīʿat-i-Mushtāqī* and probably also from the *Tārīkh-i-Daudī*, *ibid.*, 305n.
58 *Ibid.*, 257, 258.

porters and beasts of burden to transport its huge riches, most of this wealth arrived safely in Rohtas in his home country by a route through the Jharkhand hills.[59]

Other sources support the picture as given by Abbas, particularly as regards the Gaur spoils. The chronicler Muhammad Kabir says that the ransom agreed upon for lifting the first siege of Gaur in 1536–7 was nine lakhs of rupees.[60] He also reports that when Humayun occupied Gaur in 1538, after Sher Khan had left, a huge treasure that the latter had not been able to find, was discovered under a *cabūtra* and sent towards Agra on 500 mules along with a large force to escort it. This whole precious consignment, however, was seized by the Afghans and sent to Sher Khan at Sasaram.[61] The Tarikh-i-Daudi says that Sher Khan, on his return from Gaur, got hold of the huge treasures of Maharath Chero, a tribal raja of South Bihar.[62] Abul Fazl, who clearly found the subject of Sher Khan, this 'seditious impostor', exceedingly unsavoury, also mentioned the role of finance in his rise to power. According to him Sultan Bahadur of Gujarat (1526–37) sent a subsidy to Sher Khan through merchants and summoned him to his side. But Farid, he wrote, who in a short space of time 'by craft and unrighteousness surpassed the rebels of the age', did not join Bahadur, but 'made the money into capital for sedition'. Another tale, apparently written down in the seventeenth century and explaining Sher's victory over Humayun by his seizure of the latter's treasure, nicely, though erroneously, summed up ten years of Sur successes.[63] Even more striking is that stories of the kind we have been quoting from sixteenth- and early seventeenth-century historians, were apparently current for centuries in the heartland of Sher Shah's empire. There, people about 1920 still knew that the *rauza*s (gardens) of Sasaram and Chainpur were paid for from the hoarded riches which a commander of Sher Shah had seized from the Chainpur fort and which Sher had not wanted to appropriate for his own use.[64] As long as his memory lasted, his name conjured up images of unheard-of accumulations of treasure and of lavish spending.

Portuguese sources are as emphatic as Abbas Khan in pointing out Sher Khan's special interest in finance and his success in

59 *Ibid.*, 262, 274, 275. Elliot and Dowson, *History*, v, 112 (Niamatullah).
60 Quoted by Ambashthya from Kabir's Afsana, Abbās, *Tārīkh*, 295n.
61 Quoted by Ambashthya from the same source, *ibid.*, 367n, 368n.
62 Quoted by Ambashthya, *ibid.*, 363n.
63 Abu-l Faẓl, *Akbarnāma*, I, 328, 401. Rizvi, *Religious and Intellectual History*, 504.
64 Buchanan, *Journal*, 120.

obtaining treasure. In the early 1530s, they report, he quarrelled with the treasurer of the army of King Nusrat Shah of Bengal (1518–33), who then largely controlled Bihar. This resulted in an affray in which the commander of the camp was killed. Later, he was again present when the Bengal army in Bihar rebelled against the new king of Bengal, Mahmud Shah (1533–8). In the battle that followed, Mahmud was victorious, but Sher Khan got away with the treasure of the defeated army.[65] In 1536–7, as we saw, he invaded Bengal himself and got as far as Gaur, Mahmud Shah's capital. His army, on this occasion, consisted of 40,000 horsemen, 1,500 war elephants, 200,000 foot and 300 boats each of which had two rowers and three archers. Mahmud paid him thirteen lakhs of gold, valued at 525,000 *pardaus*, to get rid of him, the deal being that Sher Khan would recognise Mahmud as his lord and publicly pay him his respects. The captain of the Portuguese, who was present with the Bengalis during the negotiations, counselled against this bargain as Sher Khan, he said, would no doubt use this money to continue his war of aggression.[66] He was right, because in 1537–8 the Afghan returned, this time accompanied by 100,000 horse and 300,000 foot – inflated numbers no doubt, but interesting if compared with the lower numbers cited for the preceding expedition – demanding the same sum again from the king, telling him this was going to be an annual contribution. This time the king refused, whereupon Sher Khan plundered the city. The Portuguese could not be very exact as to the value of the jewels, pearls, *aljôfares* ('seed-pearls') and of the gold and silver that was taken from the city's palaces, but over a period of seventeen days they saw 300 'calaluzes', i.e. rather large rowing boats, carrying these treasures to the other side of the Ganges, whence they were brought to Sher Khan's stronghold Rohtas in Bihar. It was rumoured that all this was worth 60 million (pieces?) of gold.[67]

Though quantification of the accumulated wealth of diverse origin flowing towards Sher Shah in South Bihar in the 1530s is clearly impossible, the evidence of its enormity is convincing. Perhaps the best indication of its vastness and of its importance for his rise to power in Hindustan, is the fact that in Abbas' account

[65] Castanheda, *História*, Book VIII, ch. cix, 379, 380.

[66] *Ibid.*, Book VIII, ch. cxxviii, 410. Barros, *Da Asia*, Dec. IV, Book ix, ch. vii, 500, 501. I assume what is meant here is the *pardao em tanga* or *tanqat*, worth about one and a half future Mughal rupees.

[67] Castanheda, *História*, Book VIII, ch. clxxvii, 486, 487. Barros, *Da Asia*, Dec. IV, Book ix, ch. viii, 503–6.

these data become crucial explanatory ingredients. In large parts of his exposition of Sher Khan's career between 1529 and 1539, he allows these acquisitions of treasure to dominate his narrative. They must have been a conspicuous element in the reports of Sher Shah's relatives and contemporaries. Abbas knew quite a number of such men intimately and he was in an easier position to interview them as he himself was related to Sher Shah's family.[68] Chronology may have faded from their minds but the stories of how their chief acquired his gold and silver during a period when he was only reluctantly taken notice of by his fellow-Afghans, had made a lasting impression on them. To Abbas – and this is saying something about his quality as a historian – these frequent references were no bizarre tales of oriental riches. On the contrary, he emphasises the theme to tell us something essential about the polity Sher was building at the time, the so-called second Afghan empire that differed so much from the first, Lodi, sultanate.

Some of the massive resources that fell to Sher Khan were no doubt spent on *peshkash* and presents to those lords of Hindustan with whom he could as yet not cope on the battlefield. But the emphasis was on the distribution of income to his own men. We have mentioned the theme earlier. From 1529, Sher Khan was using his position amongst the Nuhanis of South Bihar almost exclusively to increase the number and discipline of his retainers. This was exactly the cause of the rupture between him and the proud Nuhani faction around the young sultan Jalal Khan.[69] 'Whatever new territories, treasures and wealth came into his hands, he spent them over appointing fresh retainers and granted to the new entrants the jagirs to their hearts' content, while he gave nothing to the Nuhanis out of his new jagir.' In the end he even told Jalal Khan quite frankly, that, as he saw it, this was in the best interests of both the king and the kingdom.[70] He thus attacked the tribal basis of the realm and replaced it by a new distributive principle that may be regarded as one of Sher Khan's main political innovations. Fixed payment and discipline replaced clannish loyalty. He is quoted as telling anyone who entered his service: 'Whatever monthly pay and stipends I will fix for you . . . I will not

68 Abbās, *Tārīkh*, 110. A sister of Sher Khan had been married to a Sarwani relative of Abbas Khan.

69 *Ibid.*, 119. Abbas does not mention Sher Khan's marriage to Dudu, the widowed queen of the Nuhanis, see Roy, 'New Light', 60.

70 Abbās, *Tārīkh*, 111, 112. *Jāgīr* is the Mughal term for what in Sher Shah's time would have been called an *iqtā*'.

reduce it even by one grain of rice. But you will not have to commit oppression and crime and quarrel with anyone.'[71] Besides their salary his soldiers also received their share of the spoils of battle. After an encounter with the Mughals in Bihar they all got at least four horses and many boxes containing valuables.[72] Thus, by the end of the 1530s, Sher Khan's name was associated with victory, treasure, good pay for soldiers and minor, well-disciplined commanders and, consequently, good service from the rank and file.

Such distributive practice attracted large numbers of horse and foot.[73] A worried Mughal commander is said to have reported that when, early in 1535, Humayun had embarked on his Gujarat campaign, Sher Khan had only 6,000 horsemen under his command, but that only a few years later he had 70,000 of them at his disposal and spent twelve crores on their pay.[74] Though, again, one can have one's doubts about the reliability of these figures, the message of the historians is clear: they draw attention to the extraordinary qualities of Sher Khan as a recruiter, disciplinarian and paymaster, in short, to his methods as an employer of men. Abbas, in his concluding chapter, is perhaps more explicit. 'All through the day', he explains, 'he distributed gold like the sun and remained busy with the scattering of pearls like [a] cloud and that was why the Afghans rallied round him and the country of Hindustan came under him.'[75]

We can accept this judgement without reserve. After 1539 Sher Khan, now entitled Sher Shah, remained keen to restrict the elite's independence and to maintain personal control of his power base, his army. But he set about perfecting his system in two respects. The aim was to preserve, under the changed circumstances, the distributive polity that had taken shape in the 1530s and of which the army was the central institution. Firstly, as the supply of the hoarded treasures of Hindustan into his coffers largely ceased with the re-establishment under his leadership of regular government, he became increasingly dependent for his income on the agrarian resources of the country, supplemented perhaps by tributary

[71] *Ibid.*, 129.

[72] Neamet Ullah, *History*, 115. Ambashthya, as so often, gives a slightly different translation, see Abbās, *Tārīkh*, 354n. See also Elliot and Dowson, *History*, v, 112 (Niamatullah).

[73] E.g. Abbās, *Tārīkh*, 206.

[74] Translated by Ambashthya from the *Waqī'at-i-Mushtāqī*, *ibid.*, 307n; see also 235n.

[75] *Ibid.*, 769.

payments from the fringes of his empire. A regularly assessed land revenue, for which he became rightly famous, became the major source of his income. Secondly, after 1539, a set of fixed rules that ensured the payment of salaries to soldiers became feasible. An essential element of the system chosen was the branding of horses to which we have already alluded.

Sher Shah, therefore, after his seizure of the sultanate, responded to the changed circumstances by effecting both a new fiscal policy and new procedures of spending. Both reforms were crucial if the kind of army built by Sher Shah was to survive in less troubled times. Indeed, the political economy that Sher Shah endeavoured to establish in Hindustan between his accession to the throne in 1539–40 and his death in 1545 was largely conditioned by the need to preserve intact the main instrument of his power: a well-recruited, well-paid, trained, and disciplined professional army of horse and foot. Abbas significantly ended his work by concluding that, as a sultan, Sher Shah gave peace and tranquillity to peasants and soldiers alike,[76] that is to say, that his new income policy worked as well as his policy of expenditure. If there is truth in this, it should be worthwhile taking a closer look at the recipients of his distributive system. Were all of them drawn from an exclusive ethnic category, the Afghans, or did some of them originate from the peasant strata that the king took so much pains to satisfy and turn into a prop of the state he built?

Afghans and non-Afghans

In other words, who were Sher Khan's soldiers? On this score our faithful historian, Abbas, fails us entirely. He describes himself as 'the author of the annals of the kingdom of the Afghans'[77] and we, therefore, cannot blame him if his bias throughout his history is clearly Afghan, though his emphasis on the role of the Sarwanis, the clan to which he himself belonged, is less excusable. Inevitably, there were things which he could or would not take notice of. But was Sher Khan's career really such an exclusively Afghan affair?

It probably was not. To begin at the beginning, Farid's – to use his proper name, for Sher was a complimentary one later acquired – father and grandfather did not enter the service of any Afghans at all except for a period immediately after their arrival from Afghanistan when they served a Sur kinsman of theirs in the Panjab. At

[76] *Ibid.*, 788. [77] *Ibid.*, 3, 4.

some point during the 1480s they, along with other Surs, joined Jamal Khan Sarangkhani, the governor of Hissar in present-day Haryana. Later, they moved as retainers of the Sarangkhanis to Jaunpur when the family was put in charge of that area. This connection with members of the Sarangkhani family would last for decades. The Sarangkhanis were Turkbachchas, i.e. they descended from the Turkoman or Mamluk slaves, who had served the Tughluq dynasty of Delhi in the fourteenth century – just as Indian slave-soldiers had served to the west of the Indus – and who, in North India, continued as an important element in military society afterwards. No doubt, these men had not lost the reputation for loyalty that characterised all slave soldiers. Their gangs must have been much in demand in the unstable and segmented warrior polity of fifteenth-century North India. In their forts they often kept great riches and military stores. When, in 1527, Ilyas Khan Turkbachcha was captured by Babur, one of the latter's followers got hold of two lakh *man* of grain, 2,000 *man* of oil and also a few thousand *man* of pearls and jewels. The Lodis used their troops in certain key posts to counterbalance the power of the unruly Afghan clans.[78]

Thus, when Sikandar Lodi in or about 1498 tightened his grip on Jaunpur, which had been an independent kingdom not long before, he sent Jamal Khan Sarangkhani there with 12,000 horsemen. The strong fort of Chunar was given to another Turkoman, a relative of Jamal Khan. So the Lodi sultan created a non-Afghan base right in the centre of Hindustan to serve as a check on the surrounding *iqtā'*s and provinces held by the Sarwani, Farmuli and Nuhani noblemen. As we saw, however, Jamal Khan Sarangkhani had a number of non-aristocratic Sur Afghans amongst his retainers. These he took with him and gave them as fiefs a number of *pargana*s in the present Mirzapur, Bhojpur and Rohtas districts south of the Ganges.[79] This narrow area formed the strategic link between Awadh and Jaunpur on the west and Bihar on the east. It had never been brought fully

78 The identification of the Sarangkhanis as Turkbachchas is taken from Qanungo, *Sher Shah*, 67n. See also Siddiqui, *Mughal Relations*, 20, and Niamatullah, *History*, 30. See for the Turkbachchas also Halim, 'Foundation', *JIH 31*, 201–09; *JIH 32*, 157–69; *JIH 33*, 32, 38; Badaoni, *Muntakhab*, I 360, 362, 365; Abū'l Faẓl, *Ā'īn*, II 176, 195, 297. In my opinion, other 'Turk' or 'Turkoman' commanders may as well have represented the Mamluk Tradition, see e.g. Siddiqui, *Sher Shah Sur*, 53, 69, 107, 136.

79 Abbās, *Tārīkh*, 12, 14, 15; Siddiqui, *Mughal Relations*, 18–20, 22, 26, 43, 46–7, 52, 179, 183. The erstwhile Shahabad District has now been partitioned into Bhojpur and Rohtas.

under the control of any of the sultans of Hindustan. The Surs, therefore, now had to safeguard the passage of troops across the Ganges ferry at Chausa as well as on the stretch of the Delhi to Bengal road that ran across their area. As one of them, Farid's father was put in charge of two *parganas*, sufficient for the maintenance of 500 men. One of the *parganas* was Sasaram, which would become the central *qasba* of Sher Khan's home counties.

So, about 1498, Farid and his father, Hasan, left the Panjab for Hindustan with the Sarangkhanis and spent twenty years in the largely Turkbachcha enclave in the east of the Lodi sultanate. During this period we may assume that, from about 1501 to 1511, Farid was a freelance soldier-administrator in the Jaunpur neighbourhood and, between 1511 and 1518, managed the family *parganas* at Sasaram. He then probably served another Sarangkhani at Agra only to return to the family base on the death of his father in 1524.[80] But even after he joined the Nuhani Afghans of South Bihar in about 1525, his association with non-Afghans remained a vital factor in his rise to power, as is shown by his service as a client of the Mughals between 1527 and 1529[81] and, most importantly, by his marriages with Guhar Gosain, who can hardly have been an Afghan, and with the Sarangkhani, i.e. Turkoman or Turkbachcha, widow Lad Malika, as well as by his alliance with Bibi Fateh Malika, a Farmuli, and therefore a member of a group of families that were *sheikhzādas*, not Afghans, though related to Afghans by marriage.[82] Inevitably, the composition of his army in the 1530s must to some extent have reflected these non-Afghan connections. It is clear, for instance, that after his alliance with the three Turkbachcha or Turkoman brothers and his marriage with their chief, Lad Malika, the Chunar contingent, which must entirely or largely have consisted of Turkbachcha professional soldiers, was henceforward part of his army.

But this does not exhaust the issue of the Sur relationship with non-Afghans. Even more striking than the Turkbachcha link are the connections that allied Hasan and Farid with Rajputs. A bardic poem from Rajasthan, the 'Qaimkhan Raso' caused one of Sher

80 See Qanungo, *Sher Shah*, 66–75. The chronology is based on Ambashthya, 'Accounts'.

81 Bābur, *Bābur-Nāma*, 652, 659. Qanungo, *Sher Shah*, 76–88. Abbās, *Tārīkh*, 103–7. The Portuguese were also told that Sher Khan had served Bābur and Humayun, Barros, *Da Asia*, Dec. IV, Book vi, ch. iii, 23, and Dec. IV, Book ix, ch. vi, 488.

82 On the identity of the Farmulis, see Siddiqui, *Rise*, 122.

Shah's biographers to surmise that Hasan's first wife, Farid's mother, was 'a daughter of the ruling Qaimkhani Rajput family of Fatehpur-Jhunjhun (Shekhawat)' near Narnaul in Haryana where Hasan's father in the late fifteenth century held an *iqtā'* for the maintenance of forty horsemen.[83] At about that time Hasan Sur was himself in the service of another Rajput in the Shekhawat area, a certain Raimal.[84] Though the Persian chronicles of the period rarely refer to these things, in medieval times there was nothing extraordinary about non-Afghan women being received in Afghan households,[85] nor about Afghan soldiers serving Rajput masters. As examples of the latter phenomenon we may cite Rana Sanga of Mewar and the Baghela raja of Bhata, both of whom received Pathans in their armies in the period after the battle of Panipat in 1526.[86] Perhaps we may go one step beyond this and suggest that Afghans and Rajputs were not really exclusive or even distinct ethnic groups at all. Fuchs found that among Indian tribes the title of Pathan, i.e. Afghan, is assumed 'by any member of the Hindu military caste who is converted to Islam', adding that 'such men find admittance into the Pathan ranks and are adopted by a clan or tribe in the same manner as some wealthy aboriginals are admitted into the Rajput caste'.[87] Similarly, if Farid's grandfather was a Rajput, this does not mean he was not an Afghan, because his being a muslim – temporarily or for good – entitled him to the name of Afghan if he should adopt that identity and live up to it, for instance by serving an Afghan lord.

This may seem quite a heretical thing to say, but I suggest that, according to the ways of the North Indian military labour market, in the pre-Mughal period, 'Afghan' as well as 'Rajput' were

83 Qanungo, *Sher Shah*, xi. See Jan Kavi, *Kayam-Khan-Raso*. The name of Qaimkhani makes one wonder whether these Rajputs were perhaps of Turkbachcha origin. In the *Waqī'at-i-Mushtāqī* an anecdote is told about a Sheikh Farid, who in Roy's opinion apparently is the future Sher Shah, in which it is said that 'Shaikh Farid Turk was a Sur', Niamatullah, *History*, 171. See also Abū'l Fażl, *Ā'īn*, II, 205, 282, where the annotator says they are Chauhans converted to Islam. Cf. the Qaim Khan, *zamīndār* of Jhunjhun, mentioned in Tikkiwal, *Jaipur*, 4–6. See also Sunita Budhwar, 'The Qayamkhani'.

84 Abu-l Fażl, *Akbarnāma*, I, 327.

85 See, for instances from Lodi family history, Hameeduddin, 'Lodis', 151n, 153n. Raja Bihar Mal Kachhwaha, the first Rajput later to enter Mughal service had a previous alliance with Hajji Khan, the Sur governor of Mewat and Ajmer to whom he offered his daughter, see Streusand, 'Formation', 120.

86 Bābur, *Bābur-Nāma*, 562. Digby, 'Dreams', 64. Niamatullah, *History*, 164n.

87 Fuchs, *Aboriginal Tribes*, 85. This practice was not restricted to tribes, see the passage from the 1911 Census Report quoted in Rowe, 'New Cauhāns', 66.

soldiers' identities rather than ethnic or genealogical denotations. It was merely to register membership of the war-band they had decided to join that, until quite late on, Indian soldiers were known by such names. It is perhaps appropriate here to quote a British recruiting officer, Garrett, who wrote on his experience during the years 1917 and 1918 in the Panjab that 'there were a large number of families of the Hindu Zamindar class of which those members who had enlisted in the army had, as a matter of course, become Sikhs'. Those staying at home remained 'hindus' until, as a result of the intensive recruitment during the later stages of the war, they were induced also to join up, in which case they also became Sikhs. 'It was', Garrett continued, 'an almost daily occurrence for – say – Ram Chand to enter our office and leave it as Ram Singh – Sikh recruit.' Finally, he observed acutely that 'conversion on other than military grounds just before the war was not common'.[88] This, in other words, was by no means 'religious conversion' as we understand the term; just as the cases of the weaver whose success made him a Sheikh and of the Muzaffarnagar farmers who became the famous Sayyids of Barha, it represented an inflection of social status or professional identity.[89] What at first sight might seem to be a change of religion, is often a device to register either recruitment or professional success whether military or otherwise. Very often the Rajput to Afghan change – and, one may add, the peasant to Rajput change – was a similar kind of affair, indicating the pervading impact of soldiering traditions on North Indian social history. The military labour market, in other words, was a major generator of socio-religious identities.

Therefore, for Sher Khan and men like him who were aiming at building up political power and entered the military labour market of North India with the treasure and the credit commensurate to their ambition, ascriptive status and ethnic identity were no barrier to recruitment. On the contrary, identities were easily adapted to and even shaped by any new alliances concluded. In this way the Turkbachchas of North India were probably entirely absorbed into the Afghan 'nation', just as was the case with many Sheikhzadas and Rajputs.

For most Rajputs, however, the switch to an Afghan identity, even under Afghan sultans, was often unnecessary, because Rajputs carried on a military tradition in their own right and they were frequently much in demand as such. Thus when Farid's father,

[88] *Census Punjab 1921*, xv, pt I, 179. [89] See chapter 1, pp. 18–9.

in about 1498, moved to the Sasaram neighbourhood of South Bihar, an understanding with the local families of Rajputs became as indispensable for him, if he was to maintain himself in his *parganas*, as it had been earlier in the Shekhawat area of Rajasthan. Fortunately, thanks to a bardic source of information dating from 1663, we know a good deal about the most important of the clans in this territory, the Rajputs of Bhojpur. A short account of their history will inevitably lead us face to face with the imposing personality of the future Sher Shah. They were a group of fighters, who had, during the course of the fourteenth century, found their identity as Ujjainiya Panwar Rajputs. They felt – or, at the latest in the seventeenth century, came to feel – that they were related to the famous Panwar royal family of Ujjain in Malwa and, indeed, they may well have migrated from that region to Hindustan as adventuring soldiers. In 1324 – their tradition has preserved the year – the clan was strong enough to successfully challenge its tribal master in South Bihar, one of the regionally dominant Chero chiefs. They now founded their own estate of Bhojput in the present-day Bhojpur district and ceased marrying their daughters to the Cheros, a decision tantamount to a declaration of political emancipation.[90] But they had to face the rulers to the north of the river Ganges, especially those of Jaunpur who coveted control of the ferry at Chausa. Manoeuvring for a position that would enable them to check traffic on the strategic Benares–Patna road just as the Cheros had done before them, they alternately met profit and disaster.

The seventeenth-century *khyāt* that is the source for the history of the Ujjainiyas of this period, records that, in 1394, the Sharqi ruler of Jaunpur crossed the ferry at Chausa with his army and halted at Baksar about twenty kilometres to the east of the ferry. Baksar was then probably, as it was 400 years later when Buchanan visited it, a holy place celebrated in Brahman legend, where assemblies of pilgrims were held several times a year in order to visit the temples and bathe in the Ganges.[91] According to the *khyāt*, some of the Sharqi ruler's 'Yavanas', i.e. foreigners, seeing a few Brahmans performing their *sandhyā* prayers on the bank of the Ganges, interfered with them. The Ujjainiya Rajputs thereupon

[90] Ambashthya, 'Accounts', 426.

[91] Buchanan, *Shahabad*, 65, 71. Bābur visited the place in 1528 and noticed 'between 40 and 50 landing-steps' on the river bank that were, however, washed away during the next monsoon, Bābur, *Bābur-Nāma*, 660. See also Cunningham, *Report 1871–72*, 64–6; C. R. P. Sinha, 'Buxar', 107–10.

took up the cause of the Brahmans of Baksar and chased the Yavanas from that place. The Sharqi ruler, however, soon defeated the Ujjainiyas and plundered Bhojpur, demolishing, the *khyāt* adds, its temples. The episode, duly emphasised in the Ujjainiya literary tradition, provided an early historical base for the social relationship which grew up between the Bhojpur Rajputs and the pilgrimage centre of Baksar.

After their defeat, the Rajputs fled to the hills and forests, began a life of pillage and plunder, and generally continued harassing the Sharqi foreigners. In 1400, as their enemy, the Jaunpur man, had died, they felt safe enough to leave the jungle and to resettle the area they considered their own. But, as with all *zamīndār*s, their negotiating position depended on their prowess as soldiers. From 1417 to 1449 and between 1455 and 1457 they again spent long years in the wilderness.[92] After these unruly years, they appear to have adjusted to paying a more or less regular tribute to the Sharqi sultans until that kingdom was merged in the Lodi empire. When Jamal Khan Sarangkhani was sent to Jaunpur as the governor of the Lodis, he soon established a hold of some kind or other over the Ujjainiya country. Once more their chief, a man by the name of Durlabh Deva, retired into the forest. This time, however, his exile did not last long. Farid's father Hasan, sent in about 1498, as we saw, by Jamal Khan to administer a stretch of half-subjugated country that was meant to yield him enough for the maintenance of 500 soldiers, knew by experience that it was best to try to come to an understanding with these Rajputs. 'Hasan Khan' the *khyāt* records, 'far from fighting with the Ujjainiyas, befriended them. Durlabh Deva accepted the suzerainty of Hasan Khan and began to rule over Bhojpur.'[93]

From this point onwards, the tone of the *khyāt* I have been quoting changes. Chronicle turns into romance. The only theme henceforward is the relationship between the Ujjainiyas and Hasan's son Farid, the future Sher Khan. I will confine myself to giving the bare facts. Badal, Durlabh Deva's eldest son, neglected by his father, who in 1500 chose the son of a younger wife as his heir-apparent, left his home accompanied by his followers and 'braved the unbearable pains of jungle-life'. Though the bard informs us that he spent his days hunting, one may assume that he kept himself going by gang warfare and pursued his feud as so many Rajputs in his situation did. In chapter 4 we shall return to the

[92] Ambashthya, 'Accounts', 427–30. [93] *Ibid.*, 431.

theme of the Rajput son, who, ostensibly as his father's rival but also as the champion of his clan, takes to the jungle and performs his *bhūmiyāvat*, his raid in search of a territory of his own. It is a role no Rajput family, it often seems, could do without for long. One day, when he was resting with his men by the side of a water-tank, Badal saw 'a young Yavan', a foreigner, on horseback coming towards him. It turned out to be Farid, who, disgusted with the hold his stepmother had gained over Hasan Khan, had left Sasaram and was now on his way to Jaunpur to try his fortune in the world. As he was all alone, Badal asked him how he would manage. Farid replied (and there is here perhaps an allusion to his later name of Sher, i.e. tiger or lion): 'Nobody teaches the art of hunting to the cub of the lion and the latter never waits for his associates in hunting.' There was plenty to eat in the forest, he said. 'Like you, I also can hunt the animals when I feel hungry and take rest by the side of the streams.' The Rajput was duly impressed. Badal and Farid had a meal sitting side by side and found their respective life stories strikingly similar. In the end, the two young men 'having swords in their hands, took vows to remain friendly to each other all through their lives and to help each other in times of misfortune. They then embraced each other and separated.'[94]

One cannot, however, help wondering whether this was all there was to it. The *khyāt* uses the incident to explain why Farid, as soon as he was called back to Sasaram in 1511 to administer his father's *parganas*, sent Badal a horse and a robe of honour and forced Durlabh Deva to allow to his eldest son his share in the management of the Ujjainiya clan estate.[95] But we know that, in 1542, Farid, then Sultan Sher Shah, told the story of how as a young man, during the same decade which Badal spent in the jungle, he had led a life that must have been in many respects similar to that of his outlawed friend. He recalled how he 'fell in with a party of thieves and highway-men, with whom he associated for some time, plundering the country all round; till one day, when seated in a boat with his new comrades, he was pursued "by his enemies", who, after a conflict, were completely victorious. Upon this, placing his bow and arrows on his head, he plunged into the water, and after swimming for three *kos* escaped with his life'.[96] It is tempting to conjecture that the bard's account of Badal and Farid's joint meal

[94] *Ibid.*, 432, 433. [95] *Ibid.*, 433, 434.
[96] Elliot and Dowson, *History*, IV, 393n. See also Abbās, *Tārīkh*, 585n, where the *Waqī'at-i-Mushtāqī* and the *Tārīkh-i-Daudī* are used.

and their oath at the water-tank telescopically sums up an association that may have been less ephemeral.

Yet it would be rash to accept Abul Fazl's view of Farid as a mere robber and to reject the report that during that same first decade of the sixteenth century, Farid must have received an administrative and even a literary training of sorts in the Jaunpur area.[97] Both some experience as an outlaw and a certain grounding in Persian documents were valuable assets for a political entrepreneur in the medieval context. The combination goes some way to explaining Farid's success after 1511 when he became the manager of the family *pargana*s. Also, the information as to Farid's liking for books is too precise to be put aside lightly and is perhaps confirmed by his being chosen about 1529 as the guardian (*atālīq*) of the Nuhani sultan's young son. On the other hand his management of his father's *pargana*s shows features that remind us of Mughal practices against the Rajputs of Western Hindustan during Jahangir's reign. 'The powerful *zamīndār*s', writes a biographer of Sher, 'were not spared, in spite of their requests. They were surrounded in their villages; the dense forests which were used by them as hide-outs were cut down; and then they were killed to the last man. It is said that not a trace was left of the old population, for the children and women who survived their men were captured and sold into slavery. And, new peasants were brought there to carry on cultivation.'[98] The evidence, therefore, seems to be that Farid, like so many of his contemporaries, owed his early achievements to a combination of soldiering and ruthless administration and that, as had been the case with his father, a friendly understanding with one or more of the local Rajput families was of great help to him.

During the 1511–18 period, as Farid lived at Sasaram, he and Badal remained allies. It was a brotherhood beyond all genealogical or ideological allegiance. Thanks to it, both prospered. Badal was in a position to collect 'thousands of Ujjainiyas' around him. The term Ujjainiya soon came in general use to denote soldiers recruited and led by members of the Ujjainiya clan. Only a few of them, however, can have belonged to the kin of the Bhojpur Rajputs; the remainder must have been mustered from the numerous men who could easily be engaged by anybody whom luck appeared to favour, especially in the so-called Purab area of Eastern Hindustan, which was, or anyway would become, a

[97] Abu-l Fazl, *Akbarnāma*, I, 327, 328. Abbās, *Tārīkh*, 14.
[98] *Ibid.*, 96, 107, 108. Siddiqi, *Sher Shah Sur*, 18, see also 72.

famous recruiting area and in whose centre Bhojpur and Sasaram were situated. 'Ujjainiya', in other words, rather than a genealogical concept or a clan name, now became a soldiers' identity, the name of an open category of fighting men whose mere recruitment under Ujjainiya leadership caused them to be labelled as Rajputs. Some of them, of course, may even earlier have considered themselves as Rajputs, but Bhumihars, Brahmans and many categories of peasants may also have been amongst them.

Badal soon had a sizeable number of auxiliaries in his pay and he must have appreciably added to Farid's strength. But when, in 1518, Farid left for Agra to try his luck there and when Durlabh Deva died soon after, a struggle for the Bhojpur *gaddī* inevitably followed. Badal was killed by one of his half-brothers. His wife with her two sons, Gajpat and Bairishal, fled and passed the traditional number – often met in ballads and folksongs for periods of adventure and hardship spent away from home – of twelve years 'amidst the jungle people in the deep ravines of the mountains'. Not until 1532, when Gajpat was eighteen years old, did his mother send the boys to serve her husband's old ally Sher Khan, who was now building up his strength in South Bihar and who received them well. Gajpat and Bairishal now collected 'two thousand Ujjainiyyas' and killed their rival uncle with Sher Khan's help whereupon Gajpat was seated on the *gaddī*.[99] The Bhojpur Rajputs, under Gajpat's leadership, amply repaid Sher Khan during the following years, rendering invaluable military assistance. During the battle of Surajgarh in which Sher Khan defeated the Bengal army, he put 3,000 picked Pathans and 2,000 Ujjainiyas in his first line.[100] The battle was won and, according to the *khyāt*, the Bengali general was killed at the hands of Gajpat. Sher Khan was much pleased. 'All the spoils of war, comprising elephants, horses and other equipments, which had fallen into the hands of Maharaja (Gajpat) were allowed to be retained by him. At the time of departure of the Maharaja (Gajpat) he (Sher Khan) tied with his own hand the bejewelled sword to hang round his (Maharaja Gajpati's) waist, bound his arm with a jewelled armlet, gave a string of pearls round his neck, fixed a bejewelled Kalangi in his Sirpech (headdress), gave a horse, head-to-foot dress and a sword for prince Bairishal, and gave Buxar as jagir to him (Maharaja Gajpat).' Again, the relationship between the Ujjainiyas and the pilgrimage centre is stressed. Soon after this, the chronicle said,

[99] Ambashthya, 'Accounts', 434, 435. [100] *Ibid.*, 437.

Gajpat brought his new fief of Baksar under his control and went to live there along with his Ujjainiyas.[101]

Though the published part of the *khyāt* unfortunately stops here, there is every reason to believe that the relationship between Sher Khan and Gajpat was a lasting one. It is reported that Sher Khan, presumably after he had become sultan, conferred the title of raja and the districts of Rohtas and Shahabad on Gajpat.[102] The relationship was indeed a necessary one from the point of view of both, firstly because they were close neighbours, their headquarters lying only some 70 kilometres apart, and secondly, because each of them compensated the weakness of the other. Since the struggle for the succession to the Bhojpur *gaddī* of 1519–20, the rivalry in the Ujjainiya family had never stopped and Gajpat, though, as we saw, with Sher Khan's help successful against his uncle in about 1533, soon found himself faced with another rival, a cousin of his by the name of Dalpat. Just like Gajpat, Dalpat had been driven out of the Bhojpur country as a young boy with his widowed mother. He had found refuge with his mother's brother at Arail in the present-day Allahabad district and stayed there until, in 1538, his uncle produced him before Humayun and got a Mughal firman for the conferment of Bhojpur issued in his favour. For a while, he became the master of the family estate and Gajpat retired to Sher Khan, his protector. Thus, Sher Khan and Humayun each had their own clientele among the Ujjainiyas; the dividing line between the great protagonists of Hindustan split even a relatively obscure Rajput family on the frontiers of the sultanate. Though Gajpat, no doubt with Sher Khan's help, recovered the *gaddī* and could maintain himself there until his death in 1577, the rivalry between the branches of the family would survive him.[103]

His lineage's factionalism rendered Gajpat dependent on continuing help from his powerful neighbour at Sasaram. But on the other hand the alliance with the Ujjainiyas proved an equally invaluable asset for Sher Shah. As Rajput chiefs and as the protectors by heritage of the Brahmans of the pilgrimage centre of Baksar, they had access to the recruiting grounds of Eastern Hindustan to an extent that complemented Sher Khan's personal style of recruitment. Though Sher Khan's entrepreneurship as a warlord allowed him to rise above the segmentary bickerings of the Afghan aristocrats, he could neither demilitarise Northern India

101 *Ibid.*, 438. 102 *Imperial Gazetteer*, XI, 378.

103 Ambashthya, 'Accounts', 439, 440, and genealogical table opposite p. 424.

nor dissolve the old ties and the security that bound locality, lineage and old identities to hundreds of leaders all over his realm. He needed these *zamīndārs* as allies as much as they needed his treasure and loot. Achievement and ascription had to strike a balance of some sort.

It is certain that Sher Khan tried hard to do just this. He had more *zamīndārī* contingents like that of the Ujjainiyas in his army. It is only because the Ujjainiya clan was to survive as an important family locally, recognised as Panwars by the Rajputs of Rajasthan, and allowed a place in a Rajasthani bardic *khyāt*, that we know so much about their association with Sher. In any case there appears to be some reason to assume that, though he emphasised the direct recruitment of individual soldiers to be disciplined and paid under his personal supervision, and though he could afford to avoid loose alliances with aristocratic Afghan warlords, Sher Khan must have made frequent use of more or less powerful non-Afghan middlemen, whether Turkbachcha, Rajput or 'tribal'. Often these men commanded resources Sher had no access to. In addition to their kinship ties and the historical identities they represented, they had patrimonial estates and forts of their own. They may also to a certain extent have engaged in trade and the asking of protection money from caravans. They may have been horse dealers as both Bahlul Lodi himself and Sher Khan's grandfather Ibrahim had once been.[104] But above all, such men were dealers in manpower. And because much of the military labour force of Hindustan was bound to remain beyond Sher's immediate control, he could not do without these men in his attempt to rearrange the best bits of it and then direct these units to empire building.

To sum up, such were the conditions of the segmented military society of sixteenth-century India, that Sher Khan was to some extent debarred from directly tapping the human resources of the Turkbachchas, the Farmulis, the Rajputs, the Bhumihars and the Brahmans of Hindustan. He needed men like the three 'Turkoman' brothers in the fort of Chunar and the Ujjainiya subcontractors. In the lower Doab, the Gautam Rajput family of Argal, to cite another example, fought several battles for Sher Khan against Humayun.[105] On the other hand, there seems to have been only a single Afghan nobleman of old respectability put in charge of a

[104] Niamatullah, *History*, 27, 28; Abu-l Faẓl, *Akbarnāma*, I, 326. Roy, however, denies that Bahlul was ever a trader, though his father and grandfather were.

[105] Growse, 'Notes', 155, 161.

sarkār and given a high *suwār* (cavalry) rank in Sher Shah's empire. Other members of the old aristocracy were only given small maintenance fiefs.[106] If, therefore, Sher's army was by no means entirely recruited by Sher himself directly from the peasantry, he was clearly in undisputed command and could choose his own companions in leadership.

As commanders, then, Sher chose quite a few Afghans, though practically all of them descended from 'obscure families the members of which never appear to have occupied any important position in . . . the Lodi period'. Amongst them were the manumitted slaves Haji Khan Sultani and Habib Khan Sultani. The Abyssinian slave or ex-slave known as Habsh Khan whom Sher employed to superintend the building of a citadel in the fort of Rohtas, is another example.[107] Then there are the three sons of one of his slaves, who cannot have been an Afghan by birth as only free men could claim that identity. Two of these sons at different times bore the title of Khawas Khan, the second of whom became Sher's most trusted and prominent commander.[108] It is possible that the soldiers of this family of slaves successfully arrogated to themselves the name of Afghans; the second Khawas Khan anyway seems to have done so. Another of Sher Shah's outstanding military leaders was Barmazid Gaur, or Kaur. Qanungo contends that this man was a Gaur Rajput called Brahmajit. Siddiqi, a later biographer, points out that this man's name was Kaur, i.e. 'one-eyed'. If this is so, then the lack of a community name may, as in the case of Khawas Khan, indicate low social origins. Anyway, we must assume that many thousands of this commander's soldiers also were 'hindus'.[109] Even in the Lodi period, for the matter, it was a common occurrence for an Afghan amir to have non-Afghan personal retainers and, as one instance shows, for hundreds of Meo tribals – from Rajasthan – to serve as guards in the contingents of an Afghan commander. One can only guess at the composition of the army of Shujaat Khan Sur, who was another of Sher Shah's great commanders, and who led the household troops of the sultan.[110] The Surs, though not as aristocratic as the Farmulis, might, like the latter, be described as spurious Afghans, in the same sense as in the

106 Siddiqi, *Sher Shah Sur*, 44. 107 *Ibid.*, 43; Buchanan, *Journal*, 51.

108 Abbās, *Tārīkh*, 100, 261 and *passim*; Abu-l Fazl, *Akbarnāma*, I, 615. Badaoni, *Muntakhab*, I, 537; Siddiqi, *Sher Shah Sur*, 66–87.

109 Qanungo, *Sher Shah*, 419–21; Abbās, *Tārīkh*, 514–18; Siddiqi, *Sher Shah Sur*, 88–95. See for Khawas Khan's 'hindu' noblemen and retainers, *ibid.* 79, 80.

110 *Ibid.*, 125–9, 252; Niamatullah, *History*, 120, 176.

nineteenth century some Rajputs were spoken of as spurious, i.e. as not answering to the then generally accepted genealogical or ethnic criteria of historical identities. I no longer accept these rigid criteria and suspect that in the ranks of these armies social identities could be achieved in a manner that was diffuse and dynamic. Indeed, if aristocratic notions about lineage had as little place in Sher's dispensation as I think they had and if so many of Sher Khan's commanders were slaves in the process of emancipation or adventurers and peasants in the process of achieving an Afghan or Rajput identity, we are far removed from the world of caste and 'ascribed' status that for so long was regarded as central to the social history of India.

Abbas Khan could be silent about his pluriformity and could present a picture of Afghan harmony, because clearly ethnic conflict was not a prominent feature in Sher Shah's camp. As we saw, Sher Shah had built his army not just as a loose confederation composed of Afghan factions and other ethnic groups but as a distributive structure of comparatively well-paid and disciplined soldiers. Badauni rightly remarks on the preciousness to Sher Shah of the individual trooper.[111] During the 1530s, luck as well as shrewd politics had made him the master of huge treasures. After 1540 an energetic fiscal policy remained a feature of his reign. And inasmuch as he succeeded in securing for his men a fair distribution of the resources of the realm, he pushed ethnic and factionalist rivalry into the background. The most important institution of Sher Shah's reign was no longer the clan or a particular tribe, nor the court, but the army camp. The physical expression of this was the earthen entrenchment with which Sher, to the surprise of his contemporaries, invariably surrounded his camp. Within this clearly defined little world, Sher Shah's word was law. The citizen of the camp was the common soldier rather than the noble confederate. Abbas Khan's history seems irrefutably to testify to Sher Shah's success in integrating widely differing groups in a polity characterised by a new distributive intensity. For these men, one might say, the opportunities of an aggressive and enterprising kingship carried more weight than any pedigree or bond of ethnicity. The challenges of ethnic loyalties, if any, and of the Lodi heritage of segmentary, aristocratic politics, were largely overcome by direct recruitment based on merit, a leadership that owed very little to ascribed status, alliances with minor commanders, and the

[111] Badaoni, *Muntakhab*, I, 477.

lavish distributions of, first, the windfall of loot, and, later, once the empire was established, of the revenues of a regular agrarian administration.

But did this really work in the end? If aristocratic solidarity and the politics of alliance that had been the props of the Lodi segmentary state were rejected in order to build a more stable – perhaps one should say 'early modern' – state, what sources of legitimacy and integrative solidarity did it depend upon? Was Sher Shah, to use the idiom of political science, as successful a creator of solidarity as he was an administrator?

Admittedly, in Indian political science – I am referring to Kautiliya's *Arthaśāstra* – treasure (*koṣ*) is one of the essential elements of kingship and, as a source of legitimacy, seems to have occupied at least as high a place as the *khutba* (the official Friday prayer in the name of the sultan) and the *sikka* (right to coinage) derived from Islamic tradition. There is indeed a political quality about Indian hoarded wealth and treasure trove as is testified by Indian folklore. Riches in Indian stories are often miraculously unearthed, almost as Sher Shah found his, and states immediately spring into existence. A hidden treasure is a hidden kingdom and its rediscovery was enough for the rays of royalty to shine again in the world. Such was the power of the treasure brought to light by Prithiraja at Nagaur in the twelfth century, 'amounting to seven millions of gold, the deposit of ancient days'. And as late as the eighteenth century, a Bihari poem proudly and at some length explained the emergence of the Darbhanga kingdom as based on the plunder of an enemy's camp.[112] To bury a hoard with one's comrades-in-arms was, inversely, the establishment of a bond that would one day find its consummation in royalty. A hidden treasure was the centre of a kingdom to come and of a political solidarity that did not require the actual distribution of its riches to be real. The results of one of Sher Khan's battles with the armies of Bengal in about 1534 was that, as an eyewitness remembered later, 'countless booty' had fallen into his hands and into those of his companions; it consisted of 400,000 gold coins (*mohurs*). Sher proposed not to send this money to Humayun, their nominal overlord, but to bury it for the time being and to covenant with an oath on the Qoran to maintain secrecy about the place of the burial. The decision amounted to the establishment of Sher's hidden kingdom, which would take many years to become manifest. One

[112] Tod, *Annals*, I, 300; Narayan Singh and Grierson, 'Battle', 16, 35.

of the friends (a non-muslim?) asked to be exempted from the oath, saying his word would be enough. And it was, because, though the allies never had an opportunity to return to the place, their four lakh covenant was not broken as long as their gold remained where it was, serving as the pledge of their faith to each other and contributing to the status of its chief even from its secret vault.[113]

Meanwhile, Sher Shah did portion out most of his hoarded and fiscal wealth. The widening circle of people sharing in the largesse of the pretender was the reality of his expanding kingdom. His gift economy seemed tantamount to a new political nation that cut across ethnic and communal boundaries. To Jaisi, the great mystic, who wrote his tale of love, the 'Padmavati', during Sher Shah's reign, this was the essence of his legitimacy as a king. None of the great rulers of former ages, he sang, equalled Sher Shah. His treasures, like the Ocean and Mount Meru, were inexhaustible. 'The kettle-drum of his generosity soundeth at his court, and the fame thereof has gone even across the ocean. The world touched this Sun, and became of gold compact, so that poverty fled and went beyond the borders of his kingdom. He who but once approacheth him and asketh, for all his life is free from hunger and from nakedness. Even that [King of old] who performed ten horse-sacrifices – even he gave not holy gifts like him. So generous hath Sultan Sher Shah been born upon the world, that none hath e'er been like him, or will be, nor doth anyone give such gifts.'[114]

Yet, though Sher made most of his wealth politically, there were problems. A large part of the next chapter will be devoted to these. In order to draw attention to the risk of distributive politics irrespective of 'primordial' identity or ethnic claims, suffice it here to mention once more Sher's general Khawas Khan. Abul Fazl said of him that he extorted money from people with one hand and distributed it with the other in order to gain popularity. There were always several hundred *faqīrs* attached to his household: '*malang* (a kind of muslim ascetic), *Langotaband* (Hindu ascetics who put on only loin cloth), *Yaran-i-Pyara* (also muslim ascetics), *jogis* and munis (Brahmins, exclusively devoted to religion) and *gibrs* (fire-worshippers)', who received daily allowances of money, grain and cooked food. Often there were lavish meals with separate menus for hindus and muslims. Sufis assembled in his house every Thursday night when there was music. Because of this, there were differences of opinion with the orthodox amongst the muslim

[113] Roy, 'New Light', 60, 61. [114] Shirreff, *Padmāvatī*, 14.

learned 'and disagreement arose with regard to the upholding of the rights of the soldiery'.[115] This case may indicate that indiscriminate distributive practice, ideologically based on heterodox eclecticism, could be found unpalatable by the orthodox *'ulamā* of Islam.

The answer could be to try and avoid an alliance with orthodox Islam, just as Sher Shah tried to avoid all alliances with powerful identities. But an understanding with *zamīndār*s and with Afghan troopers was still essential for him and to ignore the *'ulamā* later in his reign would not be easy for him, as we shall see. There are several questions suggested by Khawas Khan's predicament. What exactly was the price which one paid (and which Sher Shah tried hard to avoid paying) for an alliance in Indian medieval politics? If India's multiplicity of identities represented as many integrative concepts, as many communities of memory and expectation, what chance did Sher Shah stand of transcending this pluriformity? And if he could not altogether avoid all alliances, what channels of communication could he establish, what balance could be struck between allies whose claims clashed with each other?

These questions are relevant to Sher Shah's relationship with the learned islamic community, but they should equally be asked with reference to his attitude towards the Rajputs of Central India with whom he would clash in a dramatic way. I shall now enquire into the character of these Rajputs. So far I have, through a case study of Sher Shah, looked at the demand side of the military labour market and to the ways he struggled to overcome the restrictions the abundance of its fighting men put on any endeavour at state formation in North India. I shall now take a closer look at the supply side, i.e. at the world of the armed peasantry of Hindustan. I hope to show, that the Rajputs Sher Shah found on his way to power, represent the most articulate and characteristic identity that North India's armed peasantry produced in medieval times.

[115] Siddiqi, *Sher Shah Sur*, 76–9. See also Roy, 'Some Interesting Anecdotes', 226.

3
The Rajput of pre-Mughal North India

Settled agriculture and early urbanisation have long been regarded as important features of Indian civilisation. But recently, attention has also been drawn again to the pastoral, trekking element in North and Central Indian history.[1] The martial character of mobile groups which was an indispensable feature in their survival strategies, made them a factor in state formation and in politics generally. Though it will never be possible to fully write their history, it is clear that in Western India and in Hindustan – the area between the Panjab in the west and Bengal in the east – a large number of wandering groups of fighters rose to prominence throughout the medieval period. Some of these flourished for centuries, others fell back into obscurity much sooner. There is, however, some evidence to suggest that, between the thirteenth and fifteenth centuries, a greater number of such pastoralist bands than previously succeeded in achieving, and passing on to their heirs, some measure of landed status. The Ujjainiyas of the preceding chapter are one of them. It is possible that agricultural expansion and demographic growth during the sultanate period of North Indian history were among the causes of the emergence of these local gentries. They did not constitute endogamous castes, but formed largely open status groups of clans, lineages, or even families and individuals some of which were connected to each other by exogamous connubial ties. Inevitably, a certain group identity grew up amongst these families: it was summed up in the name of Rajput. This word literally means 'son of a king'. At first used to denote various individuals who achieved such statuses as 'horse-soldier', 'trooper' or 'headman of a village', and then pretended to be connected with the family of

[1] Bayly, *Rulers*.

some king, it became a generic name for this military and landed class as a whole.[2]

These men were by no means each other's equals in wealth and opportunity. During the sixteenth and seventeenth centuries, the top layer of Rajputs, encouraged by the openings presented by the Mughal state and helped by the expertise of their bards, tended to close ranks and to articulate new norms of Rajput behaviour. Bards had always encouraged their Rajput employers to assume aristocratic self-images closely linked with myths of origin that established their status as *kṣatriya*s and traced back their genealogies to, for instance, the great dynasties of ancient Indian history. But now the political power and social status of the more successful lineages tended to be legitimised exclusively in the language of descent and kinship. This idiom, of course, was deeply rooted in the traditions of Indian royalty, but from the sixteenth century onwards, the political opportunities of the Mughal court and the emphasis the Mughals themselves placed on genealogy gave it a new vigour and largely pushed into the background the more ancient character of the Rajputs as an open status group. The tendency to interpret Rajput history in genealogical terms was later inherited by Tod and other British Indian administrators. Recently, this historiographical tradition has been continued by Fox.[3] But it does not sum up the whole of Rajput reality. It is clear that the literary tradition of the bards and chroniclers of Rajasthan, though it preserves invaluable material, obscures a good deal of pre-seventeenth-century North Indian history and completely leaves out of consideration the survival of the original Rajput phenomenon elsewhere, particularly in Hindustan. There one finds, until late in the nineteenth century, on the farther edges of recognised Rajputhood, a large number of clans with traditions of service and fighting who were no longer recognised as fit marriage partners by the aristocracy. They were the so-called 'spurious' Rajputs, whose 'rajputisation' never seemed fully achieved and who have consequently been sadly neglected in the bardic literature which, sponsored by the elite families and codified by Tod, finally came to dominate Rajput consciousness even in Hindustan.

[2] Sircar, *Guhilas*, 16. Sircar considers the word Rajput and its derivatives as 'titles of feudatory chiefs or the nobility'. But these titles must have been the result of successful military entrepreneurship as expressed in the other meanings he quotes. Cf. Ziegler, 'Seventeenth Century Chronicles', 140, 141. See for the exogamy of the medieval aristocracy, Sircar, *Guhilas*, 18.

[3] Fox, *Kin, Clan, Raja, and Rule*.

I suggest, therefore, that, since the late sixteenth century, something like a new Rajput Great Tradition emerged which could recognise little else than unilineal kin bodies as the elements of which genuine Rajput history ought to be made up. By the middle of the seventeenth century, Rajasthan and particularly Mewar had become the seat of this new Rajput genealogical orthodoxy. Outside that region, to be accepted as fit marriage partners of the great families of Rajasthan and to be recognised as genealogically pure in Rajasthani bardic literature was valued by many as among the marks of the highest stage of rajputisation. The Baghelas of Rewa, for instance, whose most outstanding family emerged from obscurity late in the fifteenth century, later married girls from Rajasthan aristocratic families; and the Ujjainiyas of Bhojpur were, about 1665, included in a Rajasthani account of the Panwars, which entailed recognition of their claim to be connected with one of the great dynasties of ancient Indian history.[4] But, in Hindustan and Central India, there were few groups who achieved as much as the Baghelas or the Ujjainiyas, though the myths of origin and the genealogies they put forward were perhaps no more fictitious than those of their more prestigious brethren. They continued to represent, though by sheer necessity, the older, medieval tradition of soldiering, because, even if they imitated the new genealogical fashion, they were rarely allowed a full share in the prestige of the aristocracy redefined in terms of descent and finally even of caste.

The Bundelas offer an example of a clan who, despite their military prowess in the seventeenth-century Mughal armies, could never fully make the transition from the old Rajput identity to the new. Innumerable other lineages and clans, put down as Rajputs in the nineteenth-century British censuses and settlement reports, never attained the celebrity of the Ujjainiyas or even of the Bundelas and remained remote from the Great Tradition elaborated mainly at the princely courts of Rajasthan. Thus North Indian ethnohistory shows a continuum between at one end, mainly in Rajasthan, a genealogically defined Rajput aristocracy and a centre and opposite end occupied by a variety of peasant groups and tribal elites, largely in Hindustan, whose values and behaviour kept alive a more ancient layer of Rajputhood. This older, pastoralist tradition, because it did not attain bardic legitimacy and largely lost its claim to *kṣatriya* status, continued to be served by a folkloristic idiom with Puranic overtones. In this idiom the 'spurious' Rajputs,

[4] *Rewah State Gazetteer*, 13, 18, 108–11; Ambashthya, 'Accounts', 421.

but also Ahirs and other Rajputising peasants and pastoralists expressed their values. These groups retained, to a much larger degree than those of 'Rajputana', the sociological openness of the ancient Rajput character. Moreover, as the bards reinterpreted the issues of rank, values and ideals and formulated the new Great Tradition that dominates Rajput historiography to the present day, this older layer was left outside the scope of Mughal elite culture. Yet, as soldiers and peasants, they were anything but a spent force. At various moments, until far into the nineteenth century, their role would indeed prove decisive in North Indian history.

What then exactly was the character of the original Rajputs of medieval India that was lost from sight by the reinterpretation of the bards? To answer this question, let us turn to the folkloristic tradition that even today continues to express the pastoral migratory tradition we are in search of. Until as late as the nineteenth century, there was no lack of men opting for a life spent as errant soldier, migrant labourer, or pack-animal trader. Perhaps the meaning of Rajput, in this context, is not properly conveyed by the literal translation 'son of a king'; it is also the proud name of all adventuring young men, or *jawāns*, in search of a truly paternal and kingly patron. Historically, such men were far more numerous than the members of the successful aristocratic lineages of North India. I shall focus on them in this chapter and, to begin with, will consider some of the oral literature that sheds light on their values and way of life. Then, I shall turn to social reality and, particularly, to sixteenth-century Malwa and the Rajput military leaders of that area. By taking this approach I shall suggest that, whatever Fox or the historians of Rajasthan may have put forward, political structures and state–locality relations in pre-British North India were by no means exclusively, or even mainly, based on kinship.[5]

The warrior-ascetic in song, ballad, and legend

One of the most widespread motifs of Indian folklore and, for that matter, literature is that of separation, especially the separation between a travelling husband and his wife. Indian lyrics often take the woman's point of view and so the poets, though telling us all about the yearnings of women left behind in lonely homes, do not find it worth while enlightening us about their spouses' whereabouts or even about the reason for their departure.

[5] Washbrook, 'Review of Fox', 364.

Thus the *virahinī*, the woman separated from her husband, has become one of the most common heroines of medieval literature, including early Hindi literature. The *bārahmāsā*, i.e. 'twelve months', poetry which expresses her feelings of abandonment and desire, has for many centuries occupied an extraordinarily prominent place among Indo-aryan literary genres.[6] But the historian, however much enthralled by the beauty of these songs, cannot help wondering to what extent the literary theme of separation, so popular in Northern India, reflects a tradition of mobility and seasonal migration among the peasants of Hindustan. This is not to deny that the *bārahmāsā* genre, as always in literature, answers to principles that are all its own. Nevertheless, as Charlotte Vaudeville has remarked, it is also deeply rooted in peasant life and in the seasonal changes that accompany the annual agricultural cycle. Indeed, the sparse facts these songs suggest concerning the social background of separation, arouse the curiosity of the student of history.

The 'twelve months' songs seem to have developed from shorter 'four months' lyrical verses in which the *virahinīs* of the village sang about their loneliness during the rainy monsoon months. During that time of year travel had become impossible and the chances of a reunion with the beloved were dim indeed. In one of these songs a woman describes her feelings during the first month of the rains, Asadh:

> All my friends sleep with their husbands,
> But my own husband is a cloud in another land.[7]

Though not all 'twelve months' poetry would have as its motif the separation of husband and wife, almost all of the oldest songs of the type, dating from before 1600 and still closest to the original 'four months' model, were *viraha*, i.e. separation, *bārahmāsās*. The permanent background, as Vaudeville suggests, is the seasonal vagabondage of the husband: 'In a pastoralist, mercantile and soldiering society, the rainy season that brings home the husband is the season blessed and looked forward to by women.' The absent hero is generally represented as a *banijārā*, a merchant, or as a *sevaka*, a mercenary soldier in the service of a distant lord.[8] But

6 Vaudeville, *Dhola-Mārū*, 104; Vaudeville, *Bārahmāsā*, XXX.

7 Archer, 'Seasonal Songs', 247. This song is called *caumāsā*, i.e. four months, but consists of six months.

8 Vaudeville, *Bārahmāsā*, V, XII, XXV, XXVI, XXX; Grierson, 'Some Bihari Folk-songs', 200, 207, 209. *Banijārā* differs only in spelling from the better known *banjārā*.

that is about all the information the singers yield about their travelling husbands.

Other lyrical songs, however, are concerned with the same emotions and, though just as feminine in character as the 'twelve months' poetry, give a few more suggestions as to the reasons for the husband's absence. In the late nineteenth century, women of Eastern Gorakhpur knew a song in which it was said:

> The mango trees have blossomed,
> And the mahuas dropped their flowers.
> By whom shall I send a message?
> Ah, heartless one, leave thy service (*naukaria*).

The woman then tells the messenger that her beloved is to be found sitting in the *nawāb*'s assembly (*kachahrī*). The word *naukarī*, though nowadays used for more menial kinds of services, seems in traditional India generally to refer to long-distance service as a retainer, for instance in the British East India Company's army;[9] In nineteenth-century Bihar, a *nokar* was a servant paid in cash by the year.[10] Sepoys are now and then mentioned in these songs, e.g. in one, also from Eastern Gorakhpur, where a soldier (*sipāhī*) abandons his wife after a minor quarrel, whereas in yet another, Baiswari, folk-song a sepoy leaves his mistress to return home.[11]

Ballads treat the same subject. The 'Visaladevarasa', of which the written version was composed – in Old Marwari – about 1450 AD, tells of a raja who leaves his palace to perform *ūlaga* in Orissa. The editor of the text explains this term as 'service as a courtier' by one who leaves wife and home to serve a foreign king.[12] The poem is still very much written from the point of view of the raja's wife whose lyrics, including a *bārahmāsā* song, dominate the work. As so often in Indian literature, the woman of the house tries to make her travel-loving husband change his mind. She pleads:

> O Lord, who tells you to go into service as a courtier?
> (When the master is away,)
> There is no money in the house and no salt in the pitcher,
> And the low-born women quarrel in the house.
> Homes oppressed with debt are unpleasant,

9 Fraser, 'Folklore', 5–7; Sita Ram, *From Sepoy to Subadar*, 6.
10 Grierson, 'Selected Specimens', verse 494.
11 Fraser, 'Folklore', 12–14; Jogendra Nath Rae, 'Baiswari Folk Songs', 245–6.
12 Smith, *Vīsaladevarāsa*, 57. See also Vaudeville, *Dhola-Mārū*, 113–14, and *Bārahmāsā*, 22.

Whether the master goes off as a *yogī*,
Or whether he goes in shame into service as a courtier.

But the raja does set off to Orissa and in the end it turns out not to have been a dishonourable affair at all. For when, after twelve years, the two are reunited, the raja brings home 'wealth and a store of riches', swift horses and four big elephants, diamonds and precious stones.[13]

The theme of the earnings of the husband-vagabond that justify his absence from home is also found in the 'Dhola-Maru', another Old Marwari ballad. In this poem the hero, in an attempt to persuade his wife to let him go, proposes successively to go and serve the Idar raja, in present-day Gujarat, whence he will return with jewels, to go and hire himself out as an archer in Multan and bring back horses and, lastly, to go to Kutch and get hold of a camel of pure strain.[14] In these proposals it is impossible to distinguish between long-distance trade and the service of a distant lord. Indeed, the peregrinations of merchants and soldiers belong to the same cluster of pastoralist activities. And very often, it seems, these can only successfully be performed in the garb of a *yogī*, or ascetic.

As the case of the Gosains and Nagas of medieval India shows, asceticism and war are by no means incompatible. The same is true of trade and asceticism. A Bhojpuri folk-song says about Shiva, the god-ascetic:

Mahadev has gone to the East to trade (*banijiyā*),
And four months are passing away.
Gaura sits on a chair and watches the road, saying
'When will my ascetic (*tapasi*) come?'.[15]

Whatever the motive, to leave one's home and kin alone for any extended period of time, will always require an ascetic's effort and in itself almost turns a man into a *yogī*. There used to be no legend more popular throughout the whole of Northern India than the 'Song of Gopi Chand'. Versions recorded in South Bihar, a country of fighting men and a recruiting area *par excellence*, stressed that Gopi Chand was by caste (*jatiyā*) a *kṣatriya*, but at the same time 'from his birth' 'an ascetic (*jogī*) of the highest degree (*siddha*)' – a combination that, as I suggested, certainly makes sense for long-distance soldiering.[16] Rajput soldiers from the area must have fully

13 Smith, *Vīsaladevarāsa*, 125, 261, 277.
14 Vaudeville, *Dhola-Mārū*, 36, 74.
15 Grierson, 'Some Bihari Folk-Songs', 236.
16 Grierson, 'Two Versions', 40, 49.

understood the scene describing his farewell to his mother, when she caught him by his clothes and said: 'First pay me the price of my milk and then go and become an ascetic.' Gopi Chand confessed: 'Thy milk is beyond price.' His mother then gives him the milk as a free gift, whereupon Gopi Chand, in a final effort to make himself absolutely clear, restates the matter once more, saying: 'Mother, the day of meeting me again is gone far off. Say not, mother, "It is I who have given the free gift." It is God [Parameshvar] who giveth me my birth, and decideth my fate.' The ascetic *kṣatriya* now goes off to see his sister, who is married and lives away in Bengal. She does not recognise him and, as a result, at first does not treat him well. In one version of the legend, the discovery of the *yogī*'s identity makes her heart burst and she dies, which enables Gopi Chand to revive her with the help of the ambrosia (*amrit*) that has, as the result of his good deeds, accumulated in his little finger. The meaning of this episode probably is that it completes Gopi Chand's emancipation from 'primordial' and kinship ties. Another version does not leave us in doubt as to what interpretation to put on this family visit. Here, his sister, overcome by shame, curses herself and is swallowed up by the earth; the legend then terminates by remarking: 'And thus was broken the relationship of brother and sister between these two.'[17]

Surely, it was a radical decision to shave one's head and to leave home as a *sādhu*. But strong urges, either economic or psychological, pushed out many a young man. In yet another song, recorded in Rangpur, there is not even any choice. Here Gopi Chand is not only childless at the age of eighteen but, worse, it has been foretold that he will die unless he renounces his home. Yet, he wavers and is afraid that, if he becomes a wanderer (*athit*), he will easily lose his *kṣatriya* birth (*kul*) and his Baniya caste (*jāti*).[18] And it is true that the pilgrim, the wanderer, the knight bachelor, or whatever name one gives him, cannot retain his old identity, though he can take it up again after his duty is done.

The song of Gopi Chand, though here quoted from versions recorded in the nineteenth century, was already well known to Malik Muhammad Jaisi when he wrote his *Padmāvatī* in Sher Shah's reign. In this long poem, the raja left his kingdom as a *yogī* and went in search of Padmavati whom, in the end, he won after

17 *Ibid.*, 39, 46, 53–5.
18 Grierson, 'Song of Manik Chandra', verses 281, 691, 695.

many austerities. It is true that the meaning is mystical rather than sociological. Yet, the imagery used is taken from ancient folklore:

> Lover-like he took his viol in his hand,
> His body was uncared for, his mind
> was distraught and drooping: love
> was fixed [in his mind] and a
> tangled knot of hair was on his head.

He refuses to consult the astrologers about an auspicious day of departure:

> [He who is on] love's path does not
> look to days or hours. . . Does the
> distraught widow ask the wise
> men [if it is an auspicious day for
> committing Sati], and, [if not],
> remain at home and arrange the
> household utensils?

As expected, his mother beseeches him to remain seated on his throne and enjoy it, but he says: 'If kinship and enjoyment were good things, Gopi Chand would not have engaged in Yoga.' And to his queens: 'You have heard of the wise King Bharthari: he had sixteen hundred queens in his palace: they cherished the soles of his feet on their breasts: but he became a yogi and took none of them with him.' So in the palace nine *mans* of pearls were broken and ten *mans* of bangles (which women break when they become widows) were smashed. Sixteen thousand valiant youths became the king's disciples: his army of consecrated warriors, clad in red dyed clothes, who would serve him in his war of love.[19]

When the *naukar*, soldier, or mendicant begins his career and leaves his home for the first time, a change comes over him. From now on he will acquire new norms of behaviour that will set him apart from those whom he has left behind in the village. In the 'Song of Bijai Mal', recorded in the Shahabad District, the very centre of the Bhojpuri recruiting area, the hero's elder brother's wife, his *bhaujī*, tells him regretfully on the day of his departure: 'From to-day you have begun to forget me.'[20] A new life begins. The ascetic identity has taken over.

This also applies to marriage, which becomes largely dormant

[19] Shirreff, *Padmāvatī*, 87–92.

[20] Grierson, 'Song of Bijai Mal', 141.

and is only revived during the days of furlough (*chuṭi*) as in the following song:

> My lord, in what month wilt thou return?
> My beloved has gone away, and entered into *nokari*,
> Leaving me alone in the house.
> He took two or four days *chuṭi* and came,
> And went away at dawn.[21]

Obviously, there is a certain tension between a man's marriage and his *naukarī* or service to distant duties. On a religious level this is expressed in the above-quoted 'Song of Bijai Mal' by the hero himself who, asked by his wife to 'stay here but one night', tells her: 'Hear me, o slender wife. . .I have placed the goddess Durga round my neck and if I do as you desire, all the gods will be displeased with me. I would be killed in the open battle-field.'[22] Marriage and the ascetic's identity should be carefully kept apart. But they also complement each other; if the balance between the two can no longer be maintained, that means the end of a harmonious life or even of one's physical existence. On a more homely level, this was the dilemma of Bir Kuar, the Ahir cult hero of West Bihar, who was caught in the conflicting claims of his family and his herd. His wife complained to him that he treated his she-buffalo like a co-wife: 'It wakes you and takes you from me when you are sleeping.' He admits so much and says he would rather sell her, his lawful wife, than not pair his buffalo. And when she asks him how that will work: 'Who will nod to you when you talk?', he answers: 'The buffalo will nod to me as I talk' – and concludes that, if it doesn't, he will sell his buffalo, become a *sādhu* and go to a strange land. That is the risk of failure. But for those who succeed in balancing family on the one hand and *naukarī* or pastoral migration on the other, there is a fair prospect of enhanced success.

The *yogī*'s austerity, indeed, increases his potency. Provided his duty is fully accomplished, his return may be looked forward to with confidence: 'When will my ascetic come?' Indeed, the asceticism we are considering is not brahmanical and irreversible like a *saṁnyāsī*'s renunciation. When the soldier succeeds in making it home again, his just rule as a *grihastha* is guaranteed. When in the Chhattisgarhi ballad of Sitaram Naik Banjara the hero tells his mother he will go away to trade and to 'rule in another land', she at

[21] Grierson, 'Some Bihari Folk-Songs', 237.
[22] Grierson, 'Song of Bijai Mal', 145.

last consents, but asks him not to make love to anyone and to return in the end, because 'when there is a son in your lap, he will enjoy your wealth'.[23]

Before the fruits of restraint and sacrifice can be reaped, however, a long period of warrior-asceticism – often the ballads mention a period of twelve years – elapses. In folklore, more often than not, a raja – i.e. one who must always be prepared for a fight – is an ascetic. The 'brave warrior' Bir Bawan in the ballad of Lorik and Chandaini, has matted hair. In the ballad of Bakaoli, Lakhiya says: 'I am the first of great Rajas. There is no Rishi greater than I.' And later on during his adventure, his 'hair grew matted on his head'. He is in search of a flower to bring home to his *bhaujī*, his elder brother's wife: 'I have no lust for woman; it was for a flower I did my penance.' Only abstinence can protect a man against the risks of his warlike pursuits.[24]

Repeatedly, therefore, in these legends, there is mention of fighters who go to war as *yogīs*, their bodies besmeared with ashes. Though in the so-called 'Lay of Alha' this is usually explained as a disguise, there is no doubt that, rather than a traditional ruse, this seems to be reminiscent of the ancient habits of the Rajput, who was, we suggest, essentially a warrior-ascetic of the type so well remembered in folklore.[25] The phenomenon, in other words, may belong to the world of history as well as to the world of ballad and folksong. The 'Prithiraja Rasau', a chronicle-legend in Old Hindi describing twelfth-century events, is quite explicit. Here a Rajput, who must have belonged to the Tonwar clan – a clan that will figure again later on in this study – goes to battle 'with a coil of matted hair on his head, and a musical horn (in his hand), and ashes of cowdung (smeared on his body)'. His ensigns were a battle axe, a trident and a leather cloak. In short, 'he was altogether like Hara (Siva), the destroyer of all'. And further on it is said, probably about this same man, that 'by the power of his asceticism' he defeated his foes.[26] There is an even more unequivocal instance of the common identity of the ancient Rajput and the Saivite warrior-ascetic. It is found in

23 Archer, *Vertical Man*, 69, 70, 80, 81.

24 Verrier Elwin, *Folk Songs of Chhattisgarh*, 311, 312, 316, 321, 328, 343. For the important distinction, in the analysis of this phenomenon, between the asceticism of the consecrated warrior and transcendent renunciation, see Heesterman, *The King's Order*.

25 Waterfield and Grierson, *Lay of Alha*, 80, 81, 239. Cf. Shirreff, *Padmāvatī*, 168n.

26 Chand Bardāī, *Prithirāja Rāsau*, 49, 50, 57. On this theme see also pp. 29, 70, and (on Bairagi fighters) 71.

the person of the chief of all Rajputs, the *rānā* of Mewar, who derived his authority from Mahadeva (Shiva), the tutelary divinity of the Rajputs of Mewar. It was said about Rana Samarsi, who lived in the late thirteenth century, that he was the 'Regent of Mahadeva' and that 'a simple necklace of the seeds of the lotus adorned his neck; his hair was braided, and he is addressed as Jogindra, or chief of ascetics'.[27] His descendants are recognised to the present day as Rajputs of the highest status. In later medieval historical sources – as distinguished from folkloristic and lyrical traditions – only scattered traces of this aspect of Indian society can be found. It belongs to a gregarious, pastoralist pre-Mughal world that, from the sixteenth century onwards, was increasingly delegitimised by the new Rajput Great Tradition and restrained by the brahmanical emphasis on renunciation, endogamy and exclusiveness.

As hinted at, the crucial point of difference with brahmanical theory was that these Rajputs and the numerous semi-tribal clans that took to the rajputising model were not inspired by the ideal of renunciation as an other-worldly, transcendent aim worth pursuing for its own sake. For them ascetic sacrifice was the necessary complement of the politics of settlement and family life. It bore fruit, in the last analysis, at home and especially in the epitome of homely politics: the marriage alliance. Of foremost importance, therefore, for those who left home as *naukar*, or service men, was not the irrevocable renunciation of primordial ties, but the hope of earning the ability to ascetically fight one's way back home. The crucial age below which to achieve this is forty, when a man ceases to be a *jawān* (a youth, cf. Latin *iuvenis*): the word used even today for an Indian Army private. At that age at the latest he hopes to return to his farm, there to fulfil and consummate his life as a householder and a family man.

Of course, 'home' means 'married life'. Yet in order to marry one first leaves home to search for a bride. It is true that the soldier's abstinence from home and subsequent vagabondage led him to wars that were fought over issues of loot and personal honour. But according to most heroic ballads of North India, what was primarily at stake was marriage. Again, one needs only to mention the 'Lay of Alha' and the 'Prithiraja Rasau'. Marriage means alliance and the emphasis reflects the overriding importance of alliance politics in medieval Indian history. Udal, the hero of the

[27] Tod, *Annals and Antiquities*, I, 300, II, 598ff.

'Lay of Alha', refused on two occasions to countenance any marriage that was not accompanied by bloodshed. After such contests, as Grierson remarked, the parties used to become quite friendly and came to each other's assistance on the next occasion of a marriage. The creation of a new home that shares in the order created by a network of political alliances, is inconceivable unless the measure is taken of the participants' physical force and ascetic power.

The above observations, perhaps, may have a certain anthropological interest. The historian, out to reconstruct the medieval past, however, demands something more solid than the decoding of legends. Grierson himself, though thrilled by all this battle and glory, seems to have been at a loss how to proceed. He pointed out that, as far as he knew, there was no trace of such bloody marriage customs to be found in modern Rajputana, but he thought that 'the poem does contain memories of customs which were in full use in ancient times'. He left it, however, to anthropologists to explain the origin and meaning of 'this curious picture of marriage and of warfare'.[28] Similarly, Charlotte Vaudeville, when dealing with the 'Dhola-Maru', the Marwari ballad of which the oldest manuscripts relate to the ancient Rajput kingdoms of Jaisalmer and Bikaner, judged the accepted typology of the Rajput Great Tradition quite unhelpful in her analysis. The 'Dhola-Maru' was plebeian and pastoral rather than aristocratic and its hero was deprived of any genealogy whatsoever.[29] She thus found herself in the same predicament as George Grierson in his endeavour to understand the 'Lay of Alha'.

We shall contend that history, after all, does provide data that enable us to solve the dilemma, albeit only partially. On the basis of this, I suggest that there is a layer of Rajput tradition now almost hidden from view by historical myth and the paucity of sources, which is characterised by the complementarity of asceticism and settled life and by alliance politics as expressed in marriage links. This is a tradition very different indeed from what the Rajputs of the colonial period have told British scholars and administrators their history was all about. Rajput culture, according to them, was, if anything, aristocratic and based on agnatic kinship, the legitimacy of its chiefs being derived from landholding and the exclusiveness of their genealogies. Confirming the pride of their Rajputana

28 Waterfield and Grierson, *Lay of Alha*, 23, 24.
29 Vaudeville, *Dhola-Mārū*, 34, 35.

allies, the British dubbed as 'spurious' Rajput traditions that seemed to deviate from proper standards; once having given in on this point, they could no longer take cognisance of traces of an underlying layer of Rajputhood, more ancient than the well-known traditions of the Rajasthani courts, yet at least equally important for an understanding of North Indian history until far into the nineteenth century.

The oral literature we have quoted from suggests both a clue to what is wrong with this historiographical tradition and a way out of it. These lyrics and ballads certainly do not contain names and dates that can be assigned a place in a chronological narrative, but they provide the vital context that can help to interpret and put into perspective the few data, often only epigraphical or numismatical, that one has. A case in point is the *Bagaḍāvat Mahāgāthā*, another story of marriage and bloodshed, set in thirteenth-century Rajasthan and connected with Hari Raj, the last Chauhan Rajput ruler of Ajmer. The main theme is the marriage of a strongwilled Rajput princess to one of a clan of twenty-four cattle-breeders, whose father Bagh was the son of Hari Raj and a Birhamain girl, and whose twelve mothers all belonged to different non-Rajput families. It is a clash between pastoralism on the one hand and the claims of genealogical status and territorial rule on the other. *Jauhar* and *satī* are conspicuous elements in the story. There is no doubt that, as the 'Prithiraja Rasau' and the 'Lay of Alha' do, part of the ballad describes historical events.[30] More importantly, these songs add an entirely new dimension to the extremely limited number of historical sources available and, taken together as a genre, they are convincing evidence that the new Rajput Great Tradition of the seventeenth century is an unreliable guide to pre-Mughal North India. They build a stage against the background of which, as we shall see, some of the medieval actors, whose appearance otherwise would not make sense to us, come alive.

So far in this chapter, I have, with the help of an exercise in oral literature, preliminarily redefined the character of the oldest layer of Rajputhood as an open status group of warrior-ascetics in search of patronage and marriage. An awareness of the dynamics of pastoralism and alliance politics, both intimately bound up with this phenomenon, is indeed as indispensable to the interpretation of

30 B. L. Panagariya, 'The Bagadawat Maha-gatha – A Great Folk Lore of Rajasthan', paper presented to the International Seminar on Rajasthan, University of Rajasthan, Jaipur, December 1987.

pre-modern India as is an understanding of its military labour market and the peculiarities of the Indian process of state formation. Assuming that these ideas add to our tools as historians, we shall now turn to a set of data from sources that, in my view, give empirical substance and validity to our attempts at redefinition. These data are sixteenth-century and are worthy of special notice, partly because this was the last period before the Rajput character in Rajasthan, under the Mughal impact, underwent important qualitative change, and partly because a number of authors, writing during Akbar's reign, showed a special interest in, even a fascination with, the ancient Rajput traditions during the last decades of their vigour.

Rajput power in the sultanate of Malwa

One of the most celebrated figures in Rajput history (see Figure 1) as recorded by the seventeenth-century chroniclers of Rajasthan and, later on, by Tod, is Sanga Sisodiya, the *rānā* of Mewar

Sultans of Delhi
Bahlul Lodi (1451-1489)
Sikandar Lodi (1489-1517)
Ibrahim Lodi (1517-1526)
Babur, the Timurid (1526-1530)
Humayuṇ, the Timurid (1530-1540)
Sher Shah Sur (Farid Sher Khan) (1540-1545)

Sultans of Malwa
Nasir-ud-din Khilji (1500-1510)
Mahmud II Khilji (1510-1531)
Mallu Khan, Qadir Shah (1537-1542)

Ranas of Mewar
Sanga Sisodiya (1509-1528)
Ratan Sen Sisodiya (1528-1532)
Bikramajit Sisodiya (1532-1535)

Sultans of Gujarat
Muzaffar (1511-1526)
Bahadur Shah (1526-1537)

Purbiya Warlords
Medini Rai (d. 1528, *jauhar* of Chanderi)

Lakshman (d. 1532, *jauhar* of Raisen)
Silhadi x Durgavati (both d. 1532, *jauhar* of Raisen)

Bhupat (d. ± 1538)
Raja Pratap
Puran Mal x Ratnavali (both d. 1543, second *jauhar* of Raisen)
Chaturbhuj

Figure 1. Some rulers and warlords.

(1509–28). The pride his exploits inspired in the hearts of those representing the new Rajput Great Tradition of the Mughal and British periods was certainly justified. But if we read sixteenth-century historians such as Nizamuddin Ahmad who were closer in time to the events of Sanga's life and who knew nothing of later bardic legend, we notice that, as far as Rajputs go, they paid more attention to a class of men they called Purbiya Rajputs than to the history of Mewar. These Purbiyas played a conspicuous role, especially in Malwa, between 1511 and 1543. More importantly, one is struck by the difference in political behaviour and cultural outlook between these men and the Rajputs as stereotyped in the lore of Rajputana since the seventeenth century. Therefore, if, as I suspect, our view of medieval Rajputs is incomplete, even distorted, an enquiry into these Purbiya lords may prove rewarding.

I shall begin by looking at the reign of Mahmud II (1510–31), the last sultan of the Khilji kingdom of Malwa. Soon after Mahmud had succeeded his father on the throne, his position was threatened by an insurrection led by his nobles and his elder brother. Hard-pressed, he turned for help to a certain Rai Chand Purbiya, a Rajput who was then a *thānadār* – i.e. he held an official appointment – in north-eastern Malwa. This man who became known in history by the title of Medini Rai, but who was also called Medini Purbiya, on that occasion is said to have raised from various parts of India a force of 40,000 Rajputs. The chronicler Ulughkhani reports that the 'best Purbiya soldiers' were recruited in his army. Medini Rai was soon appointed *wazīr* of the realm and, through his soldiers and appointees, came to dominate the throne.[31] The sultanate had been taken over from within. In 1517, Mahmud, finding he could not check the informal hegemony of the Rajputs, escaped to Gujarat and only in the following year, thanks to the help of the Gujarati sultan, did he recover control of his capital. Not long afterwards, however, he lost the predominantly Rajput areas in the north and east of his kingdom to Medini Rai and other powerful men in that area who had allied themselves with Rana Sanga Sisodiya of Mewar. The alliance between Sanga and the eastern Malwa chiefs was consolidated by the former marrying his daughter into the family of a man who would become the most famous of all Purbiya Rajputs, Silhadi.[32]

[31] Ulughkhani, *Zafar*, I, 94, 182, 183; Bayley, *Local Dynasties*, 247, 248.

[32] Ferishta, *History*, IV, 122. According to Beveridge, 'Some Account', 395–7, two Sisodiya princesses were married into Silhadi's family.

From then onwards Mahmud maintained himself in his capital Mandu, whereas Medini Rai and Silhadi, who was the lord of Sarangpur and Raisen, were masters of the northeast of Malwa and from there kept up their relationship with Rana Sanga whose allies they were at the battle of Khanua against the Mughal conqueror Babur in 1527. After the defeat of the Rajput coalition at Khanua, Medini Rai's successes against the Mughal troops compelled Babur to come personally to eastern Malwa to attack him in his stronghold of Chanderi. There, in 1528, Medini Rai lost his last battle; he died, along with a few hundred Rajputs, performing the rite of *jauhar*.[33] But within a few years Silhadi would again show the power of the Purbiya Rajputs in Malwa by allying himself with Bahadur Shah of Gujarat, now Sultan Mahmud II's enemy, thus finally causing the collapse of the Malwa sultanate in 1531.

What was the power of these Rajput leaders based on and what kind of men were Medini Rai and Silhadi? The word Purbiya is not a clan name nor has it any genealogical meaning. Yet, the sixteenth- and early seventeenth-century authors, who thought it enough to use the term without further explanation, must thereby have conveyed to their readers a rather precise idea of what kind of men they had in mind.[34] It appears that the character of these commanders was defined not by descent but by the fame of their followers. These followers were Rajput or pseudo-Rajput migrant soldiers from Purab, a term usually meaning Awadh, Bihar, and the Varanasi region.[35] Medini Rai and Silhadi were first and foremost military commanders employing what one could call sepoys who migrated in search of service from Eastern Hindustan into Malwa, hundreds of miles to the southwest.

The two men had by no means a monopoly in this respect. The chroniclers mention several members of both Medini Rai's and Silhadi's families as commanders of Purbiyas and, besides, eight other leaders who were similarly active during the sixteenth century. Three of the latter were, at least at some stage, under

33 Ahmad Yadgar, 'Tarikh-i-Salatin-i-Afaghana' in Elliot and Dowson, *History*, v, 38, 39; Bābur, *Bābur-Nāma*, 595; Habib and Nizami, *Comprehensive History*, v, 802; Abu-l Fazl, *Akbarnāma*, I, 268; Ulughkhani, *Zafar*, II, 786; Tod, *Annals and Antiquities*, I, 357.

34 Bayley, *Local Dynasties*, 349n; Ferishta, *History*, IV, 81, 82, 114ff, 262, 270; Nizamuddin, *Tabaqāt*, III, 295n, 298ff, 599, 608ff.

35 Yule and Burnell, *Hobson-Jobson*, 724; Hodivala, *Studies*, 461. Beveridge, 'Some Account', 392, suggests that the term Purab as used in connection with Silhadi might even refer to Gwalior, because it is to the east of Rajasthan, but it seems unnecessary to stretch its meaning so far west.

Medini Rai's orders, whereas two others were in the service of the *rānā* of Mewar during periods in which the great Malwa Rajput leaders were closely allied to that chief. Then, there were Sikandar Khan Purbiya of Satwas who helped to negotiate the 1531 Purbiya–Gujarat alliance we have just alluded to, and Nar Singh Deo Tomar, who was a brother's son of Raja Man Singh of Gwalior and who likewise, with his Purbiya Rajput following, contributed to the success of Bahadur Shah Gujarati's campaign of 1531 that put an end to the Malwa sultanate. Finally, there is mention of one Dungar Rai Purbiya, who probably played a role of some importance in the confused politics of Gujarat between 1530 and 1560.[36]

With the exception of Nar Singh Deo, whose clan name was given as Tomar, these eight men are of unknown descent. Their contemporaries summed up their identity in the term Purbiya which only marks them as recruiters and leaders of Hindustani soldiers. This obscure origin applies also to Medini Rai, the earliest Purbiya warlord we are aware of. It is not known to which clan he belonged, what his father's name was or even which part of the country he came from.[37] When he died in the *jauhar* at Chanderi in 1528, after having dominated much of Malwa for seventeen years, he did not leave a successor; his Rajputs dispersed. As far as historiographical information on his person is concerned, the contrast with his contemporary and ally Rana Sanga is striking. The ancestry and clan name of the *rānā* is documented well enough, as are the names of his heirs, who are proud of him even today, but no seventeenth-century Rajput seems to have been interested in tracing his origin to Medini Rai, however awesome a lord he once must have been. About Silhadi slightly more is known. Silhadi has been 'variously described as a Gahlot, that is, a Sasodia, as Turar [i.e. a Tonwar or Tomar], and even, perhaps, as a Puar or Punwar'.[38] That he should by some have been considered a

[36] On Bhim (or Hem) Karan Purbiya, Ugar Singh (or Agar Sen) Purbiya and Shadi Khan Purbiya, see Nizamuddin, *Ṭabaqāt*, III, 307, 314, 604; Ferishta, *History*, IV, 91, 92, and Ulughkhani, *Zafar*, I, 103. On their relationship with Medini Rai see Bayley, *Local Dynasties*, 256, and Ulughkhani, *Zafar*, I, 96, 97. On Ashok and Gangu Purbiya see *ibid.*, I, 103, 194. For the identification of Sikandar Khan as a Purbiya commander see *ibid.*, I, 168. Nar Singh's name should probably be read as Bir Singh; on him see Nizamuddin, *Ṭabaqāt*, III, 346, and Bayley, *Local Dynasties*, 343, 344. For Dungar Rai (or Dungar Siv or Dungarsi) Purbiya see Ulughkhani, *Zafar*, I, 167, 355, 387.

[37] One historian has, without giving his source, written that he was Silhadi's brother, A. K. Majumdar, 'Malwa', 185.

[38] Beveridge, 'Some Account', 392.

Guhilot, can be accounted for by his family's marriage links with the *rānā* and the Sisodiyas of Mewar. Almost certainly, though, he was a Tomar Rajput from the Tonwarghar tract north of Gwalior where the rule of this clan had reached its zenith with Raja Man Singh Tomar (1486–1517).[39]

Some of these Purbiya commanders, therefore, belonged to one of the thirty-six 'royal races' of Rajputs. The Purbiya and the Sisodiya, in other words, did not relate to two irreconcilably different worlds. True, the confusion on the issue of Silhadi's family background and the silence – except in the case of Nar Singh, who was the nephew of a famous Tomar raja – surrounding the parentage of Medini Rai and the other Purbiya captains illustrate to a point the relatively minor role of kinship in the careers of these men. Yet, the Tomar connection indicates that ascriptive status was not irrelevant to their success. We are dealing with a society in which warlord and lineage chief exist side by side and where their identities, though distinct, may well overlap. These identities, in other words, were complementary and subsumed in the Rajput phenomenon. Rana Sanga and Medini Rai certainly represent a contrast, but the alliance they kept up is as significant as the difference in type of their respective careers.

So even the Purbiya leaders, though adventuring military entrepreneurs in a sense, did not lack all genealogical connections. Also some of them had a territorial base of their own in Malwa. The little evidence we have suggests that, unlike their men, some of the Purbiya leaders did not themselves come from Eastern Hindustan. If a man like Silhadi was known as Purbiya, this was because his identity and political significance was derived from the numerous Hindustani 'sepoys' who joined his standard. Silhadi was born in the neighbourhood of Gwalior and acquired what would become his family's home counties in northeastern Malwa, especially around his forts of Bhilsa (present-day Vidisha) and Raisen, and in parts of Gondwana, whereas Chanderi to the north and Sarangpur

39 Silhadi's son Puran Mal, whose mother may well have been a Mewar princess, is mentioned as a Guhilot, see Nizamuddin, *Ṭabaqāt*, II, 169, 170. Tod calls Silhadi a Tomar, see Tod, *Annals and Antiquities*, I, 104, 356. For evidence of Silhadi's family being Tomars, see note 78 below and Bayley, *Local Dynasties*, 273. See on Silhadi also Qanungo, *Sher Shah*, 329; *Gwalior Gazetteer*, I, 211; Beveridge, 'Some Account', 392–4. Bābur describes a visit, in 1528, to the birthplace, near Gwalior, of one Salahuddin. Though this seems to be the muslim name given to Silhadi only after Bābur's death, the *Bābur-Nāma* also calls him by that name in its description of the battle of Khanua in 1527, where there can be no doubt as to his identity, Bābur, *Bābur-Nāma*, 562, 614.

to the west are now and then mentioned as being in his power.[40] When, in 1511, Medini Rai began his meteoric political career in the sultanate of Malwa, he emerged from this same area. Nizamuddin makes some members of Silhadi's family at Raisen remark, in 1532, that 'for generations (*'omarhā ast*) we have de facto enjoyed (*bamā moyassar ast*) the essence (*dar ma'nī*) of the *sulṭanat*'.[41] This must perhaps be deemed an exaggeration, but it is certain that soon after Medini Rai had grasped control over Malwa, the Purbiya commanders used their newly found power to strengthen their hold on the northeastern region of that state. About 1514, according to Nizamuddin, 'all vestiges of Islam' had disappeared from Bhilsa 'and the rites of heathenism had gained currency there'.[42] Yet, territorial power for Silhadi and his like was not the mainstay of their careers.

With respect to this relative unimportance of aristocratic descent and territoriality, there is a similarity between the Purbiya warlords and Sher Shah. Sher's rule, until 1540, though very extensive, was largely informal; he openly stood forth as sultan after long delays and then only with great circumspection. The careers of these commanders was based on achievement and they felt at ease as informal, *de facto* rulers, rather than as officially enthroned kings. They held sway, as we just saw, in reality but not in name. Nizamuddin recounts how, about 1516, the Purbiya Rajputs were considering the possibility of removing the restive Sultan Mahmud of Malwa and placing the Rai Raian, Medini Rai's son, on the throne at Mandu. On that occasion Medini Rai himself reminded them of the difference between power and authority: 'At the present moment', he said, 'the *saltanat* of Mālwa is in reality in our possession. If, however, Mahmud Shāh does not remain as a buffer, Sultan Muzaffar Gujrati will come galloping along and will seize the kingdom. Therefore we should, in every way possible, endeavour to please our master.'[43] If then these great men derived their strength not from descent or from the country they ruled as their domain and if they were not in a position to assert themselves ideologically over an environment dominated by muslim aristocracies rallied around established sultanates, what was their power based on and what means did they employ to stand their ground as redoubtable participants in the political game?

[40] For Gondwana, see Nizamuddin, *Ṭabaqāt*, III, 366.

[41] Nizamuddin, *Ṭabaqāt* (Persian text), III, 225.

[42] Nizamuddin, *Ṭabaqāt*, III, 358.

[43] *Ibid.*, III, 597, 598.

To acquire and control their spoils, these Malwa warlords – like Sher Shah – relied on their swords, upon their grip upon the military labour market of Purab, the main recruitment area of Hindustan, and, crucially, upon their negotiating and diplomatic skills. Indeed, the dominant feature of Medini Rai's and Silhadi's lives appears to have been their almost continuous efforts to forge alliances and to rearticulate the terms of service of their Purbiya Rajputs (*rājputān-i-purabīya*) with actual and potential employers.[44] One is struck by the omnipresence of the alliance theme in sixteenth-century India. Politics in this period was largely synonymous with the making and unmaking of alliances. These alliances had little of the nature of sacred treaties and seem to have been regarded very much like service contracts, temporary agreements of an auxiliary character. Negotiation, alliance and – as a corollary – brokerage were the elements that largely made up medieval Indian political-military behaviour.

Nizamuddin Ahmad, writing about 1590, was still well aware of how crucial to a man's political survival a realignment of warrior bands could be. The move of gangs of soldiers from one master to another could make or break kingdoms. It is entirely in these terms that Nizamuddin accounted for the rising power of Gujarat under its sultan Bahadur Shah about 1530 and, implicitly, for the imminent victory of this ruler over the kingdom of Malwa:

> As the fame of the grandeur of Bahādur Shāh, and the report of his imperial gifts spread in the inhabited fourth part of the world, the Rāys from near and far turned their faces to his threshold, which was a seat of prosperity. The nephew of the Rāja of Gwālior with a body of *Pūrabīa* Rājpūts came, and were listed among his special attendants. Bahrūn, son of Prithī Rāj, nephew of Rānā Sānkā, also came with some notable Rājpūts, and entered his service. Some Dakinī *sardārs* also came and attained to the good fortune of an audience (of the Sultān). All of them, in accordance with their status and position, obtained a share in his favours and gifts.[45]

One is reminded here of Sher Shah, who, only a few hundred miles to the northeast, would soon be able to employ the same techniques of state formation. In both cases, there was a clear relationship between the prosperity of the sultan, his imperial largesse and the reports of his distributive habits on the one hand, and the flow of professional troops towards his camp on the other. The *Mirāt-i-*

44 Hodivala, *Studies*, 461.
45 Nizamuddin, *Ṭabaqāt*, III, 346. See also Bayley, *Local Dynasties*, 343, 344.

Sikandarī makes the same point about Bahadur Shah: 'The Sultan now opened the hand of bounty, and like a cloud rained down gold and jewels and allowances and favours all around. He was so generous to his people that the nobles and soldiers were unwilling to go to their homes, and remained near him in the hope of sharing in his bounty.'[46]

On the Malwa side things developed into a crisis when, in 1531, Sultan Mahmud again planned to get rid of the Purbiyas by putting their all too powerful leader Silhadi to death, just as he had formerly tried to escape from the Purbiya embrace by an attempt on the life of Medini Rai. Silhadi, joined by another Malwa *amīr*, Sikandar Khan Purbiya, fled to Mewar and, backed by that country's chief Rana Ratan Sen, the son of Rana Sanga, soon opened negotiations with Bahadur Shah of Gujarat. As these negotiations would lead to tremendous changes of fortune, Nizamuddin pays due attention to them. The exchanges between Bahadur Shah and Silhadi began with the former producing 'seven hundred robes woven entirely of gold thread, and seventy horses'. Silhadi felt encouraged by this and, accompanied by the *rānā*, he met Bahadur Shah on the Mewar–Gujarat border. The sultan, 'on the first day', assigned to them 'thirty elephants and one thousand five hundred robes of honour made of stuff of woven gold thread'. The new alliance was soon a fact. After a few days, Ratan Sen left for his own capital, but Silhadi stayed on to take part in Bahadur Shah's conquering expedition into Malwa that would prove the end of Sultan Mahmud and his dynasty as well as of Malwa's independence.[47]

Yet not all political dilemmas could be solved by a new choice of allies or, to put it more crudely, by changing sides. After the conquest of Malwa, in particular, a difficulty that could hardly be negotiated away became acute. This concerned the relationship of the Purbiya warlords with the muslim sultans of Gujarat and Hindustan. After the fall of Gwalior to the Lodi sultan of Delhi in 1519, followed by the defeat of the Rajput coalition under the leadership of Mewar in 1527 and 1528 and the loss in 1531 of Malwa where the Purbiya aristocrats had ruled semi-officially for a while, politics in North India were dominated by two or three muslim rulers. Rajput power and the diplomacy of the Purbiya lords were

[46] *Ibid.*, 333.
[47] Nizamuddin, *Ṭabaqāt*, III, 350, 351, 610, 611. The *Mirāt-i-Sikandarī* adds that many horses were presented to Silhadi, Bayley, *Local Dynasties*, 350.

allowed less scope and options. Silhadi, though he was still formidable as an individual commander and broker of mercenaries, had little alternative but to deal with Bahadur Shah of Gujarat whom he had helped to overthrow the Malwa state. But whether he could be compelled to become a stable element in the sultanate's system of alliances, is another question.

As Silhadi had joined the victorious Gujarati army before any other of the *amīrs* of Malwa, Nizamuddin explained, he was given, on Bahadur Shah's conquest of the country, a larger share of its resources in *iqtāʿ* than he had ever possessed before: the *sarkārs* of Ujjain and Sarangpur, i.e. the heartland of Malwa, and the fort of Raisen.[48] However generous the offer was, acceptance would, at least formally, mean a loss of his position as an independent power-broker. In order to keep his options open as a negotiator and to strike the best bargain for his sepoy Rajputs who would certainly leave him if other commanders offered more enticing prospects, he must carefully try to avoid permanent identification with any state as long as that state had any rivals left. In spite of this, he intended to accept. After all, while officially incorporated in the sultanate he could hope to continue his informal sway over Malwa just as Medini Rai had done in the 1510s. Also, his clansman Vikramajit Tomar, once raja of Gwalior and heir to the glorious tradition of Rajput leadership and largesse associated with that fortress town, had, after his defeat in 1518–19 at the hands of Sikandar Lodi, given up his independence and exchanged it for an honourable position in the Afghan kingdom accepting, as an *iqtāʿ*, the *sarkār* of Shamsabad.

But there was another issue. Though Silhadi was perhaps flexible enough with respect to the *iqtāʿ*, the negotiations went awry. He was caught on the horns of an old dilemma, to wit, whether, as Bahadur's ally and main prop in Malwa, he could claim equality with the sultan's muslim *amīrs* and official recognition as a 'pillar of the state', or whether he should stake his all on the remains of his enterprise as an independent warlord and on the fickle chances of continued informal rule. We saw that Medini Rai had resisted the temptation of a palace coup. It is said that he had 'talked about equality among the amirs',[49] i.e. he had claimed for his Rajput

48 Nizamuddin, *Ṭabaqāt*, III, 615. According to the *Mirāt-i-Sikandarī*, he received 'three *lakhs* of *tankahs* in cash, the city of Ujain, the *parganah* of Ashtah, and the district of Bhilsah as *tankhwah*, besides horses and elephants in numbers that he had never before possessed', Bayley, *Local Dynasties*, 356.

49 Ulughkhani, *Zafar*, I, 183.

captains equal status with the muslim aristocrats as sharers in the sultanate of Malwa. But he does not seem to have pressed the issue too hard, realising that also in this respect it was wisest to avoid a conflict with the proudest amongst the noblemen and the most orthodox amongst the ulema. Foolishly or not, Silhadi in 1531–2 appears to have demanded that his position at court should be equal to that of muslim nobility. When this was not granted, he soon proved unwilling to appear at court and pay his respects to the sultan, and he was said to contemplate rejoining the Rana of Mewar.

It is apparent that, in these circumstances, the sultan hesitated to return to Gujarat because that would mean abandoning Malwa to the informal rule of Silhadi and his officers. He therefore made an attempt to entice him away from Malwa towards the coast, offering him a lakh of *tanka*s, the port of Cambay and a hundred Arab horses. Silhadi now came to court, but still no agreement was reached. Bahadur Shah sent for 'artillery and troops and treasure' from Gujarat and, after having made Silhadi a virtual prisoner in his camp, marched against Raisen, then held by Silhadi's brother Lakshman Sen. The sultan's guns, directed by the celebrated expert Rumi Khan, seriously weakened the Purbiya defences. Negotiations were opened again and for a second time the possibility arose of Silhadi accepting an *iqtā*ʿ in Gujarat. He himself is alleged to have been in favour of the offer and to have told the Purbiyas that 'the town of Barōda with its dependencies had been determined upon for our residence'.[50] Yet, Silhadi never went to Cambay or to Baroda as the sultan's *muqtā*ʿ. Neither did he succeed in salvaging his independence. As in the case of Medini Rai, the problem of the place of a Purbiya Rajput warlord in the North Indian state system seemed to be insoluble. Let us mention three options.

North Indian Rajput solidarity did not really make sense. It is true that in 1518, when Medini Rai was attacked by the Gujarati sultanate and lost control of Malwa, he allied with – one could almost say 'employed' – Rana Sanga of Mewar, giving the Sisodiya 'some elephants and much gold'.[51] But, even if the allies exchanged brides and became each other's in-laws or *sagā*, there was really nothing sacred about these cooperative efforts. Now in these years,

[50] Nizamuddin, *Ṭabaqāt*, III, 355–66; Bayley, *Local Dynasties*, 356–64, esp. p. 364 which mentions the *sarkār* of Baroda being offered.
[51] Hodivala, *Studies*, 461.

as we saw, the *rānā* gave his daughter to Silhadi and the historian Nizamuddin may have had this relationship in mind when he related that in 1521 Rana Sanga, then at war with Gujarat, called on Silhadi, using Medini Rai as an intermediary, telling him that 'he should not hold himself excused from rendering his duty to his community', and that 'he should exert himself in bringing about a treaty of peace'.[52] It is not clear whether this suggestion was followed. But with the Purbiyas all alliances could be renounced and exchanged for others, even with muslims, if circumstances on the military labour market seemed to call for such a course. Silhadi was quite capable of actions that according to Tod's more modern code of Rajput honour would be treasonable. In 1527, he considered it expedient, and doubtless in the best interests of his men, to leave the army of the Rajput 'coalition', thus causing Rana Sanga's defeat against the Mughal conqueror Babur at Khanua in the same year.[53]

Another way out could be the Rajput captain's conversion to Islam, which had the advantage of rendering the alliance with a muslim court respectable in the eyes of the ulema. It was a solution often resorted to in medieval North India and was, as we shall see, experimented with also by Silhadi. Then, perhaps, there was the model of brahmanical kingship combined with genealogical legitimacy proffered by classical tradition.[54] To adopt this model, however, would require an endeavour to transcend the medieval Indian world of the war-band and of the market forces that ruled the behaviour of its military labour. It would entail the dissolution of the complementarity that was still at the basis of North Indian peasant culture: the alternation between home, marriage, and ascriptive status on the one hand, and pastoralism, *naukarī* and ascetic achievement on the other.

But let us forsake these models, options, and complementarities for a while, and return, as far as possible, to empiric history, i.e. to the predicament that faced Silhadi in 1531–2. At first sight, his problem looks rather down to earth: it concerned the composition of his household.

[52] Nizamuddin, *Ṭabaqāt*, III, 315. It is not clear what actually happened; according to one historian, Medini Rai enticed Silhadi over to the *rānā*; according to another, Silhadi made every effort to effect peace, but did not succeed. See footnotes given in Nizamuddin, *ibid*.

[53] Tod, *Annals and Antiquities*, I, 356.

[54] Heesterman, *Inner Conflict*, 108ff.

The Purbiya household

To Indian historians working as late as the reigns of Akbar and Jahangir, the fall of the great Purbiya lords in the 1530s and 1540s must have appeared as astonishing happenings. The era of which they were typical must by then have seemed gone forever. Yet, at that time, these events had taken place within the living memory of quite a number of people and this is why chroniclers were in a position to regale their readers with a fair amount of detail about them. The profuse information thus available enables us to enquire further into the complex whole of personal honour and collective doctrine that was so important to the Rajput–muslim relationship in pre-Mughal North India. Before we do so, however, a caveat is called for. The events leading up to the holocaust of Raisen are related by Persian historians of the age of Akbar as a conflict between muslim orthodoxy and Rajput honour. Yet it would be anachronistic to suggest that the episodes of 1532 and 1543 attest to the fundamental irreconcilability of two ideologies. Rather, they tell a story of Rajputs groping about for terms that would allow them to preserve their identity as exuberant and conspicuously living warriors while at the same time enabling them to be associated with the unchallenged power of the day, an assertive muslim sultanate. It would be rash to assume that this was a hopeless undertaking.

Time and again during the negotiations between muslim sultans and Purbiya warlords, an issue cropped up that was of crucial importance in their relationship and proved extremely difficult to agree upon. This concerned the composition of the domestic establishments of the Purbiya leaders. Already during the period of their rule in Malwa (1512–18) under Medini Rai, they had taken some of the members of Sultan Nasir ud-din's (1500–10) harem into their households. Later also they used in their houses to provide for muslim and even for Sayyid women.[55] Ideologically, any settlement that would publicly have left the Rajputs in possession of muslim women would erode the homogeneity of the community of muslim believers and would therefore have made a mockery of the sultanate, an institution that by definition was meant to guarantee a pure, islamic mode of life. It is easy to understand then that the sultans of Malwa and Gujarat, constantly pestered on this point by their ulema, their theologians, repeated again and again that the

[55] Nizamuddin, *Ṭabaqāt*, III, 355, 597.

Purbiya custom of keeping muslim women could no longer be tolerated. What political necessity then urged the Rajput warlords to publicly introduce muslims into their palaces and stick to their presence as tenaciously as they sometimes did? In order to answer this question we need to take a closer look at the last phase of Silhadi's life and at the significance of his women to him.

The *Mirāt-i-Sikandarī*, written about 1610, gives some details in this respect. 'It is said', the author of this work relates,

> that the expenditure in Silhadī's household on women's dresses and perfumes exceeded that in any king's palace. He had four *akhārās*, that is to say 'bands' of dancing-girls, who were each unrivalled in their special art. Forty women held the torches while the dancing-girls performed. Every dancing-girl, moreover, had two attendants, one of whom held her *pān*-box, and the other poured sweet-scented oil on the torches, for they never burned any bad-smelling oil, nor any that was not odorous, that is, not scented with rose perfume. All the women's clothes were of gold brocade, or embroidered with gold.[56]

About the origin of these women almost nothing is known. Muslim authors implied that respectable muslim women had been forced to become dancing-girls. Perhaps many of these women had been dancing-girls or slaves anyway and had simply been employed or taken prisoner by the Purbiyas. But one may also assume that the daughters of subordinate allies who depended on Silhadi for their employment and fiefs, were members of his household and added to its prestige. And then, of course, there were the princesses, the daughters of valiant lineage chiefs. Wherever they may have come from, their presence in his household and the conspicuous consumption that went with it, had, by the end of his life, become immensely important to him, perhaps more important than in the case of Medini Rai one or two decades earlier. When challenged on this point, the latter, flexible on this as well as on other issues, had not pressed his claim too hard and had surrendered his muslim women.[57] Now the say of islamic orthodoxy in the matter was perhaps more forcefully expressed. Bahadur Shah decided that it was incumbent on him as sultan, 'that he should release the Musalman women from the disgrace of *kufr* (heathenism) and the wretchedness of the slavery of *Kāfirs*'.[58] Anything less would amount to recognising Silhadi as an *amīr* of full status, a pillar of the state like the muslim grandees, rather than as an unbelieving ally of

[56] Bayley, *Local Dynasties*, 366. [57] Nizamuddin, *Ṭabaqāt*, III, 598.
[58] *Ibid.*, III, 355.

the realm. For Bahadur, to allow all the honours of the peerage of the sultanate to a heathen would no doubt have turned the learned and holy men of his realm into his enemies and would have provided his noblemen with a weapon to attack him with. It has already been explained above that the sultan's endeavour to incorporate the Purbiyas in his state by turning Silhadi into his *muqta*ʿ had also failed to yield results. The negotiations reached stalemate.

But Silhadi, who was kept under surveillance in Bahadur Shah's camp, seems personally to have been prepared to opt for radical solutions. When he saw that his men in the fort of Raisen, under the command of his brother Lakshman, were sorely put to defend themselves against the Gujarati army, he told the sultan that he wished 'to be dignified with the nobility of Islām'. The sultan was delighted, 'repeated to him the words expressing the unity of God', whereupon Silhadi accepted the faith receiving a special robe of honour and various kinds of food from the royal kitchen. By embracing Islam, Silhadi seemed to have found a definitive answer to the problem of the muslim women under his care as well as to the central problem of his place in the islamic kingdom.

He was now almost certain that he had achieved equality with the *amīr*s. In an effort to convince his brother Lakshman of this, he told him: 'As I am now included in the community of Musalmāns, Sulṭān Bahadūr will, either on account of a feeling of communal favour, or on account of his noble spirit, raise me to a high rank.' But on the other hand he admitted his loss of independence and explained: 'It is fit that after surrendering the fort to the adherents of the Sulṭān, I should bind the girdle of service strongly and should continue to render him service.' Lakshman must have known what this meant: an *iqtā*ʿ in Gujarat. He had, therefore, good reason to disagree and perhaps Silhadi secretly cooperated with him in a scheme for continued resistance. A son of Silhadi was sent with 2,000 Purbiya soldiers to meet another son of his, named Bhupat, who was assisted by the *rānā* of Mewar. The latter was by now on his way to relieve Raisen. But the Rajput rescue force was defeated and the head of Silhadi's son along with those of many comrades in arms was sent to the sultan. Silhadi fainted at the news. Soon Bahadur Shah sent him away to a Mandu prison: his conversion had not helped in reducing the Purbiya stronghold and he could thus, it seemed, be dispensed with.[59]

[59] *Ibid.*, III, 360–2.

When Lakshman, after a siege of months, saw that his situation in Raisen was hopeless, he sent a message to the sultan asking him to summon Silhadi to his presence, to forgive him and to offer him an assurance of safety. He, Lakshman, would then evacuate the fort and surrender. Bahadur Shah granted this request and gave Lakshman a firman confirming his promise as to Silhadi's safe-conduct. Again negotiations got under way in earnest. There were still about 400 women appertaining to Silhadi in the fort and the chief of them, Durgavati, who was Bhupat's mother, asked the sultan to allow her husband to come up into the fort so that he, rather than strangers, would conduct her and the other women down into the camp. So Silhadi, accompanied by one of the sultan's trusted *amīr*s, was allowed to see his family. At the meeting Lakshman and Taj Khan – another Purbiya leader and perhaps a member of his family who had accepted Islam at an earlier stage – of course asked Silhadi what *iqtāʿ* Bahadur Shah offered them 'in exchange for the fort of Rāīsēn, and the country of Gōndwāna'. As we saw earlier, the sultan had chosen the town of Baroda in Gujarat as their place of residence and Silhadi told them so. All must have realised that they were thus to be cut off from Rajasthan, the land of their Sisodiya allies, from Hindustan, which included the Purbiya recruiting grounds, and finally, from Malwa, the land where they had been able to play their role as brokers between Rajput manpower and muslim thrones. As on a former occasion, Silhadi expressed his faith in his new master, reasoning that the road to honour was not closed. 'It is likely', he told his relatives, 'that the Sulṭān would, out of his generosity, exalt me.'[60] To him, at that stage, it was enough to be able to serve, like any other *amīr* of the realm, wherever his patron would send him. But there was another side to the Rajput character that could not be dismissed as easily as that.

The chroniclers' accounts of these emotional days allow us, for the first time, to see that the Purbiyas' women were not only objects, but also subjects in the process of decision making. In this respect they remind one of Jaisi's Padmāvatī, of the women of the 'Lay of Alha', of the *Bagaḍāvat Mahāgāthā*, and of medieval Indian folk tradition in general. Durgavati and the Purbiya leaders indicated that nothing the sultan could give in recompense for their loss of freedom would really be worth considering: 'Although the Sulṭān would show us favour and kindness, still for generations the

[60] *Ibid.*, III, 366.

sulṭanat of these lands essentially is for us a real experience.' Now fate had reunited them all at home as a family and presented them with a unique chance to stick to what they had always stood for. 'The right way of bravery is this, that we should perform *jauhar* of our women and children, and should ourselves fight and be slain; and there should be no further longing left in our hearts.' Nizamuddin, who describes the scene, singles out Durgavati as the main pleader for such drastic action. Silhadi was much moved by her stand. He realised that her words expressed what was, according to the tradition he was part of, the ultimate value of life. And, once more taking charge of affairs in Raisen, he himself explained to the muslim *amīr* who was still there with him and who offered much friendly counsel, what life in the last resort meant to him:

> Every day one *krōr* of betel leaves, and some seers of camphor are consumed in my harem, and every day three hundred women put on new garments. If we are killed with our women and children, what honour and glory.

That was decisive. 'Rani Durgāwatī, taking her daughter-in-law, who was the daughter of Rānā Sānkā, with (her) two children by the hand got into the *jauhar*; and they with seven hundred beautiful women were burnt.' Silhadi, Lakshman and Taj Khan then armed themselves and died as consecrated warriors in a fight with the sultan's Dekkani infantry at the foot of the fort.[61]

Throughout the history of the sixteenth century, no solution was found to the problem of how the preponderance these Rajput adventurers and warlords now and then acquired in Malwa could be legitimised in terms of whatever political system they became associated with. The reason is clear. Because it was essential to the Purbiyas' power to be brokers, they did not fit into any stable system; and because they never really belonged to a state-like structure, no language of legitimacy supporting such a structure could have cognisance of them. What mattered to Silhadi were patrons and sepoys and terms of service, not sultans and states. The most stable element in his existence was his household. In this respect, his was not a very different world from that of his Western Rajput contemporaries. Ziegler has pointed out the importance, in Rajput politics, of alliances affirmed by marriage (*sagāī*). He has shown that, in fifteenth- and sixteenth-century Rajasthan, marriage was 'a central mechanism in Rajput society for the building of

[61] *Ibid.*, III, 366, 367. Persian text, III, 225.

alliances and the settlement of *vair* (hostilities). One's *saga* (those whom one gave daughters in marriage and from whom one received wives) were obligated to provide support and assistance, and they formed the most important group upon whom one depended outside one's *bhaibamdh* (lit. 'tie or bond of brothers') or close relations by male blood.'[62] This was even more true of Silhadi and the Purbiya chiefs like him, because, for them, agnatic ties were of minor importance. Their investment was almost exclusively in their *jawāns* and their *sagā*, i.e. their brokerage in *naukarī* and their alliance network; both were the result of negotiation, not ascription. Women served as pawns given as surety to the allies of their fathers and brothers; the number and extraction of the women in a man's fort represented the comprehensiveness and prestige of his network of alliances. Through the composition of his household he proclaimed the multiplicity of his negotiating network and his *sagā*, the richness of his portfolio of interests and, therefore, his independent status as a participant in the North Indian political process. The presence in Silhadi's household of both muslim women and a Mewar princess gave substance to his claim to have a finger in many different pies. They enabled him to handle politics in terms of all current idioms, whether muslim, Rajput, or otherwise. His household declared, over and against the states of North India, a multilingual legitimacy in its own right.

To subject himself indefinitely to a state and to derive power and prestige from it, was incompatible with his kind of vigorous and independent entrepreneurship as well as with his eternal role as a negotiator. This is what the conspicuous consumption of his household advertised: his achievement as a free agent rather than as a haggling favourite of sultans and *rānās*. *Sagāī*, i.e. the alliance network, represents a mature set of political norms in itself. As an idiom of political behaviour, it played a prime part in pre-Mughal Indian history. But, as in the ballads, these marriage relationships are complemented by the Rajput adventurer's asceticism. His asceticism is the ultimate source of his independent legitimacy; it is therefore also his ultimate resort.

As far as sixteenth-century Malwa is concerned, the ideological weight of the *sagāī* principle is shown explicitly by the historian Nizamuddin's emphasis on the plenty surrounding Silhadi's women. In the last resort, the justification of Durgavati's *jauhar* and of Silhadi's final refusal to give up his identity as a Rajput, is

62 Ziegler, 'Marvari Historical Chronicles', 240. See also Ziegler, 'Some Notes'.

put in terms of the abundance and luxury that had been a striking feature of their household. Durgavati takes a leading part at decisive moments, because as a woman she represents an essential political fact, to wit, her husband's allies. One is reminded here of the spectacular role of Rajput women throughout medieval North Indian history. The events are explained in terms not of kinship, but of *sagāī*. With Durgavati, it is not the mother–son relationship that is stressed, but her place as Silhadi's wife and even, as the text we have quoted from showed, the relationship with her daughter-in-law. The muslim historian of Akbar's time still sensed what would be beyond the grasp of later genealogists.

As the women of a man's household were the substance of his achievement, they could have no existence independent of his life's adventure. If he were to die fighting, there would be nothing for them to do but to add to the glory of his end as they had added to the honour of his career during his life. *Jauhar* emphasises that, ultimately, the household of the Rajput warlords was the most pregnant expression of their military and diplomatic entrepreneurship. This rite belongs, in other words, to the world of the war-band, which is presented so well by the Malwa Purbiya leaders and of which Ziegler saw traces in fifteenth- and sixteenth-century Rajasthan. It was, therefore, logical that *jauhar* disappeared when, as a result of Akbar's policies of empire-building, genealogy and landholding increased their hold over North Indian Rajputs. For Akbar succeeded where Bahadur Shah of Gujarat – and Sher Shah, as we shall see – failed: in the policy to incorporate the Rajputs in the sultanate.

Sher Shah's Purbiya campaign

The *jauhar* of 1532 was by no means the end of the Purbiyas nor of Silhadi's family. Silhadi's son Bhupat survived the event and joined the camp of Bahadur Shah of Gujarat, his father's great adversary, who now for a few years dominated the political scene of Central India. But he was not a very faithful servant. When, in 1535, Humayun invested Mandu, Bhupat is reported to have betrayed Bahadur. It was Rumi Khan, who had himself served Bahadur so well during the siege of Raisen, but had since joined Humayun, who persuaded Bhupat that 'the opportunity for revenge and retribution has arrived'.[63] The episode demonstrates again that for

[63] Bayley, *Local Dynasties*, 387, 388. See also Abu-l Faẓl, *Akbarnāma*, I, 305.

these Purbiya leaders serving a king never meant more than a temporary contract.

It seems that after the death, in 1537, of Bahadur Shah of Gujarat, Mallu Khan alias Qadir Shah, the new ruler of Malwa, turned for support towards the Rajput and muslim noblemen of the old Khilji regime of Malwa. Bhupat Rai and Puran Mal, the sons of Silhadi, came back from Mewar and accepted service in Malwa in exchange for the new regime's recognition of their interest in the Raisen tract. Bhupat must have died fairly soon after this and by 1540 one finds 'Puran Mal, the son of Rājā Sālhadi Purabiya' and his men as the dominant force in eastern Malwa.[64] It is perhaps significant that Nizamuddin, posthumously as it were, here confers the title of raja on Silhadi. Abbas Khan Sarwani says that 'Bhaiyā Pūran Mal held the government of Rāīsēn and Canderī as a regent for his nephew Rājā Pratāp, the son of Bhūpat Śah, the son of Salāḥuddīn. The said Rājā Pratāp was only a few years old.'[65] The use of the title of raja for a minor suggests that an element of genealogical legitimacy had now been accepted. It may be that this also represented a step towards brahminically legitimised Indian kingship. However that may be, in other respects, if we trust Abbas Khan, not much had changed since Silhadi's time.

Before we continue the story of the Purbiya chiefs, it seems proper to draw attention once more to the quality of Abbas Khan's work. For the story of Puran Mal I shall, as in chapter 2, have to depend mainly on this Afghan historian of Sher Shah's career, who wrote about 1580 under the auspices of the emperor Akbar. His account may not be an exact factual record, but as historical literature it is trustworthy in the sense that it diligently observes several of the main elements of Rajput and sultanate politics and weaves them into a coherent narrative. Like Nizamuddin in the case of Silhadi, he shows a remarkable empathy for the ambitions and susceptibilities of Puran Mal, who was, after all, a heathen warlord. Perhaps it was his patron Akbar's favourable attitude towards alliances with Rajput chiefs that made Abbas write in this way. A certain similarity of character as between Afghans and Rajputs, who, as soldiers of fortune, had similar backgrounds and shared, as we saw, in several adventures, may also have something to do with this.

In 1542, Sher Shah added Malwa to his empire. During this campaign, he ordered his *amīr* Shujaat Khan to bring Puran Mal

[64] Nizamuddin, *Ṭabaqāt*, III, 617, II, 169.

[65] Abbās, *Tārīkh*, 446; see also 540.

from Raisen to the royal presence. Shujaat Khan sent Ram Sah Tomar, the son of the ex-raja of Gwalior, to summon him. But Puran Mal demanded that Shujaat Khan should come himself and introduce him to Sher Shah. So, that nobleman came to Raisen and asked Puran Mal to accompany him to the court. By giving these details, Abbas Khan registered, first, that Puran Mal rather than being summoned through the intermediary of his clansman, the vanquished and subordinate Tomar of Gwalior, claimed a direct association with Sher Shah's premier *amīr* in Malwa and, secondly, that this claim was granted. Puran Mal was not just a non-muslim *zamīndār* or auxiliary, but a power in his own right who claimed, as his father had done, equality with the realm's *amīr*s and who was in a position to negotiate over this even with the sultan.

At the time of his departure, as Abbas continues his account of this episode, the atmopshere is that of a *bārahmāsā* song:

> Ratnāvalī, the beloved wife of Bhaiyā Pūran Mal, submitted to Śujāat Khān that she would take her food only when she would see Pūran Mal again and till his return here she would remain sitting in this bastion of the fort and would be watching his arrival. Śujāat Khān assured her that Bhaiyā Pūran Mal would come back to her the next day.

Abbas Khan here is as aware as Nizamuddin of the moral and political pressure that could be exercised by a Rajput's wife. He describes Ratnavali as successfully threatening a muslim grandee to kill herself if her husband should lose his character as a free agent and, therefore, his personal honour as a Rajput leader.

Shujaat Khan now conducted Puran Mal, who had taken with him 6,000 horsemen, 'none of whom had attained the age of forty', before Sher Shah, who at once presented his new ally with a hundred horses and a hundred splendid robes of honour and then sent him home. Puran Mal set out for the return journey to Raisen leaving his brother Chaturbhuj in the service of Sher Shah.[66] Abbas Khan here emphasises the virility and youth of Puran Mal's men – the word *jawān* comes to mind immediately – and recognises his value as a recruiter of choice troops. It is not said explicitly that the 6,000 horsemen remained with Sher Shah under Chaturbhuj, but it does not seem illogical to suppose that this was the case and that Sher Shah's liberal attitude towards Puran Mal is explained by his concern lest the recruitment of Purbiya troops from Eastern

66 *Ibid.*, 541.

Hindustan, the heartland of his kingdom, should remain outside his control.

But whatever the arrangement was, it soon went awry. In 1543, a year after the understanding between the Afghan sultan and the Purbiya lords, Sher Shah took Chanderi from Puran Mal and then laid siege to his stronghold Raisen. As his motive for this campaign Sher Shah is said to have given vent to his anger with Puran Mal, 'who had made captives the families of the Musulmāns in Canderī, had forcibly made their daughters to be the dancing-girls and had not co-operated with my son, namely Qutub Khān'.[67] Again, artillery was the decisive factor. Sher Shah ordered all copper objects that could be found in the camp and its market to be brought together and to be made into mortars. The role of artillery-man played by Rumi Khan during the siege of Raisen in 1532, here seems to have been assumed by the sultan himself. The fort suffered badly from the bombardment that now ensued and after six months had passed Puran Mal came out in person and paid his respects to Sher Shah.[68]

Once they began, the negotiations were soon successful. Sher Shah granted to Puran Mal the *iqtā'* of Benares, situated near his own heartland around Sasaram and, moreover, right in the Purbiya recruiting area. One more issue had to be agreed upon, namely Puran Mal's readmittance on a basis of equality to the *majlis*, i.e. the circle of *amīrs* who surrounded the sultan. On this issue, the Purbiya control over a large number of women of diverse origin enabled Puran Mal to put pressure on the sultan. They were used, in other words, as pawns in the negotiations. Preparations were made in the fort for a *jauhar* and then Puran asked that the sultan's son and another *amīr* of high rank 'should assure me by their oaths and vows that no injury will be caused to me and my property'. This was granted. Puran Mal's troops were now included in the imperial army, not as defeated but as allied men, the sultan himself declaring: 'On the first day when I had fixed the camping ground for my followers, I had also fixed the place for the encampment of Bhaiyā Pūran Mal which lay in the midst of my army camp.' Puran Mal and his family were now allotted this area;[69] he received a hundred horses, a robe of honour and a sum of gold from the sultan. All seemed to have ended well.[70] A major Rajput leader was incorporated in the sultanate. It very much looked like

[67] *Ibid.*, 599. [68] *Ibid.*, 604. [69] *Ibid.*, 606.
[70] Badaoni, *Muntakhab*, I, 476.

Sikandar Lodi's success with respect to the Tomars of Gwalior in 1519. Like Sikandar then, Sher Shah could now congratulate himself on a considerable increase of his forces and his camp, which was clearly what he had been after in the first place.

But, a little afterwards, a number of muslim women of Chanderi presented themselves before Sher Shah on the road-side and complained to him about Puran Mal. It is said that the *sheikhzāda*s of Chanderi had, during the preceding decades, become the proprietors of lands and gardens and now numbered more than 10,000.[71] No doubt it was for the sake of them and their wealth, that Sher had taken Chanderi under his protection. But they were not content with being rid of Puran Mal as lord of their district. 'He has killed our husbands', they said, 'put in chains our daughters whom he caused to dance along with the dancing-girls and has seized all our lands and earthly possessions.' They threatened to accuse the sultan on the day of resurrection if he did not revenge them and, when he reminded them of the 'oaths and vows' that had been taken to guarantee the safety of the infidel, they told him to consult the ulema of his camp. Apparently Sher Shah simply had to comply with this. The ulema got together and issued a *fatwā* deciding that Puran Mal deserved death. The camp of the sultan's new ally was now surrounded by elephants and troops. Seeing this, Puran Mal went into his tent 'and severed the head of his beloved wife, namely, Ratnāvalī who composed beautiful poems in Hindī, brought it before his dear and near ones' and ordered them likewise to slay their families.[72] The Rajputs were soon either put to the sword or trampled to death by the elephants. According to Badaoni they numbered nearly 10,000; Nizamuddin says there were 4,000 Rajputs of note involved.[73]

The fall of Raisen, apart from its importance to the history of Purbiya soldiering, marks Sher Shah's dependence on his ulema. The political weight of the *amīr*s in Sher Shah's council was, as we saw earlier, kept to a minimum, but it was more than rivalled by that of the learned and holy men of the realm. Qutub Khan, the *amīr* on the strength of whose oath Puran Mal had surrendered, is reported, soon after Puran Mal and Ratnavali's *jauhar*, to have left Sher Shah's service and to have become a hermit on account of his master's breach of faith in which, as he must have felt, his personal

[71] Siddiqi, *Sher Shah Sur*, 147. [72] Abbās, *Tārīkh*, 606, 607.
[73] Badaoni, *Muntakhab*, I, 476; Nizamuddin, *Ṭabaqāt*, II, 170.

honour was involved.[74] The fundamental difficulty of the choice before Sher Shah at this juncture is perhaps reflected by the persistent controversy among the early Mughal historians over the issue. Abul Fazl denounces Sher Shah for his dishonesty and calls the ulema misguided men. Abbas Khan, faithful to the memory of the sultan as well as to Akbar's views, puts the blame for the massacre exclusively on the ulema. Nizamuddin Ahmad and Ahmad Yadgar seem to carefully avoid taking sides, whereas Badaoni, who thanked God he was born during the reign of so just a king as Sher Shah, assumes an understanding attitude without feeling capable, it seems, of clearing his hero of all imputations in the matter. Finally, Niamatullah gives both the sultan and his advisers full credit for their victory over the infidel.[75] But in reality all these embarrassingly different opinions probably do more justice to the discourse of the learned men of Akbar's and Jahangir's time than to the problems before Sher Shah and Puran Mal. Let us, again, sum up the options open to both of them.

By 1542–4, Sher Shah had made himself the master of all the resources of Hindustan except one: he was as yet far removed from a dominant position as a recruiter of men in Purab, or Eastern Hindustan, though his own home counties were in that area and though he had quite a number of Ujjainiya Rajputs who came from the heart of Purab. There were, especially in Malwa, numerous Purbiya war-bands of which the most important were commanded by members of the family of Silhadi, a Tomar Rajput originating from northern Malwa. Sher was prepared to come to an agreement with this family, allow *amīr* status to its head and employ its Rajput sepoys *en masse*. Perhaps this was the wiser policy, as the destruction of its leadership, if that could be achieved at all, would not in itself guarantee that Purbiya soldiers would then flock to his standards. The alliance would apparently have pleased his *amīrs*. But it was at odds with his emphatically anti-aristocratic method of state formation.

As we saw, he endeavoured to build a broadly based political nation. The chief props of his realm, apart from his army, would be the village heads (ryots) whose position he strengthened with the help of rural settlements, and, secondly, the largely muslim gentry

74 Abu-l Fazl, *Akbarnāma*, I, 400n.
75 *Ibid.*, I, 399; Abbās, *Tārīkh*, 606–8; Nizamuddin, *Ṭabaqāt*, II, 170; for Ahmad Yadgar, see Abbās, *Tārīkh*, 637n; Badaoni, *Muntakhab*, I, 473, 476; Neamet Ullah, *History*, I, 137.

of the towns. To many of the latter were given rent-free or *in'ām* grants of a kind that later would be called *madad-i-māsh*. The deeds these men received often obliged them to train themselves in archery and other military skills so as to improve their value as recruits for the imperial camp.[76] Through these grants, Sher Shah invested a great deal in these towns as a recruiting ground. The representatives *par excellence* of this expanding *sheikhzāda* gentry were, as we saw in the case of Chanderi, the ulema: men often of comparatively humble origins who profited, like other *in'ām*-holders, from the possibilities of vertical social mobility which were a corollary of Sur politics. Logically, they supported the anti-nobility bias of Sher and clashed vehemently with him when he departed from that bias and yielded a central place in his court to a would-be *amīr* whose life-style was extremely unpalatable to them and – even worse perhaps – whose numerous retainers took the place in camp they considered to be theirs by virtue of their covenants with the sultan.

Earlier in this study, we have asked what chances Sher Shah had to transcend the pluriformity of identities in his realm, what channels of communication he could establish, what balance he could strike between allies whose claims clashed. The example given of his *amīr*, the ex-slave Khawas Khan's gifts, already showed that indiscriminate distributive practice, ideologically based on heterodox eclecticism traditionally associated with the aristocracy, could irritate the muslim learned; and perhaps in that case too they acted as the gentry's mouthpiece. Sometimes the court could not avoid taking sides however much the sultan might have hoped that the extremes of broad-based support from Hindustan and warlordism in Malwa could be reconciled. The end of Puran Mal and Ratnavali proves that gentry and ulema could compel him to make a choice. It ruined the alliance to achieve which he had considered it worthwhile immobilising his army for six months; perhaps it also shows up a basic weakness of Sher's endeavour, to wit, the impossibility as yet of finding an alternative to the power of the great lords, whether aristocrats or self-made men. It was, anyway, not easy to find a nexus, or even channels of communication, between the Sur throne and the service traditions of the Malwa Purbiyas.

As far as Puran Mal's options were concerned, they were likewise limited. I have earlier assessed the chances of effective

[76] Siddiqi, *Sher Shah Sur*, 134.

North Indian Rajput solidarity and have written about the failure of Silhadi's experiments with conversion to Islam.

Knowing as we do what Akbar achieved later in the century through his alliance and marriage politics with many Rajput clans, one wonders whether the Rajput principle of *sagāī* or alliance by marriage could not have bridged the gap. This was the principle which, however loose the bond was, held these Rajputs together amongst themselves. It was expressed in the honourable gifts they gave and received as each other's allies and in the conspicuous living in their households. We have already seen what kind of things were consumed and given: crores of betel leaves, seers of camphor, new garments, elephants, Arab horses, gold, a lakh of *tanka*s, the port city of Cambay, robes of honour and, above all, women of all origins whose radiant presence advertised the attractiveness of the Rajput household as a distributive force. The household was, as it were, the centre of a political economy based on giving. It was a place where every dancing-girl had two attendants of whom one held her *pān*-box while the other poured scented oil on the torches and where the air was filled with the odour of rose perfume. The atmosphere of all this spending of resources is that of a potlatch. When there is nobody left willing to play the recipient's role, one option still presents itself: the ultimate gift is the *jauhar*, the suicidal rite in which everything is exchanged for honour and glory. It is the apotheosis of the ancient Rajput tradition. Now, if all this works as I think it does, why could there not be common ground between a Rajput 'theatre state' based on personal alliances, *sagāī* and the exchange of gifts on the one hand, and a strong sultanate whose legitimacy was, likewise, supported by spectacular and widely acclaimed gift-giving on the other?

It needed just a few more decades for this meeting of structures and minds to take effect. Perhaps Sher Shah contributed to the process, firstly by his alliance with the Ujjainiya Rajputs of Bhojpur who were much closer to the gentry and village heads whose loyalty he preferred and sought and, secondly, by his annihilation of the semi-aristocratic Purbiya Rajput warlords of Malwa, who could never give up their role of independent brokers in the military labour market. As far as the majority of the Rajput elite lineages was concerned, their rather emphatic adoption, after the *jauhar* of Chitor in 1568, of a genealogical idiom, meant that they drifted further away from the Indian political tradition of volatile alliances and *sagāī*, a tradition which had deep roots in medieval and even ancient Indian history and of which Rajputs like Medini Rai, Silhadi and Puran Mal were among the last remarkable representatives. It would also bring them, in certain respects, within the compass of Mughal political discourse. Particularly Akbar would, helped by a liberal interpretation of islamic custom, refurbish as it were the principle of *sagāī*, and forge marriage relationships with a great number of Rajput families. In this way, *sagāī* did not disappear entirely, though its character as an exchange between equals was lost. The archaic political system, based on ever-changing networks of service, was verticalised and frozen under Mughal leadership. The *bādshāh* became the one patron of Rajput warriors, his household the ultimate destination of their sisters and daughters as well as the unrivalled nexus of the empire's political economy built on the exchange of conspicuous gifts amongst the elite. Such a hierarchical system tended to encourage among the Rajputs participating in it tendencies towards constancy, even rigidity. Genealogy, always a legitimising factor in North Indian politics, thus assumed even greater importance and soon came, under the Mughal aegis, to be equated with Rajput orthodoxy. Together with a more brahmanical interpretation of kingship, or *rājādharma*, it became the new Rajput Great Tradition.

But was that the end of the ancient 'little' tradition? If we look at the paltry traces that remained, after the *jauhar*s of Raisen, of the glory of Silhadi, Durgavati, and their children, one would almost conclude it was.

Absorption into the Mughal state

One must assume that Puran Mal's family largely perished in 1543. According to Abbas Khan, a daughter of Puran Mal, still a minor, and three brother's sons were captured by Sher Shah who 'gave away the daughter of Puran Mal to a rope-dancer in order to make her dance in the market and ordered the aforesaid three boys to be castrated in order to put an end to the line of the oppressor'. Similarly, Nizamuddin wrote that the Raisen Rajputs now 'became totally extinct'.[77] Obviously, both North Indian historians were not aware of all the details, because Silhadi's charisma was after all carried into the seventeenth century by his descendants. In the

[77] Abbās, *Tārīkh*, 609. Niamatullah has a slightly different version, see Neamet Ullah, *History*, I, 138; Nizamuddin, *Ṭabaqāt*, II, 171.

1620s, one of them occasioned the emperor Jahangir to record in his memoirs their remarkable family history. The emperor's story is that after the death of Puran Mal Tonwar his 'sons and caste fellows went off to various places'.[78] One of these, a descendant of Silhadi, entered the service of Miran Muhammad II (1566–76), the king of Khandesh, a region just to the south of Malwa. Jahangir calls this soldier Khan Jahan which may have been the title he received at the court of Khandesh in Asirgarh. It is tempting to think that this was Chaturbhuj, whom Puran Mal, his brother, brought to the camp of Sher Shah in 1542 along with 6,000 young horsemen. But whatever his real name, it is clear that he did not betray his Rajput background. A Dutch trader in Gujarat was told in the 1620s that this Khan Jahan had married five or six wives by whom he had three children, but that in addition he had in his harem more than 400 women. The latter had given him eleven children of whom two had slaves as their mothers.[79] After Muhammad II's death in 1576, Raja Ali Khan (1577/8–97), the brother of the late king, took possession of the government of Khandesh. Khan Jahan along with other servants of the late king leagued together to oppose him but without success. His plans defeated, Khan Jahan, says the emperor, 'planting his foot firmly on his good fame, took to fighting and when things went badly with him committed *Johar*'.[80] Clearly, he had kept alive the main elements of his family's Rajput traditions as we have come to know them.

But a young son who survived Khan Jahan would move in quite a different world. The facts known about his career will bring out the enormous political changes he must have witnessed during his lifetime. The boy, known in history as Nahir Khan, was after his father's death adopted first by an Abyssinian grandee of the kingdom of Khandesh who made him a muslim. After his patron's death, he was brought up by the king, Raja Ali Khan, himself. When Akbar conquered Asirgarh and annexed Khandesh in 1601, Nahir Khan went over to his service. The emperor 'discerned the signs of bravery on his forehead', raised him to a suitable *mansab* and gave him in *jāgīr* the *pargana* of Muhammadpur in the *sarkār* of

[78] H. Beveridge remarks that the mss. seem to have Puran Mal Būlūr (بولور), though the translation gives Pūran Mal Lūlū; Jahangir, *Tūzuk*, II, 268n. But there can be no doubt that Tonwar (تونور), i.e. Tomar must be the correct reading. Clearly also the reading Silhadi Deo, as suggested by Beveridge in the same footnote, should be preferred to Nar Singh Deo. See Hodivala, *Studies*, 460, 461.

[79] Geleynssen, *Remonstrantie*, 41.

[80] Jahangir, *Tūzuk*, II, 268.

Sarangpur in central Malwa.[81] In Jahangir's service, Nahir Khan 'advanced more and more'.[82] In 1618, when the emperor was in Gujarat, he was summoned from the Dekkan to appear before his presence. Soon he was promoted to a *mansab* of 1,500/1,000 and presented with an elephant.[83] In the beginning of 1623 he was governor of Patan in northern Gujarat;[84] according to Jahangir, his *mansab* was then 1,000/200. In the summer of that year, he was, with some other *amīr*s, instrumental in frustrating an attempt on behalf of Shahjahan, then a rebel against his father, to gain control of Gujarat. As a reward he received the title of Sher Khan, a *mansab* of 3,000/2,000, a horse, an elephant and a jewelled sword.[85] Shortly afterwards, one finds him as governor of the towns of Broach, Baroda and Jambusar and of the neighbouring countryside most of which was given to him in *jāgīr*. Moreover, he still administered Muhammadpur in Malwa which seems to have been given to him for life. The land revenue of these *jāgīr*s which may have been close to a million *mahmūdī*s, provided him no doubt with the bulk of his income.[86] But there was more. In 1626, Nahir Khan had taken over for the year the management of the customhouse of Broach for a price of 60,000 *mahmūdī*s and it is probable that he was involved in other similar enterprises.[87] Anyway, he enjoyed all kinds of miscellaneous receipts during this period of which it is possible to give a few examples.

On the eve of his departure from the Baroda area in the summer of 1626, Nahir Khan must have been an extremely busy man. He had heard at that time that he was going to be reappointed to his old governorship of Patan, a place where the income was less and rebellions more frequent, and where it was clearly the intention of the authorities that he should spend on military operations whatever he had amassed so far in Baroda. He was thus compelled to be

[81] *Ibid.*, Abū'l Faẓl, *Ā'īn*, II, 204. Geleynssen says that the distance between Broach and Nahir Khan's town of 'Medepoer' was 70 or 75 [Dutch] miles, i.e. about 540 km. This seems to accord with the identification of Jahangir's Muhammadpur with the town of that name near Sarangpur mentioned in the *Ā'īn*, see Geleynssen, *Remonstrantie*, 8.

[82] Jahangir, *Tūzuk*, II, 268.

[83] *Ibid.*, II, 8, 22. See for the system of *mansab* ranking e.g. Athar Ali, *Mughal Nobility*.

[84] Pelsaert, *Geschriften*, 172.

[85] Jahangir, *Tūzuk*, II, 267. See for details of this episode Pelsaert, *Geschriften*, 172–7.

[86] Geleynssen, *Remonstrantie*, 8, 9, 17, 40.

[87] ARA The Hague, Coll. Geleynssen no. 14, Geleynssen to Van den Broecke, Broach, 5.ii.1626.

a little avaricious. As far as Broach was concerned, he told his brother Nur Khan to collect as much money as he could from the place and to realise all old debts. So Nur Khan put forward claims for money against several people and imprisoned them. A *desāī* of two or three villages, who was told to pay 8,000 *mahmūdīs*, took poison, but survived. Two officers of the *alfândega* had to part with 4,000 *mahmūdīs* on some pretext. A servant of the *kotwāl* had to contribute 900, the goldsmiths 6,000, and the weavers 2–3,000 *mahmūdīs*. Altogether Nur Khan collected for his brother in two or three months 50–60,000 *mahmūdīs*. A number of people fled the town in order to escape these levies and when at last Nahir Khan's son and his uncle Nur Khan left Broach, a crowd of weavers, goldsmiths and others tried to block their way in an attempt to get back their money.[88]

Nahir Khan was a success as a politician. Though in 1623 he had fought Shahjahan's troops, that prince gave him the governorship of Gujarat as soon as he entered the province on his way north to succeed his father in December 1627. At Ahmadabad, he was favoured by Shahjahan with a robe, a dagger, a jewel-studded sword, an increased *mansab* of 5,000/5,000 and, in addition, an elephant and a horse from the royal stable with a gold saddle. His *peshkash* to the emperor on that occasion consisted of two elephants and precious textiles from Ahmadabad.[89] All this must have required different skills from Nahir Khan. His income, which at Broach had come from 4 towns and about 200 villages, now consisted of the contributions from 25 towns and 2,898 villages; it had increased almost tenfold. But whereas at Broach he had had at his disposal 1,500 horsemen and 1,500 foot to help him in his government and in the management of his *jāgīrs*, he now had to maintain 15,000 horse and to take part in the imperial campaign in the Nasik-Trimbak region of the Dekkan.[90] In the summer of 1629 he plundered that area and returned with a vast booty bringing among other things five elephants which the *zamīndār* of Baglan had agreed to pay as *peshkash* and which were forwarded to the king.[91] The Dekkan campaigns probably kept him quite busy during the following years, perhaps more than he cared for. The plunder obtained may have paid some of his expenses but part of it

88 *Ibid.*, Geleynssen to Van den Broecke, Broach, 28.vii.1626.
89 Ali Muhammad Khan, *Mirāt*, 175–7.
90 Geleynssen, *Remonstrantie*, 18, 24, 40.
91 Ali Muhammad Khan, *Mirāt*, 177, 178.

had to be handed over to be sent to court and, moreover, during all these campaigns Nahir Khan was only a subordinate of Khwaja Abul Hasan, one of the greatest *amīrs* of the realm and then the generalissimo of the southern wars. It seems that his army was still in the field when he died at the beginning of the summer of 1631.[92]

It is indeed striking that the descendant of Silhadi and Puran Mal, who had both been freebooting warlords *par excellence* and had changed sides so often, was to such an extent caught in the Mughal system of administration and served it for thirty years. Of course, the sheer size of the empire made it difficult to escape, but there were other features of the Mughal state that must have proved attractive, or at least acceptable to men of Nahir Khan's background. Supposedly, he could have retired to his *qasba* of Muhammadpur in Malwa at an early date. But the service of the emperor was honourable. It also encompassed a relationship with all who 'kissed the threshold': here at last one found an acceptable measure of equality among the *amīrs*. The Mughals under Akbar had largely overcome the opposition of the ulema to a liberal interpretation of the sultanate. They could, therefore, solve the problem that had been Bahadur Shah's and Sher Shah's undoing: how to absorb Rajput manpower into their empires. The elites of Northern India accepted the Mughal imperial idiom as their political discourse and they looked up to the throne as the fount of honour. What became crucial was the favour of the *bādshāh* as expressed in the gifts he distributed among the friends of the empire, who, in turn, offered their gifts as *peshkash* to the emperor. As seen from the point of view of the elites, the Mughal empire was a political economy based on honourable – and sometimes profitable – gifts, centred on the person of the emperor. The great achievement of the Mughals is not only to have established an apex and centre to the old system of gift distribution – in this respect a great deal had already been done by Sher Shah – but also their creation of a corresponding idiom of political communication with segments of the elite that differed greatly in culture and interests.

Nahir Khan Tomar had no territorial base he could call his own. He was almost totally dependent on the empire and had no reason to regret his conversion to Islam. His life-style does not call to mind that of his ancestors. He had five wives and eighteen or nineteen

92 *Ibid.*, 179. ARA The Hague, Coll. Geleynssen no. 31, Geleynssen to Van Hasel, Broach, 25.i.1631.

concubines, which was modest for a gentleman like him.[93] All this illustrates the fact that the Rajput tradition based on loose service alliances and pure warlordism had no more future in the Mughal empire. The *jāgīr* principle, tried in vain by Bahadur and Sher on Silhadi and Puran Mal when they offered them various *iqta*s, had won.

The break with the past, however, was perhaps not total. It is possible that Nahir Khan's contingents were still largely composed of Purbiyas. It is reported that he was very indulgent to his soldiers. He paid their wages month by month and in his contingents there were no fines for absences.[94] He seems thus to have stressed his role as an employer of men and this, of course, reminds one of the careers of his ancestors. Also, Silhadi and Puran Mal must still have been very much a family legend well-known to Nahir Khan and, what is more, recognised and respected by Akbar and Jahangir. Nahir Khan received in *jāgīr*, probably for life, Muhammadpur, a town near the old family possession of Sarangpur in Malwa. His family history was recorded by the emperor himself in his official memoirs and, perhaps most significantly, he received the title of Sher Khan: the title of Puran Mal's great adversary of 1543, which must, I suggest, be seen as a deliberate *amende honorable*, after eighty years, of Puran Mal and Ratnavali, a clear expression also of sympathy for the *amīr*s in their conflict with the ulema on that occasion.

These carefully chosen honours reflect the genius of the early Mughal empire for the absorption of the North Indian elites – and their manpower – into their system. The old values would soon become archaic. To Nahir Khan's descendants, their family lore must have appeared as an odd, even embarrassing, affair, which it seemed increasingly purposeless to preserve in memory. It is thus not surprising that we soon lose sight of his five sons and two sons-in-law whose names are known.[95] But if we lose track of Silhadi's family after the 1630s, that does not terminate our investigation into the ethnohistory of the military labour market of Hindustan. Should we really assume that the main themes of this study – Rajput *naukarī* and warrior asceticism, the military labour market, and what these phenomena meant for state and caste

93 Geleynssen, *Remonstrantie*, 41.

94 Samsam-ud-daula, *Maāthir*, II, 840.

95 Pelsaert, *Geschriften*, 176. Geleynssen, *Remonstrantie*, 41, says he had six sons. Two of his sons rose to high rank before 1631; of these, Yasin Khan died in 1634–5 with the *mansab* of 1,500/1,000, Samsam-ud-daula, *Maāthir*, II, 840.

formation in North India – should remain to be sung about in Hindustan until far into the nineteenth century, but were extinct in real life? Let us now consider the phenomenon of peasant-soldiering from another angle, that of Rajput clan leadership. The Ujjainiya Rajputs, as we saw, rose to prominence as contractors of military manpower under Sher Shah and, in the final chapter of this study, I will trace the history of their fortunes. First, however, I would like to draw attention to another Rajput family, the Bundelas. Although there were probably not many Purbiyas amongst its recruits, an investigation of its career will yield a number of insights – political, religious, as well as from the point of view of peasant studies – into the phenomenon of the North Indian military labour market.

4

Politics and entrepreneurship of a 'spurious' Rajput clan

Purbiyas, Ujjainiyas, or Bundelas were, of course, not the only identities one comes across in the history of North Indian recruitment. Just to give an impression of the extreme colourfulness and fluidity of this, often semi-pastoral, world of vagabondage and service, we mention the Baheliyas, a category of men who for long apparently were an important source of manpower in Hindustan. We are told that, perhaps during the reign of the Tughluqs at Delhi in the fourteenth century, 'a certain Sanidi, an African, and a Baheliya, with the title of hazari', were appointed to be joint governers of the fort of Chunar on the Ganges above Benares. A *jāgīr* of twenty-seven villages was conferred on them. Crooke, however, says it was Akbar who garrisoned the fort with a body of Baheliyas under a commander known as Hazari. These men remained at Chunar as a garrison until its final surrender to the British in 1772. After that they fell into obscurity and, in the 1890s, the descendant of the last *hazārī* of Chunar was a 'runner' in the government *tahsīl*.[1] But the Baheliyas in their heyday had not been restricted to Chunar. During the seventeenth century, they were conspicuous as footsoldiers fighting under Mughal commanders. Mirza Nathan mentions them as serving in Bengal in 1612.[2] And Bhimsen refers to them on two occasions. He says that, in 1692, the Mughal *faujdār* of Kanchipuram in South India had many Baheliyas in his service who, after a battle, went over to the Maratha enemy. And in 1700, hundreds of Baheliya footmen were killed as a result of an ill-timed explosion during the siege of Satara by

1 *Mirzapur Gazetteer*, 307. Crooke, *Tribes and Castes*, I, 105. See also Thomas, *Chronicles*, 196.

2 Mirza Nathan, *Bahāristān-i-Ghaybī*, I, 189 and II, 826. Borah explains 'Bahilis' as 'Bhils', but there cannot be much doubt that Baheliya is meant. However, there may be a connection between Bhils and Baheliyas, see Crooke, *Tribes and Castes*, I, 40, 104.

Aurangzeb; the survivors, enraged at the carelessness of their Mughal commander, set fire to the siege batteries as a substitute for the proper cremation of their 'brothers, sons and friends'.[3] As hirelings Baheliyas probably retained a rather bad reputation through the centuries, as is shown by the story current in Central India of a 'cunning', 'wicked' Baheliya who, for a gold piece, shot dead the great Gond hero-raja Hira Khan from behind a tree.[4] They must have come from what is now the state of Uttar Pradesh. There, they were later well-known as a 'caste' of hunters, numbering in 1896, 34,000. The Karauls, who, according to Crooke, belonged to the Baheliya category, contained several sub-identities, hindu as well as muslim, e.g. Hazari (commanders of thousand), Purbiya (Eastern), Uttariya (Northern) and, among the muslims, Turkiya. The names Hazari and Purbiya suggest a military tradition and one is therefore not surprised to find that the Karauls of the Benares area as described by Sherring in 1872, were largely employed as sepoys by the families of the native nobility and gentry of Benares. The common British essentialist view of identities and 'caste' prevented Sherring from seeing how this profession induced them, in a way that was absolutely justifed, to claim and to profess the identity especially associated with their kind of service. 'Although only Sudras', he observed, they indulged 'the habit of affixing "Sing" to their names as though they were Rajpoots.'[5]

'Possibly allied', according to Crooke, with the Baheliyas were the Pasis, of whom in 1891 there were 1.2 million in the United Provinces. Pasi was a merely occupational identity and included a number of distinct groups whose only obvious connection was the occupation of extracting the juice of the date palm. There were 305 subdivisions, among the most important of which were Baheliyas, Bhils, Baniyas and Bhadauriyas.[6] In nineteenth-century Awadh, the Pasis were 'village watchmen but inveterate thieves and robbers, when not employed as such'. They were experts in archery and formidable especially at night. All refractory landholders used to hire bodies of Pasis to fight for them. They cost little as they paid themselves out of their plunder. Apart from these, there were also independent gangs; Sleeman describes the genesis of such a Pasi group under Brahman leadership. Some Pasis became Rajputs by

[3] Bhimsen, *Tarikh-i-Dilkasha*, 186, 222. [4] Hivale, *Pradhans*, 97, 98.

[5] Crooke, *Tribes and Castes*, I, 105. Sherring, *Hindu Tribes and Castes*, 353. See also Russell and Hīra Lāl, *Tribes and Castes*, IV, 359–70.

[6] Crooke, *Tribes and Castes*, IV, 142, 143, 152.

giving their daughters to Panwars and other Rajput families, 'when, by robbery and murder, they have acquired wealth and landed property'. A great many of the Indian officers and sepoys of the Bengal Army, Sleeman added, got such wives while they were home on furlough and 'pressed for time'.[7] In one version of the legend of Alha and Udal, perhaps the best-known epic of Hindustan, a Pasi figured prominently, which means that the heroic character of this category of 'thieves' was generally acknowledged by the peasantry.[8]

The cases of the Baheliyas and Pasis are symptomatic of the casual treatment these mainly hindu, spurious Rajput infantrymen have received in historiography, a modern historian even disbelieving a Persian chronicler's reference to the Baheliyas.[9] Yet it appears that we are dealing here with quite a glorious tradition of service or *naukarī* that lasted over many centuries. It is practically impossible to analyse the tribal-pastoralist or peasant background of such groups 'from below'. Only when their commanders try to acquire a territorial power base of their own or acquire fame in the service of empire do the sources of history allow more than a glimpse of them. But it is clear that the service tradition of Hindustan came out in many statures and colours, and that, for all its shared culture of soldiering and its continuity at the local and 'folk' level, it manifested itself in a multitude of groupings, a variety of origins and identities. The limitations of the sources are not such, though, that we must leave it at this. The history of the fighting men's leadership does after all yield a number of insights into the conditions of their service. It is to one of the families of peasant warlords, the Bundela Rajput one, that we now turn. The role of the Bundelas in Mughal military history and in regional agrarian exploitation has rendered available information of a kind that is lacking with regard to other categories of soldiers. Partly, these data concern the folk culture of the recruiting areas and the social origin of the recruits themselves. They also illustrate something of the politics on the employers' side of the military labour market as well as the tensions to which a family wrestling with the problem of

[7] Sleeman, *Journey*, 59, 170, 177, 180, 181, 266–8, 274, 278, 282. Sharar, *Lucknow*, 115.

[8] Crooke, *Tribes and Castes*, IV, 141.

[9] Jadunath Sarkar thought that 'Baheliya' was a mistake for 'Māvlē', but his only reason seems to have been that he was unfamiliar with the name, Jadunath Sarkar, *History of Aurangzib*, V, 170, 173. See also Samsam-ud-daula, *Maāṯhir*, II, 937.

being both territorial lord and military entrepreneur was subject under Mughal rule.

The *mansabdār* and the *yuva rāja*

It is indeed impossible, in a study like this one, to ignore the Bundelas. A late seventeenth-century manuscript, enumerating the divisions of the Mughal imperial army, sums up its infantry in the phrase 'Baksariyahs [about whom later] and Bundelahs'. And Manucci wrote that the footsoldiers of the empire were commonly either 'of the Bundelah tribe or Purbiyas from the direction of Allahabad'. The Bundelas were a clan of Rajputs who, in the sixteenth and early seventeenth centuries, came to dominate the region to the south of the Yamuna between Gwalior in the west and Rewa in the east. They gave their name to a category of soldiers in much the same way as the Ujjainiya Rajputs did. There can be little doubt that the Bundela or Ujjainiya infantrymen as a rule were not Bundelas or Ujjainiyas in a genealogical sense. They were only engaged by commanders and jemadars who were members of these two clans. Both these landholding clans thus specialised as military employers. But whereas about the year 1600 the Ujjainiyas would lose their dominant position in the Bhojpuri recruiting area to the Mughals, the several branches of the Bundela Rajput family struggled on to serve the empire, actively recruiting soldiers in North India and leading them into war for the Mughals until the middle of the eighteenth century.[10]

There was another difference between the two clans. The Ujjainiya Rajputs gave the name of their capital Bhojpur to the dialect of Hindi spoken over an entire region, but the Bundela Rajputs' fame not only survives in the dialect of their area, Bundeli, they also put the stamp of their name on what indisputably became their country, Bundelkhand. As landholders, indeed, the Bundelas were more successful than the Ujjainiyas. Partly at least, the explanation is that their role as *zamīndārs* and rajas was intimately connected with military recruitment in the service of an empire that found it difficult to dislodge them from their jungly home country. The two occupations of service and landholding could be pursued independently but, if circumstances and a man's skills permitted him to combine the two, great wealth and power could result. On the

[10] Yule and Burnell, *Hobson-Jobson*, 136a. Manucci, *Storia*, II, 459. Tikkiwal, *Jaipur*, 63, 83, 87, 88, 125.

other hand, such ventures at subordinate state formation during the heyday of empire were not without risks as the story of the Bundelas under Akbar, Jahangir and Shahjahan would show dramatically.

It seems that, as early as the thirteenth century, the Bundelas had acquired a foothold in the area where today the Jhansi (UP) and Tikamgarh (MP) districts meet. There is a tradition which tells of altercations, in that period, with the Khangar chiefs in Garh Kundar ending in the extermination of the latter and the birth of a 'Bundela endogamous group' consisting of Bundelas, Dhandheras – who claimed Chauhan status – and a number of Panwar families in the region. Other major Rajput clans would later refuse matrimonial alliances with this small cluster, thus relegating it to a position of relative isolation in terms of the doctrine of Rajput genealogical orthodoxy that would increasingly rule behaviour from Mughal times onwards. The Bundelas, in other words, became a 'spurious' Rajput clan which was not allowed a share in the modern Rajput development towards ascribed status.

The history, as distinguished from legend, of the Bundelas properly begins with Rudra Pratap who managed to maintain his independence in wranglings with the Lodis and then, after Babur's invasion had put an end to Lodi power, extended his territory as much as he could. In 1531, he descended from the relatively inaccessible fort of Kundar to found a new capital on the river Betwa. This was Orchha, the city after which the leading Bundela state would be called. Perhaps this change of residence also represents a Bundela endeavour to leave their reputation as jungle robbers behind them and to win a share of the prizes of the big politics of Hindustan. The family's change-over from Saivism to Vaishnavism, which also dates from the sixteenth century, probably reflects a similar move towards participation in all-India concerns.

Soon after the foundation of Orchha, Rudra Pratap was killed 'by a tiger from whose clutches he was rescuing a cow', to which the *Orchha State Gazetteer* painstakingly adds: 'though he slew the beast and saved the sacred animal, he died of his injuries'.[11] Rudra Pratap, clearly, was an immaculate Rajput. The story is perhaps akin to later reports that tell about similar events in which the Mughal emperor's rather than a cow's life is saved by a brave

[11] *Orchha Gazetteer*, 14–17.

Rajput.[12] But it would be some time before the service of Vishnu and that of the Mughal *bādshāh* merged into a natural service ideal in Bundela Rajput consciousness. The interval largely coincides with the reign of Madhukar Shah, Rudra Pratap's son, which lasted from 1554 to 1592.

Madhukar Shah, it was said, was by inclination 'a religious recluse' rather than a king and his *rānī* was 'of much the same temperament'. The latter was once apprised in a dream of the fact that a statue of Ram Chandra lay on the bottom of the river Sarju at Ayodhya. Thus honestly found, the statue was carried to Orchha where it would be reverently kept in the palace for centuries. It is clear from anecdotes like these, long-cherished in the Bundela family, that the recognition in Awadh and elsewhere in Hindustan of their piety and courage according to the tenets of *kṣatriya-dharma* was one of their main preoccupations. The Bundelas seem, moreover, to have stressed that their relationship with the Mughal royal family not only did not stand in the way of their careers as Rajputs, but was based on a Mughal declaration of explicit faith in their *dharma*. The Rajput legitimacy that would be denied them by the great clans of Rajasthan, was bestowed on them by the Delhi dynasty. Madhukar Sah, it is said, only once waited on the emperor Akbar whom, according to the poet Keshav Das, he considered 'a common Khān', but he succeeded in making this one visit into something unforgettable. 'Akbar', the story goes, 'in order to try his piety, of which he had heard much, issued an order prohibiting the wearing of a *māla* (rosary) or Hindu sect marks in *darbār*. Madhukar, however, went in with both, the *tīka* being painted on even more conspicuously than usual. Akbar was pleased at his courage and the particular mark the Rājā wore on that day is called the *Madhukar Shāhī Tīka* to this day.'[13] The result of the meeting could indeed not have been more satisfactory. Of course, as the anecdote implies, Akbar was interested in courage rather than peity. By allowing the test to be conducted in a religious non-muslim idiom, the Mughal publicly recognised the obscure Rajput chief's claim to Kshatriyahood as well as allowing him, through his service, a share in the empire's all-India campaigns and profits.

Another incident, long-preserved in Bundela memory, reflects a

[12] *Ibid.*, 33, where it is said that, one day, Udot Singh, raja of Orchha, when in attendance on Bahadur Shah (1707–12), killed a tiger singlehanded. Most famous is the case of Anirai Singh Dalan, Jahangir, *Tūzuk*, 1, 185–8.

[13] Keśavadāsa, 'Kavipriyā', 1, 25. *Orchha Gazetteer*, 19.

few more elements that were to become essential to the Mughal–Bundela relationship. On one occasion Madhukar, having practically lost a battle against the Mughals, succeeded in wounding Murad, Akbar's second son. Murad fell from his horse and lost hold of his weapons. The Bundela asked him to get up, take his weapon and fight, whereupon the prince wanted to know why his adversary did not kill him now he had the chance. Madhukar Shah replied: 'I am a Kshattri, it is contrary to the custom of Kshattris to kill a weaponless man.' This was the turning point of the story which, as told by a Bundela chief in about the year 1900, continued as follows: 'Murad was so struck at this that he exclaimed "I pardon you." The Raja said: "I will make peace if you promise to restore my kingdom to me." Murad replied: "Such part of the kingdom as has been in your possession up to this date shall be restored to you and a sanad to this effect shall be given to you, but you will have to accept conditions." ' The condition turned out to be that the Bundelas 'should assist the Emperor with 7,000 Sawars when the latter required them for war'.[14] The engagement thus concluded foreshadowed the later recognition of so-called '*watan-jāgīrs*', the empire's prebendal service tenures (*jāgīr*) that were coterminous with a chief's patrimonial lands (*watan*), but the undisturbed possession of which obliged the holder to put part of its resources to the service of the emperor.

What exactly was the emperor's due was determined by the process of rivalry and negotiation that was the essence of medieval Indian politics. The term '*watan-jāgīr*' sharply exposed the undecided character of the relationship between a suzerain lord, always far removed from achieving a monopoly on the exercise of armed violence in his nominal territory, on the one hand, and the allodial rajas, warlords and peasant chiefs on the other. Though there was lasting agreement of the significance of Rajput virtue to both the empire and the martial *zamīndār*s and peasants of Hindustan, a fixed formula that settled the question of the extent of the *zamīndārs*' control of the agrarian as well as the human resources of their *watan*s *vis-à-vis* the empire could never be found. *Mansabdārī* and *jāgīrdārī* systems notwithstanding, the tussle for the sharing of these resources would last until the end of empire. Everything depended on the shifts in the balance of power between the parties and the unending negotiating process that from time to time reformulated the terms of the alliance. But this admirably suited

[14] Silberrad, 'Contribution', 110.

so-called 'spurious' Rajputs like the Bundelas who, after doctrinal genealogy had gained a foothold further to the west, continued the ancient Rajput service tradition. Surrounded by sultanates and rival clans, political survival to them, as to the Purbiyas, had always meant open recruitment and an ongoing series of accommodations and alliances.

Under the Mughals, however, a certain pattern would gradually emerge. Madhukar Shah never did achieve much in this respect and spent much time as a rebel and a fugitive. In 1592, he died in the jungles of Bundelkhand.[15] His son Ram Sah then went to court and presented his case to Akbar. But he turned out to be one among many claimants for the Bundela patrimony. After two years of uncertainty, such of his rivals as had acquired their rights under Madhukar Shah were allowed to continue to enjoy them. This meant that of 22 *jāgīr*s in the Bundela area, eight were those of Madhukar's sons, twelve were held by a number of allied clans and tribes such as the Kachhwahas, Panwars and Gonds, while two others, Kalpi and Bhander, were given to muslims who may have been local Afghan *amīrs*, remnants of a former dynasty. Jointly, these sharers were bound to furnish the force of 7,000 suwars which was settled upon in a former agreement. The figure twenty-two may well, as it often does, express the joint responsibility of a number of commanders in the service of empire.[16]

The compiler of the *Jhansi District Gazetteer*, however, speaking about Akbar's reign, felt there was 'little reason to doubt that, in the systematic distribution into *sūbah*s and *sarkār*s undertaken by the Delhi monarch, the whole of Bundelkhand was reckoned in the imperial dominions and paid its contributions to the imperial exchequer'.[17] So much is clear that, throughout this period, the jostling for power and position went on unabated and a settlement seemed unreachable. Madhukar Shah's son Ram Sah was not capable of controlling his seven brothers, least of all the most turbulent among them, Bir Singh Deo. Akbar's command to Ram Sah to bring his brother to order produced no result. Bir Singh Deo and some of his brothers made themselves the masters of a number of strongholds as well as of Erachh, the headquarters of one of the two Mughal *sarkār*s in the region. One of these brothers of Bir Singh Deo was one Indrajit about whom Keshav Das, a poet

15 *Jhansi Gazetteer*, 192(n). Samsam-ud-daula, *Maathir*, II 105–07.
16 *Jhansi Gazetteer*, 191(n). Silberrad, 'Contribution', 111. *Orchha Gazetteer*, 19.
17 *Jhansi Gazetteer*, 191.

employed at his court, said in 1601, perhaps not without ground: 'Although there is a great family of the sons and brothers of king Ram [Sah], nevertheless the whole burden of upholding the kingdom rests on the head of Indrajit.'[18] Ram Sah, prodded by Akbar to put an end to his clan brethren's land-grabbing – or to use the term chosen by W. H. Sleeman, a nineteenth-century connoisseur of traditional Bundela politics, their *bhūmiyāvat* – succeeded in compelling Bir Singh to join a Mughal expedition to the Dekkan. The latter, however, without asking permission soon returned home and then fled to Allahabad, the residence of Akbar's rebellious son Salim. This new alliance had far-reaching consequences. In 1602, Bir Singh Deo murdered Akbar's favourite minister Shaikh Abul Fazl just after the latter had made arrangements for an attack to be launched against Indrajit. The Shaikh's head was sent to Salim's court at Allahabad. This affront was too severe to be atoned for without bloody vengeance. Pursued relentlessly by imperial troops, Bir Singh Deo would in the end no doubt have been hunted down and killed if Akbar's sudden death in 1605 had not saved him.[19]

Rajput clan factionalism and Mughal family quarrels were inextricably interwoven in these years. But whereas the latter was a periodical phenomenon, the first was permanent and provided the Mughal with the only effective leverage short of brute force in their dealings with the clan. The settlement that was now arrived at did away with the non-Bundela share in the *jāgīrs* of the area: the internal wranglings of the clan brethren guaranteed to the imperial court the possibility of access to the power resources of the clan anyway. Soon after his accession, Jahangir ousted Ram Sah from the Orchha *gaddī* and granted the chiefship of the clan to Bir Singh Deo. Ram Sah and Indrajit made some show of resistance but had to yield to Abdullah Khan, then in charge of Kalpi and sent by the emperor to install Bir Singh Deo. In 1607, Ram Sah was taken to Agra where Jahangir gave him a robe of honour. Eventually the emperor would not only grant him a *jāgīr* yielding an income of three lakhs of rupees, but would also marry his daughter, thus cementing his bond with his friend Bir Singh Deo's rival. Indeed, Mughal use of Rajput factionalism for their own ends would be a constant feature of the relationship. Yet the

18 Keśavadāsa, *Kavipriyā*, I 38.

19 *Jhansi Gazetteer*, 191. Silberrad, 'Contribution', 112. Asad Beg in Elliot and Dowson, *History of India*, IV, 150.

Rajputs were not at a loss to respond to the Mughal thrusts aimed at their weakest spot.

One factor, no doubt, in the honourable outcome achieved by Ram Sah had been that his grandson Bharat Sah, in spite of Bir Singh Deo's efforts, had held out for several years in the jungles of Bundelkhand championing his grandfather's cause. Later also, Bharat would remain an enterprising soldier who would never allow his imperial interests to get the better of his concern for his patrimony, or '*watan*'. In 1612, he succeeded Ram Sah and received the title of raja. He generally extended his territory and conquered Chanderi, the fortress that would lend its name to the kingdom of his descendants. Shahjahan gave him 'the present of a drum' and a *sanad* conferring on him the *jāgīr* of Chanderi, whereas Bharat Sah, for his part, served the empire as *faujdār* of a town in the royal domain and as a military commander, dying in Telangana as a *mansabdār*, according to one source, of 4,000/3,500.[20] The Chanderi case illustrates very well the complementary character of the *naukarī*, or service, and the *zamīndāri*, or landholding, principles in medieval Indian politics. This complementarity, as we saw, is admirably summarised in the concept of '*watan-jāgīr*'. It was a major feature of the Rajput–Mughal relationship and particularly of the part played by Bundelas in imperial history.

Yet another manifestation of this complementarity that seems to be the essence of the seventeenth-century Mughal–Rajput relationship, is what one would like to call the pattern of the *yuva rāja* and the *mansabdār*. The *yuva rāja* is the crown prince and champion of the clan. Often, while the raja is absorbed in negotiations with the Mughal throne or in the duties his imperial *mansab* demands of him either in the Dekkan wars or at court where he stands in attendance with the rivalling lords, a rebel son will raise his head in the jungles back home. These internecine *bhūmiyāvat*s would occur anyway, independently of empire, but with the Mughals at Delhi they became part of a wider institutional framework. The Rajput *mansabdār* may openly disavow, yet secretly encourage, his son, maintaining his respectability in the capital and at the same time making the most of his regional power. The *yuva rāja* may either yield to or resist the temptation to set himself up as a chief. But whatever the outcome is, the performance of both these roles – that of the *yuva rāja* and that of the *mansabdār* – is a corollary of the

[20] *Orchha Gazetteer*, 21. *Jhansi Gazetteer*, 194. Samsam-ud-daula, *Maāthir*, 1, 407, 408. Jahangir, *Tūzuk*, 1, 87, 160, 231. Silberrad, 'Contribution', 114.

clan's participation in empire. It is possible that others than father and son perform them, as in the case of Ram Sah and his grandson Bharat Sah. It may also be that both roles are alternately taken up by the same man and even that the clan champion and the imperial *amīr* swap places as the game proceeds. Still the pattern remains the same and basically represents the response of the Rajputs to the empire's divisive strategies that continuously threaten to disrupt their brotherhoods.

The terms *mansabdār* and *yuva rāja* belong to distinct political systems that exist independently of each other. Admittedly, *yuva rāja* is not a term that clan society itself selects for the specific role we have in view. In the language of the clan his activity is implicit in a term like *bhūmiyāvat* and more emphatically in the word Rajput itself as we interpreted it in the preceding chapter: the princely son indefatigably in search of land, honour, and a lord to serve. What we should like to stress is that the imperial and Rajput systems were at the same time rivals and partners in empire, a relationship that made perfect sense in practice, even though European political grammar may be at a loss to find words for it. Thus the Mughal–Rajput negotiating game was the result of the interplay of two strategies. Sometimes, they may have seemed indistinguishable, as when the Mughal court, exploiting the Rajput division of roles as between court and patrimony, attempted to foment a factionalist division of interests between clan segments[21] or when the Rajputs fought their internecine quarrels with the help of Mughal resources. However, what is clear is, firstly, that both strategies are recognisable in all the great clashes between Bundelas and Mughals and, secondly, that these collisions seemed to erupt into warfare at least once a generation, as every generation of clan brethren worked out its own factionalist constellation as well as its own schemes to make the most of both the *watan*'s and the *bādshāhī* resources. Basic to all this is that access to manpower, not land revenue, was the clan's main asset, whereas the attractiveness of the empire consisted in the wide field of opportunities its campaigns presented to all professional fighters.

In spite of the creation of a separate Bundela *rāj* at Chanderi, which he had to tolerate, no Bundela leader was ever as spectacularly successful in his handling of the resources of clan and empire as Bir Singh Deo. It was his genius that set in motion the Bundela

21 See, for instance, the case of Gopal Singh Chandrawat, mentioned in Bhimsen *Tarikh-i-Dilkasha*, 218.

tradition of military entrepreneurship and imperial *naukarī*. There can be little doubt that he managed to put numerous Rajput contingents at the disposal of Jahangir without, on the other hand, ever having to relinquish his personal command over them. Little is known about his early campaigns in the service of the empire. One is tempted to think that he followed in the footsteps of Man Singh Kachhwaha, who was perhaps the first to demonstrate the wonderful openings to Rajput soldiering offered by the Mughal state. After an appointment with Mahabat Khan against Mewar and with Khan Jahan to the Dekkan, in about 1612 Bir Singh Deo's *mansabdārī* rank was 4,000/2,200. In 1615 Jahangir, as he noted in his memoirs, increased his *mansab* by 700 horse and gave him leave to go to his own country 'directing that he should present himself at court at stated periods'.[22] In Agra, Bir Singh Deo maintained a palace on the Yamuna, situated to the south of the fort and next to Man Singh's mansion. But, during the 1620s, he must only rarely have been present at court. From 1620 to 1622 he was in the South with Prince Khurram fighting Malik Ambar, whose capital city of Khirki (now: Aurangabad) he had the luck to destroy. In the beginning of 1623, when Khurram rebelled, he was summoned to the presence and reported himself at Thanesar in the Panjab with an army that 'elicited great praise'. Within a few weeks he received even greater honour. It was recorded in Jahangir's memoirs: 'I dignified Rājā Bīr Singh Deo, than whom in the Rajput caste there is no greater Amir, with the title of Maharaja.' Soon Maharaja Bir Singh could return to Bundelkhand. In 1624, he had to leave again and joined Prince Parwiz and Mahabat Khan in their campaign against Khurram in eastern Hindustan. On this occasion, he first contributed two or three lakhs to the costs of the campaign, and in the end plundered Khurram's camp seizing many golden *ashrāfīs*, jewels, 3,000 horses and 40 elephants as booty.[23] Or perhaps one should say that he prevented Khurram's enemies from getting hold of all this, because a Dutch chronicler has remarked that Bir was 'a great friend of Khurram'. Not long after this he was back in his own country where he died in September/October 1627, a few weeks before Jahangir.[24] A later Persian source would state that, towards the end of his life, he had

22 Jahangir, *Tūzuk*, I, 231, 281. Samsam-ud-daula, *Maāthir*, I, 424.
23 Pelsaert, *Geschriften*, 155, 156, 160, 169, 180–1, 187, 189, 191–2, 196, 249.
24 *Ibid.*, 225. B. D. Gupta, *Maharaja Chhatrasal*, 6. Jahangir, *Tūzuk*, II, 159, 247, 250, 253. Pelsaert, *Geschriften*, 225; Bir Singh died in Muharram 1037 AH.

wielded 'such power as scarcely any other of the Rajahs of India had attained to'.[25]

Though no explicit information on the point has come down to us, it is clear that Bir Singh Deo's power was based on an impressive ability to recruit, organise and lead armies that received the label 'Rajput' and lived up to the reputation implied by that name. It is also obvious that his brokerage on the military labour market of Hindustan yielded a fabulous wealth of which he spent a great deal, though by no means all, during his lifetime. It is interesting to try and investigate what kind of expenses proved attractive to this businesslike man. Of course, there were first of all the military expenses that were a corollary of his career as a commander, such as the two or three lakhs he invested in the 1624 campaign. Then there must have been costly gifts to the emperor, though the white cheetah once transported to court was perhaps acquired rather cheaply from the Bundelkhand jungles. The presents received in return – robes of honour, special horses, from Kutch for example, a jewelled sword – must have been of less value than the *nazar*s and contributions that loyalty and expediency demanded from him as well as from all the great men gathered around the throne.[26]

Yet, it is quite possible that the sums Bir Singh Deo laid out in Bundelkhand and in a number of centres of pilgrimage in his North Indian recruiting areas exceeded his spending at court. It was recorded in the memory of the clan – we depend here on two late nineteenth-century versions[27] – that he was a mighty builder who not only built the great palace forts at Orchha and Datiya, the latter at a cost of 36,90,980 rupees, but also many other edifices 'within and without the limits of Central India'. Some of these suggest agrarian and commercial expansion, others are proof of conspicuous investment in religious merit. One tradition has it that on a Sunday in December 1618, the foundations of fifty-two buildings were laid, whereas the other account says that he built the famous tanks of Bir Sagar and Barwa Sagar and many others, fifty-two in all. At Orchha, part of his Chaturbhuj Vishnu temple still stands. An even greater achievement of his perhaps was the building, at a cost of 33 lakhs of rupees, of the Keshavadeva temple, devoted to Krishna, at Mathura. Tavernier wrote about this building that it was 'one of the most sumptuous buildings in all India'. It was built of the same red sandstone as used by the Mughals for the red fort,

25 Samsam-ud-daula, *Maāthir*, I 424. 26 Jahangir, *Tūzuk*, I, 147, 204, II, 12.
27 Silberrad, 'Contribution', 114, 115. *Orchha Gazetteer*, 22, 23.

for a number of mosques, and for the houses of the great nobles at Agra. After those of Jagannath and Benares, it was the most considerable temple in India and was, though the numbers had much decreased in Tavernier's time, for a while 'visited by the greatest concourse of pilgrims'.[28] But this doesn't sum up Bir Singh Deo's investment in his relationship with the holy city of Mathura. In 1614, he is said to have gone there on a pilgrimage and have weighed himself against an amount of gold which, together with an additional 81 *man* of gold, he distributed in charity. The ceremony of weighing one's body and then giving away its equivalent in grain, silver, or gold is called *tulādān*. It ritually replaces an inauspicious or impure person and restores his harmony with the cosmic world. The 81 *man* of gold may well have represented the 81 *pargana*s (districts) which, as we shall see, constituted Bir Singh Deo's realm. The ritual, therefore, ensured a lasting future for both the king and his realm by bringing them into line with the principles of dharmic order. For centuries, the Orchha family would cherish the fact that the balance prepared to weigh the great king was still kept at Mathura on the Vishrant Ghat, dedicated to Krishna. His munificent gifts were mentioned in *sanad*s held by priests at that place. Tradition also has it that Bir Singh Deo 'made nine pilgrimages and offered innumerable sacrifices', which again is an indication, if any is needed in addition to what has been brought forward already, that in terms of time and money enormous sums, amounting to many crores of rupees, must have been spent by the maharaja on military business as well as on the dignity of his rule in Bundelkhand and a share in the religious affairs of Hindustan, his main recruiting area.

Of course, what was at stake here was the legitimacy of the hindu king and of his *rāj*. What kind of king was Bir Singh Deo in this respect? Surely, his legitimacy as a raja was of a composite character. Territoriality, for one thing, had a share in it. He was said to have built fifty-two buildings in one day, his kingdom consisted of 81 *pargana*s and 12,500 – one and a quarter (*sawā*) of

[28] Growse, *Mathurā*, 36, 117–20. Tavernier, *Travels*, I, 85, II, 175, 186ff. See also Bernier, *Travels*, 284. The account published by Silberrad says that Bir Singh Deo in 1613 built a temple at Vrindavan at a cost of 30 lakhs, but probably the temple at Mathura is meant, Silberrad, 'Contribution', 114. In 1670, the temple was destroyed by Aurangzeb and its richly jewelled images were brought to Agra and desecrated; see Muhammad Saki Mustaidd Khan in Elliot and Dowson, *History of India*, VII, 184. See, on the remains of this temple, Bute, *Private Journal*, I, 339, 340.

10,000 – villages: the figures express the completeness and sanctity of the realm. But there were many other elements: the *bādshāhī* relationship – extremely well developed – the association with the Krishna cult at the all-India pilgrimage centre at Mathura – achieved at great cost, but successful – and a more general tendency, apparently also quite effective, to conform to royal dharma. To elaborate the last point, Bir Singh Deo, according to later legend, was well acquainted with the *dharmaśāstra*s and once listened for seven days to recitations from the Mahapuranas. He was famed for his strict justice and it is said of him that 'one day his eldest son Jagat Deva when hunting, allowed his hound to kill a Brahma-chāri or hermit. On hearing thereof the Raja summoned his son to him, and put him to death for having caused the death of an innocent devotee.'

Many tales centred round the personality of the maharaja, some of them connected with his building activities, made the same point. The Jahangir Mahal at Orchha, so-called because the emperor reputedly stayed in it – a story that, though almost certainly erroneous, correctly professed the special relationship between the Orchha raja and Jahangir – was said to have been built on an island in the river Betwa selected for the purpose in the following manner. First, a pregnant Brahman woman with a load on her head, who endeavoured to cross the river at a particular spot, had to stop half-way as the pains of delivery came on her, whereupon Bir Singh Deo saw to it that his servants safely delivered her of a son, an act which earned him the blessings of the woman. Then a *sādhu* disclosed that the island on which the happy event had taken place, concealed hitherto invisible, but substantial, merit: it was the dwelling place of a great sage and if Bir Singh would build his palace there and reside in it, the rule of his family would be forever secured. Of course when, during the excavations that preceded the founding ceremonies, the great sage himself appeared from his underground hermitage and asked to be left in peace, his desires were complied with.[29] Henceforth he helped to uphold the Delhi–Bundela alliance, or at least the building now raised above his head, which proclaimed that alliance.

Bir Singh Deo's claim to legitimacy as a raja was thus clearly put forward in a variety of geographical directions and ideological

[29] *Orchha Gazetteer*, 22, 23. It was also remembered that he performed the 'Tāraian Birt', a fast for a month during which eating was only allowed when the stars were visible, which reminds one of the muslim fast of Ramadan, Silberrad, 'Contribution', 114.

idioms. But in one respect, the genealogical, it could not help but remain weak. He came to the *gaddī* by ousting his elder brother from Orchha, a fact never forgotten by the other branches of the family. More importantly, the status of the Bundelas as Rajputs was doubtful in a more general sense. This is particularly reflected in their marriages. Even Bir Singh Deo himself married only two Dhandhera – they were girls from the same village – and a Panwar wife.[30] The acceptance of Bundela girls by the Mughal royal family stands in sharp contrast to the isolated position the Bundelas occupied among the great Rajput lineages of North India. The 'achieved' nature of their prominence must have contributed something both to the value of the Bundelas in the judgement of the Mughals as well as to the efforts of the Bundelas themselves to acquire legitimising attributes and make up for their lack of good births and marriages. To the Mughals, the genealogical spuriousness of the Bundelas was an advantage rather than an embarrassment. The emperor must, in this respect, have argued much as he did in the case of the Barha Sayyids about whom he wrote, as we saw, that 'some people make remarks about their lineage, but their bravery is a convincing proof of their being Saiyids'.[31] The ultimate arbitrators of honour and virtue were the Timurids on the Delhi throne who seemed to many Rajputs to have espoused the cause of upholding their *dharma*. Thus men like Madhukar Shah and Bir Singh Deo could ignore the odious rules now construed by genealogical experts and the new marriage taboo of the Rajasthan aristocracy. In Hindustan there was a king and *bādshāh* who would determine their mettle both as Rajputs and as *amīr*s of the empire. Jahangir, finding among all the Rajputs of his realm no greater *amīr* than Bir Singh Deo, created him a maharaja and allowed him to bring together the resources with which ritually to underpin his proclamation as a king and an upholder of *dharma*. In this way it was made clear that performance in the service of Timur's dynasty could take precedence over any genealogical status, though such ascribed statuses might have a certain validity at a less exalted level of politics. This Mughal view of political expediency *vis-à-vis* the warlike adventurers of Hindustan perfectly suited the ancient soldiering traditions so pervasive in North India. And it particularly suited a hindu raja like Bir Singh, who with Mughal support grew into a great patron or father of Rajputs, i.e. 'princely sons', a term that, though apparently belonging to an idiom of kinship, should,

30 *Orchha Gazetteer*, 23.

31 Jahangir, *Tūzuk*, II, 269.

as we suggested, not be understood in an exclusively genealogical sense but as the proud name of all adventurers in search of a truly paternal and kingly employer.

When Jahangir in 1623 elevated Bir Singh Deo, the premier of Rajputs as he understood them, to the title of maharaja, he also increased the *mansab* of his son Jujhar Singh. This man then received, or had received on an earlier occasion, from the emperor the title of 'Jogrāj', as the term is spelled in Jahangir's 'memoirs'. As an English and several Dutch sources attest he soon became known as such in India at large. The latter mention him as 'Joogradia', 'Iugeras', 'Sjougeras' or 'Joegeraes'. I suspect the title was Yuga-Rāja, meaning 'Raja of the Age', brahmanised Persian idiom that took its inspiration from titles like Maryam Zamani (Mary of the Age), Khan Zaman (Lord of the Age) or Rustam Zaman (Rustam of the Age).[32] By conferring this title, Jahangir once more proclaimed himself the sole judge of true raja-hood, at the same time stressing its 'achieved' character: it was the emperor, and no one else, who at a particular juncture of time recognised the marks of princeliness on a man's forehead. Whether the clans of Mewar and Marwar were prepared to marry their daughters to such a man, was immaterial to the issue as seen from the imperial throne. On the contrary, the disdain of the lineages of the west reinforced rather than weakened the role of Timurid arbitration.

During the 1620s, though, Bundela ritual entrepreneurship, Vaishnava propaganda and Timurid inventiveness added more to the glory of the Bundela service tradition than to that of the Mughal state. One cannot help thinking, indeed, that the proceeds of Jahangir's Bundela alliance flowed in the direction of Bir Singh Deo's *watan* rather than into the imperial coffers. Bundela power in the empire was not adequately balanced with that of other Rajput clans, the Kachhwahas of Amber having been pushed into the background as Bir rose to favour. From the point of view of the maharaja, this meant there was no need to activate the *mansabdār*

[32] *Ibid.*, II, 253. ARA, VOC 1100 f. 224 v° ('Memorie gehouden bij forme van journaal', Surat 7.i.1629); VOC 1116 f. 89 (B. Pietersen to Heeren xvii, Surat 10.i.1636); VOC 1117 f. 728 v° (F. Timmers to B. Pietersen, Agra 3.i.1636); VOC 1119 p.1766 (B. Pietersen to A. van Diemen and Council, aboard 'Vere', 23.iv.1636). ARA, Collectie Geleynssen no.103 (W. Geleynssen to B. Pietersen, Agra 26.ii.1639). Foster, *English Factories*, 155. See for titles of the '-Zaman' type, Samsam-ud-daula, *Maāthir*, III s.v. Malikauz-Zamani, Rustam Zaman, Khan Zaman, etc. A comparable case of Jahangir conferring a Hindi title modelled on a Persian one is 'Singh-dalan' (tiger slayer) from 'Sher-afgan' (tiger thrower), Jahangir, *Tūzuk*, I, 113–14, 188.

versus *yuva rāja* clan strategy. The centre now had to make a move if it wanted to restore the balance. It would, however, only be in a position to regain the initiative if clan factionalism, long suppressed by Bir Singh's phenomenal success raised its head again. This inevitably happened towards the end of the maharaja's life.

Jujhar Singh and the Bundela inheritance

As Bir Singh grew more powerful and awe-inspiring, he became a potential danger to the empire that had set him up in the first place. But he was also increasingly troubled by his family affairs. The resulting tensions led to the beginnings of what, after Orchha and Chanderi, would become the third Bundela princely state, Datiya. When, in 1626, Mahabat Khan with his Rajput army made himself the master of the person of Jahangir in the Panjab, the Bundelas did not come to his help. Instead, Bir Singh Deo sent his son Bhagwan Rao to the emperor's camp, while he himself to a certain extent assisted Nur Jahan Begum's party by affording hospitality to Fidai Khan, one of her loyal noblemen.[33] Bir Singh by this time felt the weight of his years; he was estranged from the court he no longer frequented and was troubled by the rivalry between his sons who became ever more difficult to control. Towards 1626, he entrusted the management of the state to his eldest son Jujhar Singh, the Yuga-Raja, and distributed *jāgīrs* to his remaining sons, of whom there were at least ten. As Bhagwan Rao was then at court, his share was given to two of his sons. One of the latter was a certain Dhurmangad, a brave Rajput champion who once, after swimming a river, met a lion on the other bank which he killed with one blow of his fist – a man, in other words, unlikely to be prepared to share his father's *jāgīr* with his brothers. Bhagwan Rao, who was the more incensed at all this as he was, though younger than Jujhar Singh, the son of a senior *rānī*, returned to Orchha and, finding he did not get very far, left again for the imperial camp to put his case before Jahangir. As Bhagwan Rao had meanwhile won many friends at court, his departure seriously jeopardised Bir Singh's family arrangements. The old maharaja made a futile attempt to arrest his son *en route* and then decided to make terms. A separate *jāgīr*, including the town of Datiya with its palace, was granted to him and to this were added one hundred *Madhukarsāhī* lancers, three swords received from the emperor, an image of Lakshmi

33 Pelsaert, *Geschriften*, 209, 218, 225.

Narayan, formerly belonging to Madhukar Shah, and other gifts. The day that Bhagwan Rao took up his residence at Datiya, 20 October 1626, would later be reckoned to be the date of the foundation of the Datiya state. But that was hindsight. It would take decades and another spell of Mughal arbitration before the state could be established on a reasonably secure footing. When Bhagwan Rao died in 1656, after having served Shahjahan in several campaigns, his sons went to court and petitioned the emperor to allow them to keep their father's *jāgīr*. In the end Subha Karan, one of these sons, received a *jāgīr* of 12 lakhs including Datiya out of the kingdom of Orchha in recognition of his services with the Mughal army in Balkh and Badakhshan.[34]

The interplay between the imperial connection and the rivalry of the clan brethren had led to the formation of the Datiya state. The division of roles we have pointed at earlier as a recurrent phenomenon of Rajput–Mughal relations was found at play here again. In Bhagwan Rao's family, the father – Bhagwan Rao himself – and some of his sons represented the *mansabdāri* element of Bundela power, whereas Dhurmangad, the lion killer, and his brother championed the clan's local roots, taking upon themselves what we have called the role of the *yuva rāja*. Though the foundation of the Datiya state went partly at the expense of Orchha, the interests of the Bundela clan as a whole did not suffer from it. On the contrary, for a new nexus of Bundela brokerage between the imperial need for manpower and the military labour force of Hindustan was added to those of Chanderi and Orchha and this would strengthen the clan's position among the jobber-captains of the empire. The Datiya *gaddī* became another place to which Mughal honourable gifts and titles flowed, another regional locus of hindu kingship, another centre for the recruitment of peasant soldiers.

Thus Bundelkhand became a landscape strewn with an amalgam of kingly features and imperial honours. The *Maāṯẖir ul-Umarā*, an eighteenth-century biographical source, frequently mentions Bundelas, rajas as well as minor commanders, who received 'a robe of honour', 'the gift of a flag and a horse', 'the present of a drum', 'an ornamented sword', 'a jewelled dagger with Phūl Katārah', or 'a standard and a kettledrum'.[35] These honours were cherished for centuries and as late as the beginning of the twentieth century the

34 Silberrad, 'Contribution', 120. *Datia Gazetteer*, 4.
35 Samsam-ud-daula, *Maāṯẖir*, I, 408, 472, 728, 756; II, 882. Phul Katara literally means 'flower dagger'.

State Gazetteers duly stressed the exclusive character of some of them. One of the stories related is that once Rao Dalpat Rao of Datiya (1683–1707) was deputed to escort Husain Mir, one of Aurangzeb's begums, to Agra and took his own *rānī* along on the trip.

On the way his Rānī's elephant became troublesome while crossing a river and could not get over. Dalpat Rao, fearing that his Rānī's *pardah* would be broken, determined to kill her. The *begam*, however, hearing of this at once sent her own *chondel* (closed *pālki*) in which the Rānī was able to escape off the elephant. In remembrance of this event the Rānīs of Datiā still travel in a *chondel* when proceeding in State, a unique honour not enjoyed by any other State in Bundelkhand.[36]

The spell of the Mughal name continued for a long time. Once, during Muhammad Shah's reign (1719–48), the Orchha raja Udot Singh (1689–1736) and his son Prithvi Singh were attached to the emperor's retinue when he visited a Delhi mosque on the occasion of the Id festival. 'Udot Singh', the State Gazetteer says, 'received a *khilat* and Prithvī Singh a royal palanquin which is still preserved and is always used by the Chief at the *Id* festival to this day'. Even the powerless Shah Alam II was judged capable of adding to Orchha's glory. It must have been in 1762 that he passed through the state's capital and presented its ruler with 'a royal banner, and the title of *Mahendra* which is still borne by the Orchhā chief'.[37] As late as the nineteenth century, the states of Orchha and Datiya prided themselves on being *bādshāhī*, i.e. imperial. By thus emphasising their *reichsunmittelbar* character, to use the German term, they openly took as their point of reference their service to the centre rather than any allodial autonomy or genealogical self-righteousness. This, of course, was in perfect keeping with their significant role as brokers between the empire and the manpower of the imperial *sarkārs* of Hindustan, a region far beyond the territories they ruled.

Yet, neither the honours from a muslim monarch, nor the intensive nature of their service relationship with the Timurid dynasty, affected the hindu character of Bundela kingship in the least. In the seventeenth century, Raja Devi Singh of Chanderi was renowned for his knowledge of the *dharmaśāstras*, of astronomy, medicine and literature, while he was, our source adds as if to stress

[36] *Datia Gazetteer*, 5.
[37] *Orchha Gazetteer*, 33, 35. Jadunath Sarkar, *Fall*, II, 544.

that these things were by no means incompatible, 'at the same time an excellent shot'. Of other rajas it was remembered that they heard the recitation of the eighteen *Purāṇas* or presented gifts to brahmans: Udot Singh of Orchha gave a statue of a *man* in gold to brahmans and was then blessed with a son and successor, while Ram Chandra of Datiya, before setting out on a campaign in the service of the Mughal, offered 108 cows and a *man* of gold. Similarly, Pahar Singh of Orchha, hearing during the siege of Raisen in 1644 that the Gonds of the region employed cows in ploughing, moved into Gondwana to punish those responsible for this blasphemy and then proceeded to his duties in the Dekkan. Also not lacking is the phenomenon – frequently met with in Indian history – of the raja who, 'disgusted with this world', retired to devote himself to religious exercises, in this case at Chitrakut.[38]

Some of these *bādshāhī* rajas virtually spent their lives campaigning for the empire as was the case with Subha Karan (1656–83) and Dalpat Rao (1683–1707), both of Datiya, and Pahar Singh (1641–53) of Orchha. The completeness of Subha Karan's service is expressed in the tradition that he fought twenty-two battles for the emperor.[39] Dalpat Rao likewise took a leading part in all the major campaigns of his time. Of course, such total surrender to the role of imperial *mansabdār* held its risks. Dalpat Rao could only with great difficulty control his son Ramchandra, who joined Chhatrasal Bundela in his rebellious *bhūmiyāvat*. Dalpat had to instruct his agents at home to enlist a local force and much money had to be spent to prevent the over-eager '*yuva rāja*' from taking over control of Datiya.[40] Of Pahar Singh's Orchha it has been remarked that it suffered because of its chief's continued absence in the wars.[41] The problem of striking the balance between the 'mansabdār' and the '*yuva rāja*' roles never ceased to trouble these lineages as long as the empire lasted, for all arrangements of necessity depended a good deal on the changing personal relationships of clansmen with each other and with the parties at court.

Certainly, it was seldom enough that a local chief contented

38 Silberrad, 'Contribution', 117, 118, 121, 122, 125. *Orchha Gazetteer*, 31, 32.

39 *Datia Gazetteer*, 4. Silberrad, 'Contribution', 121. The figure 22 is frequently used to denote a certain completeness, especially of armies. See *ibid.*, where Dalpat Rao is with a force of 22 rajas, and *Orchha Gazetteer*, 32, where a Sengar Rajput attacks Orchha with 22,000 men. Also, Mirza Nathan, *Bahāristān-i-Ghaybī*, I, 13, 172, 221, 223, 230, 415, II, 757, Pelsaert, *Geschriften*, 97, 174, and I. H. Siddiqi, *Sher Shah Sur*, 80, 153.

40 Bhimsen, *Tarikh-i-Dilkasha*, 200, 201, 211, 214. *Datia Gazetteer*, 6.

41 *Orchha Gazetteer*, 32.

himself with the *pargana*s the emperor was pleased to grant him. To win respect and a somewhat redoubtable following, it was necessary to make an effort oneself, either in the shape of connived at *bhūmiyāvat* or of open confrontation with the centre. A large part of the territory – in all yielding two crores of rupees – that Bir Singh Deo acquired must have been the result of his own conquests, angrily put up with by some, but never by all. After Bharat Sah Bundela had, in 1616, seized the town of Chanderi, which would become his capital, he went to meet Prince Khurram who was then on his way to the Dekkan. The prince was pleased with the report of the storming of the fortress and granted his visitor a *sanad*.[42] But as a rule the Mughal was bound to put some kind of check on such initiatives and to assert his superior rights, if only by claiming a share of the spoils secured by his subject. Indeed the management of the resources of India often looks like a kind of political sharecropping between the Mughals and the imperial armies on the one hand and regional landed powers on the other. Maintaining the joint character of the venture and securing its share of the proceeds of regional military entrepreneurship consumed much of the energies of the centre.

With regard to the Bundelas, a crucial period in this respect began with Bir Singh Deo's decline and death (1627); it would last until 1641. Bir, as we saw, had been a great friend of Khurram, Jahangir's rebellious son in the early 1620s. And the historian Khafi Khan says that, during his last years, he 'preferred the path of rebellion', attacking the imperial domains, looting caravans and, of course, collecting 'immense treasure'. His successor Jujhar Singh, the Yuga-Raja of 1623, another source recounts, was attending Shahjahan (the erstwhile Prince Khurram) at Agra in 1628 when he found that an addition was made in the books of the imperial treasury to the tribute due from his father. There were no doubt good reasons for this increased assessment, but these things required perhaps more tact than Shahjahan could spare during the first months of his reign. Anyway, Jujhar Singh at once took up the challenge, left court without taking leave of the emperor and returned to Orchha where he had an army consisting of 15,000 men. He then held the rank of 4,000/4,000 and had recently, on

42 Silberrad, 'Contribution', 124. See for Bir Singh Deo's oppression of the *zamīndārs* in his neighbourhood, Abul Hamid Lahori in Elliot and Dowson, *History of India*, VII, 7.

paying homage to Shahjahan, received a robe of honour, a jewelled dagger with *phūl katārā*, a flag and drums. What he wanted above all, however, was to reassert the position of the Bundela clan in imperial affairs and in particular the primacy of the Orchha *gaddī* over the upstart *gaddī*s of his cousin and brother at Chanderi and Datiya. He garrisoned his fortress and occupied the passes that led to his country.[43]

It seems that Shahjahan regarded the concentration of Bundela power claimed by Jujhar Singh as a major challenge to his reputation and he decided to make a vigorous stand at the commencement of his reign. He left Agra in December 1628 and, after a tiger hunt lasting a week, took the Gwalior road. Mahabat Khan, the Khan-i-Khanan, was directed to attack Jujhar Singh with 10,000 horse, 5,000 musketeers, and 5,000 sappers and miners. In January 1629, the Dutch in Surat recorded the news of a letter in which Mahabat Khan implored Shahjahan not to march against the rebel himself. It would be beneath His Majesty to take the field against 'a crowd of peasants or defenceless people' (*eenen hoop boeren ofte weerloose luyden*). Mahabat Khan would rather himself bring the Yuga-Raja (*Joogradia*) to heel and to obedience to His Majesty.[44] About the peasant origin of many of Jujhar Singh's men there can, indeed, be little doubt; but defenceless they were certainly not, as is clear from the magnitude of the mobilisation thought necessary against them:

Saiyyid Muzaffar Khan Barha, Islam Khan, Dilawar Khan, Sardar Khan, Raja Ram Das [Kachhwaha of Narwar, a place on Jujhar's borders], Nazar Bahadur and ten other *amirs* were also appointed. . . A *lakh* of rupees and other gifts were bestowed upon Mahabat Khan. . . An order was sent to Khan-i Jahan Lodi, the *subedar* of Malwa, directing him to come to the help of Mahabat Khan, along with his officers. Bharat Singh Bundela [i.e. Bharat Sah of Chanderi], who was hostile to the rebel because he had claims of inheritance to his homeland, was also appointed against him. Abdullah Khan Firoz Jung was ordered to advance against Jhujhar's principality from the side of Kalpi and Bahadur Khan Rohilla, with a body

43 See for the 1628–9 campaign against Jujhar Sing, Syed, *Aurangzeb*, 5–7. *Orchha Gazetteer*, 24, 25. Dow, *History*, III, 119–21.

44 ARA, VOC 1100 f. 224 v° ('Memorie gehouden bij forme van journaal', Surat 7.i.1629). Mahabat Khan was then encamped at a serai called Mania or Mende serai, one stage to the Agra side of Gwalior (see also Mundy, *Travels*, II, 63, and Pelsaert, *Geschriften*, 29). The figures given for Mahabat Khan's army are those of Khafi Khan; Dow gives 12,000 horse and 3,000 foot.

of warriors, two thousand musketeers and plenty of sappers and miners from the north. A body of Asaf Khan's soldiers were also appointed under one of his own officers.[45]

Soon Jujhar Singh realised he had better yield before the imperial onslaught. He made his submission before Mahabat Khan, who was, like him, a great commander of Rajputs. Mahabat Khan brought him to Agra and for three days interceded for him with the emperor after which the latter pardoned him. He now paid a *nazar* of a thousand *ashrāfīs* and had to give as a fine a further fifteen lakhs of rupees and forty elephants. His *mansab* of 4,000/4,000 was not reduced and a *jāgīr* corresponding to his rank was granted him, according to Khafi Khan, out of the *mahal* (estates) he had without permission acquired by force, the rest of his personal conquests being annexed to the empire and granted in *jāgīr* to Abdullah Khan and Khan Jahan Lodi.[46] It is difficult to estimate exactly how hard the terms imposed on him were, but subsequent events showed that he still controlled considerable resources.[47]

Jujhar Singh now proceeded on service to the Dekkan. In due course, he was, along with several other Bundela chiefs, rewarded for his efforts in the south. Jujhar's son Vikramajit acquired even greater fame during these years. He distinguished himself particularly during the campaigns of 1630–1 against the rebellious *amīr* Khan Jahan Lodi, whose son he killed. This earned him the title of Yuga-Raja (Jograj), or Raja of the Age, the same title his father, as we saw, had earlier received in Jahangir's reign.[48] The compiler of the *Orchha Gazetteer*, published in 1907, thought that Vikramajit was awarded the title of *yuva rāja* on this occasion.[49] The mistake is telling. The idea of the *yuva rāja*, the champion who embodied the hopes of the local lineage, still had a familiar ring to it after almost three centuries but the notion of the Mughal as the ultimate judge of *kṣatriya* qualities – a notion implicit in the emperor's conferment of the title of Yuga-Raja – had by then been forgotten.

Like Bir Singh Deo, both Jujhar Singh and Vikramajit must have

[45] A. J. Syed, *Aurangzeb*, 6, 7. The campaign, as described by Khafi Khan, was led by 22 commanders, cf. note 39. According to Dow, *History*, 120, Khan Jahan had 12,000 men and Abdullah Khan 7,000 horse.

[46] Dow, *History*, 121. A. J. Syed, *Aurangzeb*, 7.

[47] Khafi Khan's implication seems to be that his ancestral domains – still extensive in spite of the secession of Datiya – were left undisturbed, but Dow says that he had been handled severely. Dow, *History*, 145.

[48] Abdul Hamid Lahori in Elliot and Dowson, *History of India*, VII, 10, 20.

[49] *Orchha Gazetteer*, 26.

been fully aware of the operational value of both these concepts. But to strike a balance between the two during Shahjahan's stern rule in the 1630s was even more difficult than during Jahangir's long decline. For several years, Jujhar Singh fought the emperor's wars in the Dekkan. Then, in 1634, he took leave of Mahabat Khan to attend to his affairs at home. Vikramajit, the newly created Yuga-Raja was left behind with a contingent of men to further exert himself in the imperialist cause. Back home, Jujhar Singh found it necessary to re-assert his regional territorial claims and, as the Mughal chronicler Khafi Khan would put it, 'took to his old mischievous ways'.[50] He attacked Raja Prem Narayan, the Gond *zamīndār* of Garha-Mandla and induced him by a treaty and promises to surrender the fort of Chauragarh, some 100 kilometres to the east of Raisen. After this, he killed Prem Narayan and a number of his followers, and seized all his property and the fort's treasure of ten lakhs of rupees. Prem Narayan held an imperial *mansab* and had sent a number of elephants to the royal stables. Yet Shahjahan does not seem to have told Jujhar Singh in an unequivocal manner to restore the Gond raja's property to his successor. Instead, the emperor probably would have settled for a share in the spoils for himself. What happened next, however, was that Vikramajit suddenly left the Dekkan to join his father in Bundelkhand. It was a desperate attempt by the Bundelas of the Orchha branch to regain the eminence that had been theirs in Bir Singh Deo's time. Vikramajit was hotly pursued by some of the chief commanders of the Dekkan who were also accompanied by a number of prominent Bundela *sardārs*, rivals of Jujhar. He was beaten in Malwa and wounded, but he escaped and joined his father. Huge preparations were once more set on foot against Orchha. Jujhar Singh asked for a re-opening of negotiations; the emperor in response sent Sundar Kaviraj, a hindi poet and grandee of the court, with the demand that Jujhar hand over a *mahal* yielding three lakhs of rupees, send Vikramajit to court and go himself to serve in the Dekkan as before. Jujhar refused. Apparently he had staked too much on his bid for regional dominance in Bundelkhand. After the rains of 1635 were over, an imperial army of 20,000 men, under the nominal command of Prince Aurangzeb, moved against Orchha; with it were a large number of Rajputs, Bundelas as well as others, amongst them being two of Jujhar Singh's own brothers.

It serves no purpose to retell the dramatic story of how Jujhar

[50] Syed, *Aurangzeb*, 8.

and Vikramajit, their army of 5,000 horse and 10,000 foot, their women and their sixty elephants, 'some of which were loaded with gold and silver money and gold and silver vessels', were brought to bay in the wilds of Gondwana. The pursuit allowed them no time to perform *jauhar*, both chiefs at last being cruelly killed by the Gonds. By then the hectic search around Orchha for the buried treasures collected by Bir Singh Deo was already largely over. Much silver and gold was found in wells; plenty of it was plundered and scattered, but in the end, according to one report, a crore of rupees was put into the imperial treasury. The members of Bir Singh Deo's family at Orchha were either killed or converted to Islam and the town itself was handed over to Raja Devi Singh Bundela of Chanderi.[51] These events are to some extent reminiscent of the Purbiya defeats in Malwa about a century earlier. They represent yet another defeat for the pre-Mughal entrepreneurship of warlords and the medieval Rajput traditions of recruitment described in the preceding chapter.

Shahjahan attached great importance to his Bundela victory. His superiority over Jujhar Singh was celebrated more than once in court paintings and, in 1637, in a haughty letter to Shah Safi of Iran, he gave an account of the campaign, stressing his triumph over heathendom.[52] He himself visited Orchha in December 1635 and there ordered a large part of the temple of Chaturbhuj, one of Bir Singh Deo's proud achievements, to be pulled down, the chronicler of the emperor's reign noticing that 'among the Hindu Rajputs who assisted at this pious work fighting under the Mughal banner were Sisodias and Rathors, Kachhwahas and Hadas'.[53] This latter remark seems to stress the division of interests between these clans on the one hand and their Bundela competitors on the other. It perhaps provides, in other words, a clue to the political importance of the fall of Orchha as seen from the point of view of the military labour market and the Rajput soldiering profession.

To grasp this it is necessary to realise that the share of the Rajputs in the resources of the Mughal empire fluctuated with time and that within the Rajput category different groups were employed at different times. Thus it has been remarked that the Kachhwaha *mansabdārs* of Akbar's reign, who continued to serve

51 *Ibid.*, 8–14. Elliot and Dowson, *History of India*, VII, 47–50. Samsam-ud-daula, *Maāthir*, I, 615. *Orchha Gazetteer*, 26–9. On Prem Narayan, see Jahangir, *Tūzuk*, I,. 379n, 388, and Sleeman, 'Gurha Mundala'. 631, 632.

52 Skelton, *The Indian Heritage*, 42. Riazul Islam, *Calendar*, 254, 255.

53 *Orchha Gazetteer*, 29, B. D. Gupta, *Maharaja Chhatrasal*, 8.

under Jahangir, held ranks altogether amounting to 26,100 *suwār*, whereas in the tenth regnal year of Shahjahan (1637–8) the total of the *suwār* ranks of the Kachhwahas came to only 11,000.[54] During Jahangir's reign, a man like Mahabat Khan, himself not a Rajput, had been able to attract thousands of Rajputs to his camp. But even greater had been the success of Bir Singh Deo and his Bundelas who had gradually built up a position similar to that which Man Singh Kachhwaha and his relations occupied towards the end of Akbar's reign. Jujhar Singh had endeavoured to retain this eminence and to translate it into the consolidated territorial dominance of the Orchha lineage over a large part of Central India. When the empire strove to prevent this, it was joined by those at whose expense the Orchha *gaddī* had built up its strength; *sardār*s from the Bundela branches other than that of Orchha and, more important, the clan chiefs of the west such as the Kachhwahas.

The emperor seems to have wavered in his attitude towards Jujhar Singh, both in 1629, when he eventually pardoned him, and in 1635, when, after several attempts at negotiation, he at last decided to crush him. The Mughal empire, indeed, would never find a constitutional solution to the problem of what measure of territorial power to grant to its *zamīndār*s. As the latter knew that they would only become attractive as imperial subjects to the degree they gathered strength as careful rebels, an ever-changing mix of *bhūmiyāvat* and negotiation would continue to be the most efficient method of registering the relative strength of all parties. Jujhar Singh's death did not render the Mughal–Bundela relationship any less problematic. Devi Singh, the head of the rival lineage of Chanderi, was a failure at Orchha. A young son of Jujhar and, later, one of his old associates by the name of Champat Rai Bundela, continued to champion the Orchha case, in the end compelling Shahjahan to restore a son of Bir Singh Deo to the *gaddī*. After this, Champat Rai would only for short periods serve the empire or at least desist from causing trouble. After his death in 1661, his son Chhatrasal (1649–1731), a most distinguished rebel as well as *mansabdār*, would, founding his own state at Panna, firmly establish the turbulent tradition of yet another Bundela branch. Whereas the descendants of Champat Rai in Eastern Bundelkhand would be known as the Dangahi Bundelas (from *dangā*: row, mutiny), the Bundela families at Orchha, Chanderi and Datiya in Western Bundelkhand would continue to serve the languishing

[54] S. I. A. Zaidi, 'Kachawaha Troopers', 60.

empire and be known as *bādshāhi* (from *bādshāh*: emperor). So these two wings of the Bundela clan, though differently labelled and without the complementarity so vital to Rajput survival during the days of Mughal dominance, can be seen as the post-Mughal descendants of the principles of the *yuva rāja* and the *mansabdār* respectively.[55]

Chhatrasal, indeed, in many respects conformed to the ideal of the *yuva rāja*. First, he stayed some time in the Dekkan with Shivaji with whom he had much in common. Then, in 1671, he entered Bundelkhand accompanied by five horsemen and twenty-five foot-soldiers only. The legitimacy on which he founded his rule at Panna represents a blend of elements that was new in Bundela Rajput history. He became a follower of Pran Nath, a guru of the Pranami sect who was inspired by great Sants like Kabir and Nanak. Pran Nath is said to have prompted Chhatrasal to perform the coronation ceremony (presumably the *abhiṣeka* consecration rite is meant) and to have imparted to him the secret of the diamond mines of Panna, which would supply the sinews of war to his followers. Pran Nath's anti-brahman piety struck root in Panna and to this day it is said in Bundelkhand:

> Krishna, Muhammad, Dev Chandra, Pran Nath, Chhatrasal,
> Whoever names these five, at once removes distress.[56]

Yet it is worth noticing that Chhatrasal never completely withdrew from the empire. Time and again, he accepted *mansab*s and titles from the Mughals, exchanged presents with them and participated in their campaigns, only to extricate himself every so often from their affairs.[57] Chhatrasal's career again shows that the pursuit of *kṣatriyadharma* and loyalty to an India presided over by Mughals were often complementary rather than incompatible.

But by the end of Aurangzeb's reign the times were changing. The proceeds of imperialist campaigning must have diminished at a fast rate. Moreover, the long absences of the Rajput chiefs in the wars in Afghanistan and on the Dekkan were detrimental to their role as owners of estates that could, with good management, bring an increasing income. Military service for the empire was increas-

[55] *Orchha Gazetteer*, 29–31. Silberrad, 'Contribution', 116. Pogson, *Boondelas*, 11ff. B. D. Gupta, *Maharaja Chhatrasal*, 123n, however, derives the name of the eastern Bundelas from *dāng*: mountain top.

[56] *Ibid.*, 22, 98, 143n. Dev Chandra was Pran Nath's guru. See on the Pranamis also *Panna Gazetteer*, 37, 38.

[57] B. D. Gupta, *Maharaja Chhatrasal*, 45n, 53–64.

ingly unprofitable as compared to agrarian and town-based entrepreneurship and those commanders who were chiefs of regionally dominant clans ran the risk of ruining their concerns at home in order to preserve their honour as *amīrs* of the empire. This seems to be the current interpretation of a complaint by Bhimsen, an officer of Dalpat Rao Bundela. Writing about the events of the year 1702, he remarked; 'At this time, only three men have homes, viz., Rao Dalpat and Ram Singh Hada in Nusrat Jang's army and Raja Jai Singh Kachhwaha ... a subordinate of Prince Bidar Bakht. They maintain their contingents for preserving their honour. Besides these three men with homes, nobody looks to keeping troops.' None of the other captains in the army had *watans*, or 'homes'.[58]

Once, there had been a number of men who had been devoted equally to *mansabdāri* service and to the energetic management of their *watans*, and who had, not without success, striven towards a symbiosis of these two roles. The empire had depended on them a great deal and, as we saw, the Mughal had explicitly recognised their services as being of great importance. A title like that of 'Raja of the Age', conferred on two Bundela chiefs, exemplified this. Now, however, as the empire overstretched itself whereas the agrarian economy slowly continued to grow, service and regional state formation became separate roles again. Those choosing the former came to be called *jama'dārs*; they would, as we shall see, occupy an important place in eighteenth-century Indian military and political history as well as in pre-mutiny British India. Those turning to the role of *watandār* laid the foundation of the multi-state system of eighteenth-century India.

Hardaul Lala

In Bundelkhand, Bir Singh Deo and Jujhar Singh, the aggressive builders of a Bundela state, would be well remembered. Bir Singh would be viewed as a man who was 'mindful of the sin he had committed in usurping his brother's kingdom' and felt 'great remorse'. This was the reason, according to local tradition, why he made his nine pilgrimages and offered his innumerable sacrifices. Bir Singh's efforts to clear his reputation of the embarrassing memories of his behaviour towards his brothers seem to have been partly successful.[59] Jujhar Singh's, however, was a different case altogether. Towards the end of the nineteenth century, there were

[58] Bhimsen, *Tarikh-i-Dilkasha*, 232, 233. [59] Silberrad, 'Contribution', 114.

several versions current in the region of his poisoning his younger brother Har Deva or Hardaul. The Orchha State Gazetteer says that Hardaul and Jujhar Singh's wife had long been friends 'he addressing her as a mother, she him as a son'. When Jujhar Singh, during his absence from home, heard tales about their intimacy, he returned 'and ordered his wife to administer poison to Hardaul, a command which if she were a chaste wife she was bound to obey'. Hardaul, seeing her tears, asked the cause of her grief. So she told him, whereupon he comforted her as follows: 'Mother dear, any food from your hand must ever be as nectar to me. This proof of your innocence is of more value than life, and will but immortalise my name.' Several of his friends joined him in eating the poisoned food. He then went to the temple of Ramchandra, where he prayed for a short time and died. Thakur Mazbut Singh, a representative of the rival Chanderi lineage of Bundelas, wrote in his history that the *rānī* felt such remorse that she poisoned herself too.

Whatever the exact truth, the story was sufficiently moving for it to earn a place in the collective memory of the region. But the matter did not end there. Vincent Smith, who recorded the tale in the Hamirpur District of Bundelkhand where he served in the early 1870s, heard the fullest account of subsequent events. After the tragedy, the daughter of Kunjavati, a sister of Jujhar and Hardaul, was to be married,

> Kunjāvatī accordingly sent an invitation to Jhajhār Singh, requesting him to attend the wedding. He refused and mockingly replied that she had better invite her favourite brother Hardaul. Thereupon she went in despair to his tomb and lamented aloud. Hardaul from below answered her cries, and said that he would come to the wedding and make all arrangements. The ghost kept his promise and arranged the nuptials as befitted the honour of his house. Subsequently, he visited at night the bedside of Akbar, and besought the emperor to command *chabūtras* to be erected and honour paid to him in every village throughout the empire, promising that if he were duly honoured, a wedding should never be marred by storm or rain, and that no one who first presented a share of his meal to Hardaul should ever want for food. Akbar complied with these requests and since that time Hardaul's ghost has been worshipped in every village.[60]

In Bundelkhand, Jujhar Singh would become – as a British civil servant, who knew the UP well, would put it – 'an object of

[60] *Ibid.*, 115. *Orchha Gazetteer*, 24, 25. Smith, 'Popular Songs', 389, 390.

execration'.[61] Local tradition remembered that he had recourse to 'Agmarshanyug' (*aghamarṣana*: sin effacing) to purge himself of the sin of murdering his brother, but the exercise did not restore his reputation.[62] The people's choice of Hardaul, as we just saw, received official sanction from Akbar, here apparently an almost mythical emperor who united in one person the functions of just sultan or *'ādilshāh* and of the ultimate judge of hindu *dharma*. Here one is reminded of Akbar's reputed recognition, referred to above, of Madhukar Shah Bundela's hindu pride, and of Jahangir's appointment of Bundela 'Rajas of the Age'. Thakur Mazbut Singh wrote, only slightly less mythically, that it was Shahjahan who issued a proclamation dethroning Jujhar Singh and directing *cabūtra*s to be built in honour of Har Deva.[63] The deification of Hardaul, or Hardaul Lala as he became affectionately known, is thus directly connected with a refutation of Orchha anti-Mughal megalomania as represented by Jujhar Singh. Significantly, Hardaul was said to have been born at Datiya, the town that stood for resistance against Orchha's territorial aggrandisement and centralism.[64] What then did people expect of Hardaul that Jujhar Singh denied them? What, in other words, did the new village god, installed through the patronage of the Mughal emperor, Jujhar's enemy, stand for amongst the peasants of Hindustan?

The numerous shrines dedicated to Hardaul in North India always represented him on horseback as a Rajput. Sometimes the stones on which his figure appeared were inscribed and Cunningham found one near Gwalior dated 1779. The image of Hardaul as a Rajput soldier also finds expression in the songs addressed to his spirit. A song recorded in Malwa had Hardaul ask: 'If my brother wished for my death, why did he not let me die in battle?'[65] And in a song from the Hamirpur district it is said: 'Beloved son of the Bundela country's chief of chiefs (*Bundelā deshā ke raiya rāv ke lālā*), in the south (*dakhin*) your sword has been busy.'[66] In Hardaul, apparently, we are dealing with a god closely connected with the Bundela soldiering tradition instituted by Bir Singh Deo, the song's 'chief of chiefs', that led so many North Indian men to a

61 Haig and Burn, *Cambridge History of India*, 185. Richard Burn, whom we quote here, had been a member of the Uttar Pradesh Board of Revenue.
62 Silberrad, 'Contribution', 115. 63 *Ibid.*
64 Smith, 'Popular Songs', 389.
65 Cunningham, *Report 1881–82*, 164, 165.
66 Smith, 'Popular Songs', 390–2. Hardaul's father was also called by the name of *lālā*, darling, Pelsaert, *Geschriften*, 155, 165, 180, 187, 225.

hazardous existence in the incessant Dekkan wars of the empire. It was this tradition of *naukarī* that Jujhar Singh's immoderate clash with Shahjahan and his attempts to increase his *watan*, his home counties, had put in jeopardy.

Apart from the political issues involved, it appears that, as a soldier-god, Hardaul stands for several issues that must have vexed the minds of the soldier as well as those of his family back home. Firstly, as the antagonist of his perfidious, but legitimately enthroned brother, he personifies the superiority of Rajput virtue over the principle of genealogical precedence. In the Malwa song, just quoted, Jujhar Singh says that 'There is no enemy in the world like a brother', thus as it were pronouncing the utter insufficiency of ascribed status as an ordering principle among Rajputs. As we saw earlier when considering the Purbiyas and their political idiom, what these Rajputs asserted again and again was their freedom to live and fight according to the *dharma* of Indian soldiering, independent of genealogical prescriptions and with complete freedom to serve and enter into alliances with whomever allowed scope to a virtuous bearing in life. Such freedom, we found, is not incompatible with service to a muslim ruler; on the contrary, the Mughal *bādshāh* is emphatically seen as the benevolent supervisor of Rajput virtue.

A second aspect, it seems, is connected with the problems caused by the long absence of the soldier from home. Hardaul was chiefly honoured at weddings and women had an important part in worship. After his death, as we saw, he had helped his sister Kunjavati in doing the honours of her daughter's wedding when Jujhar Singh, the family chief, refused to do so, and the Hamirpur song has 'Lala' as the brother of the bride's mother (*māmā*) come out and offer boiled rice (*bhāt*) to his sister's daughter on the occasion of her wedding as was the custom on the first day of wedding ceremonies. To the women of the Bundela recruitment areas the thought of Hardaul must have been consoling. Hardaul cared. Admonishing the bullock that carried the wedding gifts of the bride's family, he told the animal to hurry because 'my sister is getting worried'. Hardaul Darling, which is what Hardaul Lala means, could be depended upon to preserve the women of his *birādarī* from disgrace. Moreover, he not only took the place of the brother whose service with far-away armies did not permit him to attend to family affairs, he also stepped in the place of the absent husband. He was the ideal type of the *dewar*, the husband's younger brother, whom tradition had always allowed a degree of intimacy with his *bhaujī*, his elder brother's wife. Had not his loving sister-in-law been more dear to him than life? He was indeed, to quote the Hamirpur song again, 'the best support of his brother's wife (*bhaujī ke param adhār*)', i.e. of the wife of any 'Bundela' brother-soldier, however long his absence from home.[67] Thus there is reason to interpret the cult of Hardaul as an expression of a crucial aspect of the ancient Rajput tradition of long-distance freebooting and armed service. Hardaul, we suggest, was a typical Rajput god, not in the modern genealogical sense of the term Rajput, but according to its original denotation, stressed repeatedly in this study, of the *dharma* of young soldiers who would follow whatever king or sultan gave them an honourable place in their realms.

It stands to reason then that Hardaul was not worshipped only by Bundelas in the strict kinship sense of the term, but by all so-called 'Bundelas' who, though recruited from several identities, tribes or 'castes', served under Bundela *jama'dār*s and thus came to partake of the Bundela Rajput identity. Vincent Smith noticed that in Hamirpur he was chiefly honoured by the lower castes.[68] Towards the end of the last century, Crooke made available material referring to the many castes that worshipped Hardaul at that time. It is true that then Hardaul's character had changed; since 1817 he had come to preside over all kinds of epidemic diseases.[69] But it is clear that the association of many castes with Hardaul predates this development.

The inventory made by Crooke provides an – albeit limited – insight into the various adventuring and occupational groups that contributed to the phenomenon of Bundela military entrepreneurship. One is not surprised to find among the worshippers of Hardaul the Baheliyas of Oudh, whom earlier in this chapter, we got to know for their long-standing tradition of service as infantrymen with the Mughals and others. The Banjaras of Kanpur also paid homage to the Bundela hero-god; the association of these long-distance traders with the military camps of the Mughals may well have been responsible for this. Amongst the worshippers of Hardaul one also finds the Churihars, glass bangle makers. This may seem striking at first sight, but of course they were marriage specialists, often itinerant, and the suspicion of a link with military

[67] Smith, 'Popular Songs', 390–2. [68] *Ibid.*, 390.
[69] Sleeman, *Rambles*, 162–67, 232.

business is reinforced by some of the names of subsections of this professional group, for amongst these we find Baksariyas, Bhojpuriyas and Purbiyas, of which at least the first designation points unmistakably to a connection with soldiering.[70] In addition, there are the Gond tribals of Jhansi about whom we also know that some of them joined Chhatrasal Bundela as members of his war-band and who bring to mind Sher Shah's tribal Cheros and their contribution to Ujjainiya soldiering.

More numerous among the worshippers of Hardaul, however, are caste groups whose association was probably with the peasant-soldiers' marriage celebrations and with the army camp rather than with actual soldiering. Thus there are the Barais (*pān* cultivators) of the east of the province and South Mirzapur, the Baris (makers of leaf-platters) equally of South Mirzapur, the Bharbhunjas (grain-parchers) of eastern Uttar Pradesh, the Halwais (sweetmeat makers), the Kahars (palanquin bearers, servants) of Jhansi, the Kalwars (distillers) of eastern Uttar Pradesh, the Patwas (silk fringe makers) of eastern Uttar Pradesh and Hamirpur, the Rastaogi Baniyas, Sonars (goldsmiths), the Tarkihars (ear ornament makers) of South Mirzapur, and the Telis (oil pressers) of eastern Bihar.[71] And in the late 1960s, an anthropologist working in the Mainpuri District in the Doab recorded the 'myth' of Hardaul from the mouth of a middle-aged water carrier.[72] It is not unlikely that a number of these servant and petty *baniyā* castes picked up their taste for the worship of Hardaul in the army camps in which services such as they could offer must always have been in demand.

The figure of Hardaul has allowed us a glimpse of the 'folk' culture associated with the Bundela military service tradition. It is possible that field research in Malwa and Bundelkhand may yield more material about him even today. Moreover, the data on Hardaul's followers showed what kind of groups possibly joined the camps and contingents of Bundela *jama'dārs* as recruits. It should be noticed that, popular as a saint though he was, no sect formed around Hardaul. Yet, the case of the Pranamis, associated with Chhatrasal Bundela – himself, as we saw, received into the Pranami pantheon – suggests that sect formation in the context of the activities of war-gangs like those of the Bundelas, is not out of the question. The Pranamis themselves were a kind of *bairāgī* or

70 Crooke, *Tribes and Castes*, I, 109, 163, II, 231–2, 436.

71 *Ibid.*, I, 180, 203, II, 15, 487, III, 98, 111, IV, 173, 234, 338, 363, 374.

72 Wadley, *Shakti*, 65, 72–4, 88.

sectarian monks and possibly came close to the phenomenon of the famous 'fighting ascetics' of North India.[73] So far it is clear that many sorts of different identities could grow around the soldiering profession. One may even wonder whether the long-term employment of diverse groups under Bundela auspices could be a step towards the formation of a new endogamous caste. This question is dealt with in the next section of this chapter.

Gathered in the cave of Adullam

More often than not peasant society is a melting pot of diverse elements and the peasant armies and war-bands I have dealt with reflected this multiplicity of origins. Service could open up paths to members of the peasantry that would lead to careers far removed from agriculture, whereas, conversely, many must have found their way into the peasantry via service in army camps. For centuries, armed service of one kind or another may well have been accountable for the lion's share of social mobility in North India.

It must be admitted, however, that hardly any substantial, direct evidence about the social origins of particular Hindustani soldiers is forthcoming. The only exception to this is a short list enumerating the thirty men who followed Chhatrasal into Bundelkhand in 1671. Some of these were Rajputs, but there was also a barber, a Dhimar (fisherman) and a muslim; later on a number of Gond tribesmen joined him, whereas among other recruits of his are mentioned Brahmans, Baniyas, a Chhipi (dyer), an Ahir and more muslims.[74] The composition of this gang seems not to have been very dissimilar to that of the worshippers of Hardaul; in both cases, anyway, the diversity of recruitment is the most striking characteristic. This was a general feature of Hindustani war-bands. I am the more confident of this as, though we know little for sure about Bhojpuri and Avadhi soldiering, a mere coincidence enables us, in an indirect way, to take the measure of the great diversity of Bundela infantry recruitment.

In 1672, the French took the town of San Thomé, which nowadays forms part of Madras City, from the Qutbshahi king of Golkonda. The king responded by sending an army consisting of 10,000 foot and 500 horse to reconquer the town, but did not meet

[73] *Panna Gazetteer*, 37, where it is said that, about 1742, Pran Nath arrived near Panna with a following of 1,100 bairagis.

[74] B. D. Gupta, *Maharaja Chhatrasal*, 25n, 28, 130.

with success. Next year, a Dutch fleet laid siege to San Thomé from the sea side, while a joint Qutbshahi–Dutch force surrounded the French from the land side. The Golkonda army counted 3,000 foot and from 300 to 500 horse, whereas by June 1674 the Dutch force consisted of 583 Germans ('*Duytsen*'), 98 topasses and 1,049 peons. Among the latter were some 600 Rajput musketeers, hired in Golkonda. At the beginning of the siege, the Dutch had asked the king for '10,000 experienced and courageous marksmen, Mughals, Rajputs as well as other martial and brave races', but 600 was all they had been able to obtain from the royal capital.[75] In September, the French at last surrendered. For our purposes, the only interesting aspect of the episode is the presence of North Indian Rajput mercenaries in the 1670s not only at the siege of San Thomé, but apparently over much of Golkonda and the Coromandel coast. Still, I would not have mentioned this, if the EIC had not been a little more precise than the VOC as to the character of these Rajputs. The English correspondence noted them down as 'Pundelis', i.e. Bundelas. Troops of the same description served the English in the Masulipatam area.[76] The Mughals in South India employed them as well, as evidenced by the mention of 'Bundalar' who served in a village in imperial hands just outside Fort St George in 1697.[77] And in January 1748 200 'Bondilis' were sent into Pondichéry on the understanding they would be taken into the service of the French there, which turned out not to be the case. That Bundela soldiers from North India served far from home in the South, we knew already. But it is striking to see that here in the South, where the Mughals did not have a monopoly of power, they went from one employer to another quite as easily as the sixteenth-century Purbiyas had done in Malwa. It is further significant that, though identified as Rajputs, they were also explicitly recognised and registered as Bundelas, i.e. by the clan name of their jemadars, to use the common designation of their jobber-commanders.

Though one must assume that many of these soldiers in the end returned to their North Indian homes, some of them settled in the South, either being joined by their own womenfolk or taking wives from the Telugu- and Tamil-speaking peasants among whom they

[75] Coolhaas, *Generale Missiven*, III, 828. Van der Chijs, *Dagh-Register 1673*, 322, and *Dagh-Register 1674*, 79. ARA, VOC 1295 f. 122 v°; VOC 1299 f. 497, 509 v°, 516 v°; VOC 1302 f. 368 v°. For a remark on the Dutch using Indian troops, see also Tavernier, *Travels*, I, 188.

[76] Fawcett, *English Factories, 1670–77*, 100, 114.

[77] Love, *Vestiges*, I, 377, 581. Dodwell, *Ananda Ranga Pillai*, IV, 336.

chose to live. In the nineteenth century these so-called Bondilis or Bondiliars still lived scattered over most districts of the presidency, particularly in the Andhra districts such as Kistna, Godavari, Nellore, and North Arcot, while further to the south there were many of them in Tirunelveli, South Kanara, and Madurai. Their language then was still mainly Hindustani and to a large extent they had stuck to their old profession. The census taken in the Madras Presidency in 1871 – and this is the first we hear of these southern 'Bundelas' since 1748 – lists 15,000 of them. Generally, they were cultivators, peons, or the body-guards of *zamīndārs*.

The 1871 census commissioner called these men Rajputs and grouped them among the *kṣatriyas*. Yet, by the end of the nineteenth century, to be a mercenary servant no longer entitled a man to gentlemanly status. The manual of the North Arcot district, published in 1895, denied their Rajput character and said that Shudras formed a majority amongst the Bondiliars while a minority was Vaishya. The Shudras were mostly sepoys, constables, or revenue peons. They had the termination 'Ram' to their names, though the author of the manual had noticed that, in his time, many 'improperly' took the title Singh and said they were Rajputs. On the other hand, it had to be admitted, he added, that in their marriage customs they did indeed resemble Rajputs. The Vaishya Bondilis, of whom there were few, added 'Lala' to their names; in the districts where they were found, they were usually moneylenders. They can undoubtedly be regarded as the descendants of the campfollowing shopkeepers and moneylenders who are indispensable to the mercenary soldier whether he maintains a financial relationship with home or not. Thus, the Shudra Bondiliars in particular were at this time struggling to retain the Rajput status that was theirs by inherited adoption. What most census officers could not understand was that their claim was based on a professional tradition, not on purity of blood. The author of the North Arcot manual wrote that some people said 'that they are not even Sūdras, but the descendants of Rājputs by women of the country, and probably many of them are such'. There can indeed be no doubt about this point of miscegenation, but the common British definition of Rajputs as an exclusively ascriptive category misses a point that, to us, must be of prime importance. Sociologically, the *Kṣatriya*, or rather Rajput, and the Shudra *varṇa*s are the least ascriptive of the four *varṇa*s and the Bondiliar Rajputs were not at all a homogeneous group of families.

They themselves were acutely aware of this. All were 'very particular with respect to eating with another professed Bondili, and refuse to do so unless they are quite certain that he is of their class'.[78] Apart from the distinction between Shudras and Vaishyas, there was the difference between a majority of Vaishnavas, who burned their dead, and a minority of Saivites, who buried them.[79] The census reports present us with an even more segmented picture. After centuries of Bundela service all over South Asia, the 1891 census allows us for the first time an idea of the complex recruiting pattern of this category of soldiers. Underneath the common professional denominator of Bondiliar or Bondili now suddenly appear many additional group identities. The census report enumerates sixty-four of them. It seems worthwhile to present a rather full analysis of these names. They tell us something of the social origins of the original, seventeenth-century, Bundela Rajputs who served in the armies of the Mughal and Golkonda kings and, occasionally, in those of the European companies. Also, they have something to communicate on the history of the Bondiliars since the time of their arrival in the South.

Of the sixty-four 'subcaste' names, some twenty remained largely unintelligible to this author; others were rather vague such as 'Dēsa' (of the country), 'Villaye' (foreign), 'Sūdra', 'Lāla', and 'Varnabrashtu' (vānaprastha), or very uncertain such as 'Jātar' (Jat?), 'Nandabaniya' (Nandbansi?), 'Sākto' (Sakta, Chamar?) and 'Vaidīki' (Bengali Brahmans?). But most other names are clear enough, presenting, as so often with the subdivisions of North Indian caste categories, a mixture of regional and place names and names of other castes. Thus we find 'Hindustāni', 'Gujarāti', 'Marāthi', 'Are' (Marathi), but also 'Kanōjan' and 'Kānukubja' which may well refer to the branch of Brahmans known by that name, 'Agarvāla', the name of a North Indian caste of traders, and 'Sribastu', probably indicating a Kayasth origin. Among the North Indian caste names one further finds 'Bhatrāja', referring to the Bhats, a caste of bards; 'Sunnārlu', goldsmiths and moneylenders; 'Muc'chi', leather workers; 'Kayast', writers; 'Bairāgi' and 'Udasi', i.e. members of religious orders and a number of names that convey a direct claim to Rajput status such as 'Rajaput', 'Kshatriya', 'Raghubasi', 'Sūryavamsam' and even 'Singh'.

78 *Census Madras 1871*, I, 140, 141, II, 66–8. Cox and Stuart, *North Arcot*, 209.
79 Thurston, *Castes and Tribes*, I, 257.

One cannot but conclude from this that the so-called Bundela Rajput soldiers of the seventeenth century must have been of the most diverse origin. True, with a large number of them, memories of their precise social background were gradually obscured by vague territorial identities or claims to *kṣatriya* status. But in ancient times, recruitment by Bundela jobber-commanders had not taken social origin into account. Instead, it overlaid old identities with a new 'Bundela Rajput' veneer. Those that, after years of service, returned again to their homes in North India, resumed the membership of the brotherhoods they came from, however much their soldiering careers may have 'rajputised' them. But the case of the Bundela soldiers and camp followers that stayed behind in the South to become 'Bondiliar', 'Bondili' or 'Bondililu' was a different one. Their awareness of themselves remained pluriform for centuries. Wanting the relatively safe niche in society such as the northern returnees found, they naturally continued to fight and serve and admitted to their number whoever would appear to improve the group's position on the labour market of Southeast India.

Of course, those accepted amongst them were now mainly of southern origin. The 1901 census mentions the 'Guvālo', traders of Sambalpur in Orissa, as a 'subcaste' of the Bondiliar. The 1891 list of 'subcastes' gives the names of cultivating as well as of 'military and dominant' groups of both the Telugu and the Tamil area, such as 'Agamudaiyam', 'Kamma', 'Kāpu', 'Rāju', and 'Telaga'. But there are also traders ('Balija', 'Kōmati'), oil pressers ('Gāndla', 'Vāniyan'), weavers ('Sala'), shepherds ('Idaiyan' or 'Yādava'), leather workers ('Mādiga'), artisans ('Kamsale'), earth workers ('Odde'), and others. The impression is that these relatively late arrivals from southern Indian peasant society were still a little clearer in their minds about the social origins of their families and, of course, one can think of several reasons why this should be so. But even here one meets a group vaguely called 'Tamil', indicating a more unequivocal turning towards the acquired Bondili Rajput status.

Meanwhile, the Bondiliars did not only receive recruits. There were also centrifugal forces at work. In the 1891 census one finds a fair number of castes that had by that time acquired a Bondili 'subcaste'. This concerns mainly castes of which the names are by now familiar to us: Kapu, Raju and Telaga among the castes of a thoroughly South Indian character and Kshatriya, Rajaput, Kanojan and Lala among the others. So the Bondilis had a subdivision called Kapu, whereas the Kapus had a subdivision called Bondili, etc. There were, moreover, the Kuruman and the Nayudu, caste names that are new to us but which also had a Bondili 'subcaste'.[80]

Here in the South, in all the complex dynamics of open 'caste' identities as revealed by nomenclature one senses the processes of patronage and clientship. Until early in the twentieth century the name of Bondiliar stood for a service tradition, maintained as well as they might by bodies of sepoys, peons, body-guards and peasants, who continued, though to a diminishing degree, to be in demand among landed patrons in many districts of the Madras Presidency. The Bondili identity would continue to be valued by those who had inherited it as long as there were pride and earnings in this kind of clientship. Under twentieth-century conditions this could have meant the formation of a caste. But by 1891 such ritual rigidity had not been acquired by the Bondiliars. The census commissioner of that year wrote: 'The Bondilis, too, are sometimes treated as a caste, but I find that the name is used to denote a group of several castes.'[81] Even this, however, seems too precise; in Indian social history, endogamous castehood was no more than an option, realised by perhaps only a minority of the group identities that emerged from society. Therefore, the term 'caste system', as a description of the social reality of India in its entirety, obscures rather than illuminates Indian social dynamics. What is preferable for the moment is imagery, the imagery, for instance, resorted to by Alfred Lyall, a close observer of nineteenth-century Indian society. He wrote about 1875 – at a time when terms like clan, race, tribe and caste had not yet become the distinct sociological labels that would later contribute so much to distorting Indian reality, past and present – on the Minas of Central India that the whole of these people was 'nothing else but a cave of Adullam which has stood open for centuries, and has sheltered generation after generation of adventurers, outlaws, outcasts, and refugees generally'. Lyall here refers to the Old Testament figure of David whose first step on the road to royalty was his captaincy over 400 adventurer-soldiers.[82]

80 *Census Madras 1881*, IV, 247; see for Brahman Bondilis and Krishna Bondilis *ibid.*, 223. *Census Madras 1891*, XV, Caste Index, 11, and *passim*. *Census Madras* 1901, XV, pt I, 155. Balijas are mentioned as soldiers as early as 1697, Love, *Vestiges*, I, 582.

81 *Census Madras 1891*, XIII, 310.

82 Lyall, *Asiatic Studies*, 162. The biblical passage Lyall refers to is this: 'David departed from there and escaped to the cave of Adullam; and when his brothers

The census data cited so far have shown that, seen over a period of time, such bands or clusters of men were not closed shops: they were open categories attracting members but also losing them. The ability of the patron, whether he was a military jobber, a South Indian *zamīndār*, or a rebel like David, to support his clients and recruits, was the crucial factor regulating the survival as a group of the Bondiliars as well as of those gathered in any other cave of Adullam.

We must assume, however, that in this respect things gradually began to change after 1800. The military labour market as an independent part of India's social structure uncontrolled by, though complementary to the state, disappeared under British colonial rule. And, as a corollary, the Bondiliar identity could either dissolve among the peasant castes and be largely lost, it could merge into a more general 'caste' of *Kṣatriyas*, or, thirdly, it could become a caste itself. In fact all these three courses are discernible. Already in 1891, the Bondiliars in the deep South of the Madras Presidency had practically disappeared. In Tirunelveli, where in 1871 more of them were found than in any other district, none were registered twenty years later. In North Arcot and in Madras City, however, they appear to have maintained themselves, as they did in a fair number of Telugu districts and especially in their stronghold, the Kistna-Godavari delta. It is possible that elsewhere some Bondiliars, in an attempt to preserve their memories of Rajput service and to support their idea of themselves in modern caste society, opted for *Kṣatriya* status. Others did the same. Whereas the Madras census of 1911 still counted 158,000 *Kṣatriyas*, in 1921 the number rose steeply to 318,000. Yet, in 1921, there were still 11,064 Bondilis and it is possible that in the hinterland of Masulipatam, the town where they had served as North Indian migrant soldiers as early as the seventeenth century, a more exclusive Bondili identity developed, in other words a Bondili caste.[83] The present author, regrettably, was not in a position to make local enquiries in the Kistna-

and all his father's house heard it, they went down there to him. And every one who was in distress, and every one who was in debt, and every one who was discontented, gathered to him; and he became captain over them. And there were with him about four hundred men' *Bible (Revised Standard Version)*, I Samuel 22.1–3. Lyall, *Asiatic Studies*, I, 186, also points to 'the nucleus of a successful chief' as the probable factor responsible for clan formation.

83 *Census Madras 1871*, II, 66–8. *Census Madras 1891*, XIV, 354, 377. *Census Madras 1901*, XV–A, pt II, 190. *Census Madras 1921*, XIII, pt I, 161.

Godavari area and so perhaps trace the Bondilis to the present day.

In one respect at least it is clear that the amalgamation of the Bondilis in South Indian, and especially Andhra, society proceeded rapidly in modern times. Whereas, according to the census reports, they had kept to the Hindustani language – and, in the case of a small minority amongst them, to Marathi – until the beginning of the twentieth century, the 1921 census registered more Telugu than Hindustani speakers among them.[84] Linguistic distinctiveness, useful at a time when, in the district towns and among the landed elites, their name was a household word for armed service, lost its function when the profession they represented faded away. Gradually they were absorbed into peasant society, just as, centuries earlier, in another region of India, they had emerged from it.

84 *Census Madras 1891*, XIII, 193. *Census Madras 1901*, XV, pt I, 146. *Census Madras 1921*, XIII, pt II, 110.

5
Bhojpuri soldiering and the vicissitudes of empire

Throughout Indian history, the soldiers of the North of the country formed by no means an undifferentiated mass. There were great differences in origin, culture and economic circumstances. The central concern of this study is the historical role and political culture of peasant-soldiers in North India. This implicitly assumes that a distinction of sociological significance can be made between, on the one hand, those groups which, being largely of immigrant origin, lacked an inherited village base, and, on the other hand, men who were more firmly rooted in landholding and rural pursuits. True, some foreign warriors, perhaps within a few generations of their arrival in India, obtained a stake in agrarian lordship. On the other hand, the Afghans – the most characteristic representatives of the immigrant category – did not lose their vagrant identity for centuries. Clinging to their nomadic traditions, they remained a numerous and extremely mobile element in North India and even far into the South. In 1666 one finds, for instance, a majority of Afghans in the army of Bijapur in South India. In that same army there were, moreover, 2,000 black soldiers, so-called Abyssinians.[1] Originally slaves from the Horn of Africa, they had formed the mainstay of the Nizamshahi kingdom of Ahmadnagar until its final subjugation by Shahjahan in 1633. A generation later, apparently, they were still a clearly identifiable military category in South Indian society.[2] Often, it seems, it took centuries for such groups gradually to lose their character as migrant adventurers. I will, however, restrict myself to a consideration of soldiers of undoubted Indian peasant origin.

It may have struck the reader of the preceding chapters that

1 J. N. Sarkar, *Military Despatches*, 105, 118, 119.

2 They were not Christian Ethiopians but captured rebels or enemies of the Ethiopian empire, see Van Donzel, *Foreign Relations*, 79, 80.

several times already the area of Eastern Hindustan seemed to have a special importance as a recruiting area of peasant-soldiers. The Ujjainiyas who were Sher Shah's allies had their base in southwestern Bihar and the Purbiyas, as their name indicates, must have hailed from the same broad area. This is no coincidence. The soldiering tradition of this region of North India deserves, we suggest, to be treated as a whole. It yielded fighting men to Sher Shah, the Mughal emperors and the British as well as to numerous minor rulers, warlords and *zamīndārs*.

Eastern Hindustan or Purab, to use a more suitable name, can be defined as the linguistic region of the Bhojpuri dialect of Bihari and the Avadhi dialect of eastern Hindi. The Bhojpuri region received its name after the town of Bhojpur, the ancient headquarters of the Ujjainiya Rajputs of the erstwhile Shahabad district of Bihar (now split up into a northern district called Bhojpur and a southern one called Rohtas). It further includes the Champaran and Saran districts of Bihar and the most easterly districts of Uttar Pradesh up to the limit of the Avadhi-speaking area. Avadhi is spoken in the central districts of Uttar Pradesh. Its western boundary is a line just west of Lucknow.[3] It is the aim of this chapter to document and analyse the tenacious importance, during a period of almost four centuries, of this peasant area for the recruitment of infantry and, as a corollary, for the history of imperial and regional state formation.

The war-bands of the *zamīndārs*: Bachgotis and Ujjainiyas

During most of the fifteenth century, Eastern Hindustan was a sultanate in itself, the so-called Sharqi sultanate of Jaunpur. It was a state founded on the success of an imperial officer sent from Delhi to conciliate the local rebellious hindu chiefs in the 1390s. It is not surprising, therefore, that Mubarak Shah (1399–1402), the second of the Sharqi dynasty, is reported to have had a large army consisting of Afghans, Mughals, Tajiks and, significantly, Rajputs. Throughout the fifteenth century, 'innumerable *zamīndārs*' followed the Sharqi sultans in their campaigns. Jaunpur appears to have had troops numerically superior to those of its neighbours and there can be no doubt that a great number of Rajput vassals owed these sultans tribute and served them with their peasant war-bands.[4]

3 Grierson, *Linguistic Survey*, v, pt II, 40, 41; and *ibid.*, VI, 9, 10.

4 Abbās, *Tārīkh*, 7. Niamatullah, *History*, 68. Saeed, *Sharqi Sultanate*, xxiii, 30, 31, 39, 72, 87, 88n, 93, 101. I. H. Siddiqi, *Rise*, 117. Ferishta, *History*, IV, 361. Lal, *Twilight*, 9. See for one of these *zamīndārs* Nizami, 'Biramdeo', 145, 146.

The last of the Sharqi dynasty was Husain. He lost control of the city of Jaunpur to the Lodi Afghans of Delhi in the 1480s, but the war dragged on for several more years. Even after the loss of his main city, Husain was capable of forming a large-scale insurrection of *zamīndārs* throughout the Jaunpur country. This movement was spearheaded by the Bachgotis, a clan of Rajputs from the Awadh region. Their leader Juga is said to have collected a force of 200,000 or even 300,000 footsoldiers – inflated figures no doubt but clearly intending to convey the impression of exceptionally large numbers – and 15,000 horsemen and to have temporarily ousted the Lodis from Jaunpur city. It is clear that, already in the fifteenth century, the Rajput *zamīndārs* of Eastern Hindustan mustered enormous manpower from the regional peasantries.[5]

As far as their relationship to the Jaunpur sultan was concerned, I suggest that these Rajput lords were not just peripheral auxiliaries, but that they were intimately allied to the muslim state in a manner that is familiar to the reader of this study. The accusation, directed at Sultan Mahmud Sharqi (1436–58), that he had handed over muslim women to *kāfirs*, calls to mind the muslim women from the palace of the Malwa sultan who, between 1512 and 1518, entered the household of his *nāyak* Medini Rai.[6] I suggest that Mahmud Sharqi was, *vis-à-vis* the regional non-muslim power brokers, in the same position as the Malwa sultans, as was, for that matter, the muslim ruler of Kalpi and Chanderi who, shortly after 1443, had made over muslim women to some of his hindu *nāyaks*, i.e. captains.[7] Clearly Malwa was not an exception. All these sultanates to the east and south of Delhi in essence consisted of a sultan's intimate alliances with the Rajput warlords of North India whom they allowed an honourable share in their states. These fifteenth- and sixteenth-century princes were dependent both on Rajput-led Hindustani peasant infantry and on the supply of war elephants from Eastern and Central India. Their overriding interest in recruitment alliances and a consensus with Rajput chiefs were expressed, ideologically, in the syncretist, conciliatory idiom that dominated their courts, and physically by the exchange of women between the participants in their political enterprise. The Lodis of Agra and Delhi, on the other hand, depended to a much larger

5 Saeed, *Sharqi Sultanate*, 101–7. Niamatullah, *History*, 72, 73, 136, 139, 140.

6 See chapter 3.

7 Saeed, *Sharqi Sultanate*, 66, 67. Nizamuddin, *Tabaqāt*, III, 453–6. Ferishta, *History*, IV, 210, 367. Kalpi also had a large army; the number of its troops alarmed Sikandar Lodi of Delhi, I. H. Siddiqi, *Rise*, 129.

degree on their control of the supply of horses and Afghans from Central Asia which inevitably led them to adopt a less unorthodox approach to Islam. It is thus that the distinction we have made between the foreign warrior-adventurer and the indigenous *soldatesques* of peasant origin found expression, at the level of state formation, in two different types of power as well as of authority. Any attempt at empire in North India would have to include formulas that fused these two types of authority so as to bind both Rajputs and Central Asian immigrants. Only Akbar's genius achieved, though to an imperfect degree, this fusion and on it the Mughal empire would be built. But I am running too far ahead in time.

During the 1490s the Lodi Afghans succeeded in gradually putting an end to the Bachgoti rising in the Purab region. It does not seem to be going too far to conjecture that the conquest of Eastern Hindustan by these Afghan sultans who were accompanied by dependents of largely non-Hindustani ethnic origin, reduced the chances of military employment for the local levies of Purbiya soldiers. The migration of hindu soldiers over great distances in search of service had, as we saw, been a common feature of Indian history for centuries, but it is probable that the demise of the Jaunpur sultanate compelled an increasing number of men from the Awadh and Bhojpur areas to set out in search of *naukarī*. One tends to think that the good fortune of the Tomar Rajputs of Gwalior under Man Singh (1485–1517) as well as the increase in power of the Baghela Rajputs of Bhata (later of Bandhogarh and Rewa) under Bhaidachandra (1470–95), who had been Husain Sharqi's most important ally, was based, militarily speaking, on drafts of Hindustani soldiers who moved south on the collapse of their erstwhile employers' sultanate at Jaunpur.[8] The conspicuous largesse of these courts – the court culture from which Tansen emerged – reminds one of the syncretist atmosphere of Mandu and Raisen. Further south, in Malwa, as analysed in chapter 3, the presence of such troops came to be the characteristic feature of the political system. There, during the first decades of the sixteenth century, a number of Purbiya contingents, led frequently by members of the Tomar Rajput family from the Gwalior area, became central component elements in the sultanate. In this sense,

[8] *Gwalior Gazetteer*, I, 233, 234. *Rewah Gazetteer*, 13. Niamatullah, *History*, 73n. Saeed, *Sharqi Sultanate*, 96, 105–7.

Gwalior, Bhata, and Malwa may be considered Jaunpur's successor states.

But was it possible for these traditions of military service to be carried over into the Mughal empire? We saw that the descendants of one of their most spectacular leaders, Silhadi, gradually lost their distinct character to become absorbed into the muslim elites of the imperial provinces. Also, both in pre-Mughal and in Mughal times, a constant trickle of Hindustani Rajput soldiers turned muslim. Modern ethnographic data clearly illustrate the process. Yet I will argue that there were many more Hindustani Rajputs and members of groups associated with the military profession who continued the tradition of Purbiya soldiering in a much less adulterated manner. The reason is not that conversion to Islam did not necessarily entail a break with the old Rajput way of life. There is, as I hope to show, evidence that a large part of the infantry of the Mughal armies and even of the British East India Company's Bengal army was recruited from amongst classes that carried on the tradition of *naukarī* we have become acquainted with since the beginning of this enquiry through the songs of the Purab peasantry and through the accounts of the *jauhar*s of Raisen.

On the eve of Akbar's reign, the Jaunpur area was in the hands of Adil Shah Sur, a nephew and successor of Sher Shah. His main points of support were Gwalior and Chunar, strong fortresses near the southern limits of his kingdom.[9] By 1555, Hemu, Adil Shah's hindu general, had become the most powerful man in this region. The troops of this talented leader, who were 'numerous as ants and locusts', were recruited 'from the eastern districts', as Abul Fazl writes; from the Unao District of Awadh too a host of Rajput clans flocked to join his standard.[10] At the battle of Panipat, in 1556, his forces are reported to have been twice as numerous as those of the Mughals and he was, it was observed, 'extremely arrogant' on account of them.[11] He had 'Rajputs and Afghans' as horsemen, musketeers, many elephants, and one of his commanders was a brave hindu called Bhagwan Das.[12] Though this appears to be about all that is known concerning Hemu's army, it is enough to support the hypothesis that in it the Purbiya Rajput element was well-represented. It is true that Hemu himself was a Baniya entrepreneur. But his commanders were probably not. When Adil

[9] Ahmad Yadgar's 'Tarikh', in Elliot and Dowson, *History*, v, 47, 48, 56, 57.
[10] *Ibid.*, 62. Abu-l Faẓl, *Akbarnāma*, II, 45. *Unao Gazetteer*, 123.
[11] Ahmad Yadgar, 'Tarikh', 64, 65. [12] Abu-l Faẓl, *Akbarnāma*, II, 60, 64.

Shah lavishly rewarded him for his services, Hemu reminded him that 'the swords and bravery of these soldiers' were the means to accomplish the king's fortune. They should, therefore, be recompensed first. Adil Shah agreed to the largesse expected of him as an employer of Purbiyas and rewarded all those who had distinguished themselves, giving them 'high *mansab*s and splendid dresses of honour'.[13] Hemu's position in the Sur sultanate, as a warlord and an entrepreneur, seems similar to that of Medini Rai in Malwa forty years earlier. And, in a way, perhaps, Hemi achieved what Puran Mal had failed to accomplish: a place for the Purbiyas in the sultanate of the Surs.

Though the data presented so far often lack precision, it is clear that in Eastern Hindustan a category of peasant-soldiers, prepared to fight at great distances from their home region and, therefore, well placed to participate in the imperialist Mughal venture, was available for service if the demand for them arose. These men were also familiar with local service as retainers of *zamīndār*s such as the Bachgotis of the Jaunpur region or the Ujjainiyas who had served Sher Shah so well in his rise to power. Now, if the Mughals did decide to engage Purbiya infantrymen in their service, would they recruit them individually, or through the brokerage of jobbers (*jamaʿdār*s) or warlords (*nāyak*s), or would they call on the lineage chiefs of the region who could boast such a long tradition of military patronage? As far as the latter approach is concerned, local *zamīndāri* leadership was by no meant extinct in the Bhojpur region during Akbar's reign, or even much later. The Ujjainiya family, as we saw, was most conspicuous in this respect and would continue to yield military entrepreneurs and brokers for many generations. Indeed, the family's history shows an unbroken tradition first of confrontation, then of rebellion and troublesome service. In this way it is illustrative of the qualitative change the Mughal empire brought about in the conditions governing the military labour market and, therefore, in matters of recruitment and Purbiya patronage. To trace this change I shall first try and examine the slow decline of the Ujjainiya family as it is observable in the Mughal period.

In chapter 2 a survey of the lineage's rise to prominence was given which concluded with Gajpat who, as a young man, was a

[13] Ahmad Yadgar, 'Tarikh', 51. Interesting, in this respect, is the alliance, during Akbar's reign, between the Afghan Jalal Khan Sur and the converted Purbiya leader Hasan Khan Bachgoti, Joshi, *Afghan Nobility*, 58.

neighbour of Sher Shah in Bihar and became an important ally of this Afghan king. But Gajpat's authority as a leader and territorial chief was not unchallenged amongst the Ujjainiyas. About 1539, his cousin Dalpat, with the help of Emperor Humayun, drove him out of Bhojpur for a while. Sher Shah, however, reinstated him soon afterwards, recognised his title of raja and strengthened his position in other respects as well. When the Mughals made their comeback as rulers of Hindustan in the 1560s, Gajpat first resisted them and, for two years, kept a Mughal general 'uselessly employed in jungle-cutting and fighting'.[14] At last, in 1568–9, he was won over by Munim Khan, the Mughal governor of Jaunpur, with whom he would remain associated during the aggressive campaigns of the empire against the Afghans of Bihar and Bengal. By then he was, according to Abul Fazl, 'one of the noted landholders of the province of Bihar'.[15] During the siege of Patna, in 1574, Akbar did not achieve a breakthrough until Gajpat was sent for to reinforce the besiegers.[16] But after Munim Khan had died in Bengal, Gajpat 'took a sort of leave and went off to his own country'. There, no Mughal force was present for a while to stop him as the Bihar governor was in Bengal fighting the Afghans. The Ujjainiyas looted towns and imprisoned imperial officers who travelled by boat between Hindustan and Bengal. The strategic roads between the two provinces were also closed. Though Gajpat's fleet was defeated on the river, he drove the troops of the Mughals out of the Ujjainiya area and killed their main officers. In 1576, he even crossed the Ganges to proceed against Ghazipur, but he had to flee back across the Chausa ferry, was beaten and again lost a number of boats. The Mughals, however, never got hold of him. Abul Fazl ascribes this failure of the imperialists to the 'heights and hollows' of the Bhojpur forest and 'the broken nature of the ground, and the ravines'. For two months the soldiers of the empire were busy cutting down the trees around the fort of Jagdispur, the strongest of Gajpat's palaces. Gajpat again escaped and seems to have died a rebel in 1577. His brother Bairishal, who had been his companion in the early days of service with Sher Shah and who had also put his trust in the jungle, was killed fighting.

14 Badaoni, *Muntakhab*, II, 183. I. A. Khan, 'Tazkirat', 43, 52–4; Rafi'uddin says that, during the siege of Jagdispur in 1561/2, its Ujjainiya raja died and was survived by a seventeen-year-old son, *ibid.*, 53.

15 Abu-l Fazl, *Akbarnāma*, III, 239, 240. Abū'l Fazl, *Ā'īn*, I, , 334, 437. I. A. Khan, *Political Biography*, 109.

16 Nizamuddin, *Ṭabaqāt*, II, 443, 444. Badaoni, *Muntakhab*, II, 182, 183.

Gajpat's son Ram Singh now kept up the struggle for a while but had to submit when Akbar acquired the fort of Rohtas which was, then as in Sher Shah's time, the key to the area;[17] he seems to have died without direct heirs in 1584.[18]

The frequent notice taken of Gajpat by the major historians of Akbar's time reflects the redoubtable force he represented both as an auxiliary and as a rebel. His death did not spell the end of Ujjainiya refractoriness, but the atmosphere now becomes one of intrigue rather than straightforward confrontation and negotiation in an open power game. In 1579–80, Dalpat, Gajpat's old cousin and rival, had taken up arms against imperial authority. He killed at least one Mughal officer in a fight and cooperated with Arab Bahadur, a rebel of note in the early 1580s. In a pattern already familiar from Bundela history, he then served again as a Mughal ally, revolted anew, was caught and kept prisoner till 1599 when, on payment of a heavy *peshkash*, he was allowed to return to his home. It must have been at about this time that Prince Daniyal, Akbar's third son, married Dalpat's daughter by whom he would have a son. Dalpat, in other words, had become associated with a royal prince but it was by no means an alliance between equals; in the few years that were left to him, he lost his way in the jungle of Mughal elite rivalry. Akbar protected him against the wrath of one Barkhurdar, a Mughal officer whose father he had killed, but even imperial patronage would not save him from the mess he apparently was in. In about 1601 he was murdered in Allahabad by Mahabat Khan who acted on the orders of Prince Salim, the crown prince who had been a friend of Barkhurdar.[19]

Whereas Gajpat had still been largely successful as an autonomous military broker, Dalpat's services as such seem no longer to have been in demand at the imperial centre. In 1610 there was another desperate attempt by the clansmen to regain their old position as the unchallenged patrons of the regional military labour market. In that year, an unknown man by the name of Qutb 'with the look of a dervish and the clothes of a beggar', who gave out that he was Jahangir's son Khusru and had escaped from his father's prison, came to 'the province of Ujjainiya' and gathered a following

17 Abu-l Faẓl, *Akbarnāma*, III, 260–6. Nizamuddin, *Ṭabaqāt*, II, 490, 491. Abū'l Faẓl, *Ā'īn*, I, 437, 466, 489, 558, 581. Badaoni, *Muntakhab*, II, 244.

18 Ambashthya, 'Accounts', genealogical table opposite page 424.

19 Abu-l Faẓl, *Akbarnāma*, III, 474. Nizamuddin, *Ṭabaqāt*, II, 538; one must assume that Nizamuddin, who mentions Gajpat here, refers to Dalpat. Abū'l Faẓl, *Ā'īn*, I, 438, 517, 577. Hodivala, *Studies*, 572, 573.

around him from the 'always seditious' population of the area. With the help of these men he took the fort of Patna by surprise and made himself the master of the imperial treasury and of the treasuries of the nobles there.[20] 'Trayfuls of gold' were distributed to his followers and, as always with successful warlords, soon a number of merchants, 'greedy like flies', were running about him in the hope of securing a profit. Then he marched out with a well-equipped army and some elephants to meet the Mughal *sūbahdār* of Bihar. Raja Madhukar Ujjainiya, the grandson and successor of Dalpat, who had been promised the ministership by the pseudo-Khusru, led his vanguard just as his ancestors had done in Sher Shah's battles. For a while the Mughal *amīrs* in Bihar seem really to have believed that they were dealing with Khusru. But the insurrection was speedily suppressed and the Ujjainiyas found themselves again defeated by the empire to which they were so ill-adapted.[21]

Just as with the Bundelas, bitter hostility continued to keep the lineages of the clan divided.[22] And like the later Bundelas or the descendants of Silhadi, they were now increasingly absorbed as minor *mansabdārs* and jemadars into the Mughal empire. Yet, among those who led the family, Narayan Mal (d. 1624) and his brother Rudra Pratap (d. 1638) were still formidable *zamīndārs*. They strove to populate the land and, without depriving the ryots of their share of the harvest – as a much later, eighteenth-century account assures us – increased the revenue from about ten to fifteen lakhs of rupees, whereas the *mālguzāri* (land tax) to be paid to government remained at five lakhs. In all this they seem to have succeeded in keeping the imperial *qānūngos* out. Narayan Mal was the last to stand out as a redoubtable fighter rendering military assistance to the governor of Bengal and suppressing various refractory chiefs in his own region. In all this his ambition seems to have been that of a Mughal *mansabdār*; his exploits were chronicled in Persian by a local *qāzi*. But as soon as civil war broke out, he again reverted to old patterns of ambition. In 1624 at Patna he rejoined the rebellious crown prince Shahjahan with, according to Pelsaert, 5,000 horse and 20,000 foot. Mirza Nathan says that he received the very exalted *mansab* of 5,000/5,000 whereas his

20 Jahangir, *Tūzuk*, I, 173, 174.
21 Mirza Nathan, *Bahāristān-i-Ghaybī*, I, 89–91; II, 816, 817. Samsam-ud-daula, *Maāthir*, I, 67, 68.
22 Hasan Askari, 'Ujjainia Ancestors', *passim*.

brother Rudra Pratap was raised to the rank of 3,000/2,000 and the rest of his brothers to ranks of 2,000/1,000, all of them receiving robes of honour and horses.

It appears that Narayan Mal was killed during the rebellion. Rudra Pratap was now recognised as the manager of his estates in view of his 'kind treatment' of the ryots, which probably means that his branch of the Ujjainiyas was too well entrenched in southwestern Bihar for the Mughals to ignore them. The clan's autonomy, however, was clearly restricted and forced back into narrow patrimonial agrarian boundaries. Rudra Pratap had to pay an annual *nazrāna* of two lakhs over and above the old-established *mālguzāri* and his *mansab* under Shahjahan was a meagre 1,500. But a Rajput's dreams of his family's past could easily deprive it of a future. Inevitably, the time came when Rudra Pratap too turned rebel. For six months, he was besieged in the fort of Bhojpur by Abdullah Khan, one of the most ruthless officers the Mughal empire knew, who then, i.e. in 1638, was governor of Bihar. When he felt he had to give up, he 'put on a "Lungi" (waist cloth) and took his wife by her hands, and through the mediation of one of the eunuchs of Firuz Jang [i.e. Abdullah Khan] made his appearance'. Shahjahan soon ordered him to be put to death; Abdullah Khan then made his wife a muslim and married her to his grandson.[23] The warlord tradition he represented, so clearly reminiscent of the Purbiya *jauhar*s of Malwa and, more recently, of Jujhar Singh Bundela's megalomania and death, had outlived itself by a century.

Rudra Pratap's estates were now confiscated and put under the management of an imperial agent. Only after eighteen years, a son of Narayan Mal, on condition of his accepting Islam, was granted a firman of restoration. The Ujjainiyas continued to yield great rebels against the imperial administration without for a moment relenting in their internecine quarrels. In fact, an unbroken series of outbreaks and family events links the Ujjainiya rebels of Akbar's time with the famous Kunwar Singh, a descendant of Narayan Mal and one of the leaders of the wars of 1857–9.[24] But by then the tradition of Purbiya *naukarī* they had once so conspicuou-

[23] Nurul Hasan, 'Three Studies', 236. Blochmann, 'Notes', 111, 120. Pelsaert, *Geschriften*, 186. Mirza Nathan, *Bahāristān-i-Ghaybī*, II, 722. Hasan Askari, 'Ujjainia Ancestors', 113, 114. Datta, *Biography*, 5, 6.

[24] Hasan Askari, 'Ujjainia Ancestors', 115–18. Datta, *Biography*, 6ff. Syed Hasan Askari, 'Bihar', *passim*.

sly represented, had long since asserted itself in new forms that in no way depended on the entrepreneurship of Rajput warlords.

Baksariyas and the rise of the jobber-commander

Though the Ujjainiyas maintained themselves for centuries as the managers of extensive agricultural tracts largely coterminous with the present-day Bhojpur district and as pugnacious leaders of undoubted regional notoriety in Eastern Hindustan, by the time of Shahjahan's reign they had lost out in one important respect. They had been compelled to give up their crucial role as the principal recruiters of the Bhojpur military and as brokers between the imperial armies on the one hand and the military labour force of a large part of Hindustan on the other. The emerging divorce of land management and military brokerage did not affect the military labour market as a *longue durée* historical phenomenon. Yet, it reflected important changes on the demand side of the market. It signalled the heyday of the Mughal Empire in North India and the end of the multistate system of sultanates.

The Mughals, in other words, entered the market in full force; soon the brahmanical pilgrimage centre of Baksar on the Ganges rather than the Rajput strongholds of Gwalior, Orchha, etc. became the main locus of recruitment for the Purab area. In 1580, soon after Gajpat's death, the sources allow us a glimpse of a certain Purushottam, the *dīwān* of the Mughal province of Bihar, attempting to collect soldiers at Baksar. One day, as the twice-born man was performing his devotions on the bank of the Ganges, Dalpat's friend Arab Bahadur attacked and killed him.[25] The emergence of Qutb, the impostor, from the Bhojpur area in 1610, mentioned above, may perhaps be cited as another example of successful recruitment by an outsider-entrepreneur, though in this case apparently Ujjainiya brokerage still had a role to play. Anyway soon large numbers of soldiers drafted into the Mughal armies derived their identity from a real or supposed connection with Baksar. Significantly, they became known as Baksariyas, a name which, until the end of the eighteenth century, was almost a synonym for Hindustani matchlockmen.

What was it that equipped this pilgrimage centre for its pivotal role in the recruitment process of the Purab area? Though situated on the river Ganges, it was not the river that gave the place its

25 Samsam-ud-daula, *Maāt͟hir*, I, 266, 267.

distinctive quality. Of special fame was a tank near the temple of Gauri-Shankar, i.e. Shiva. According to legend, the ancient name of this tank was Aghasaras, or sin tank. During a visit to this place in the cold season of 1871/2, Cunningham, the Director-General of the Archaeological Survey of India, was told the following account explaining the name. Once a rishi – others said it was a raja – transformed himself into a tiger to frighten another rishi by the name of Durvasa. But Durvasa was the more powerful of the two and doomed the tiger-man to retain the face of a tiger. He was only restored to his proper form by bathing, at the suggestion of Shiva's bull Nandi, in the magic pool Aghasaras and then worshipping Gauri-Shankar. In remembrance of this event the sin tank was afterwards called by a new name: Baksar, from Vyaghrasaras. i.e. Tiger Tank.[26] Its qualities must have recommended the place to many, pilgrims and soldiers alike. But for the recruit there was something extra and unique involved: the association of the tank with identity change, first the change into the tiger role and then, thanks to Shiva, back to civility again. Did not young men become recruits at Baksar hoping that in the end divine grace would allow them a return to village and family? These *jawāns* recall the yogi-soldiers so frequently mentioned in the folksongs of Bihar. Of course, one might object that, according to custom, newly enlisted soldiers added Singh, i.e. lion, to their names: they became lions, not tigers. But in Indian consciousness tigers and lions have often been treated as one, e.g. in the word *sher* which is used for both. And in the Bhojpuri version of the 'Lay of Alha', an extremely popular song that, more than any other epic, reflects the heroic service traditions of Hindustan, the greatest warrior of all is constantly called Bagh Rudal, i.e. Tiger Rudal.[27] I suggest, therefore, that a component part of the Baksariya identity was the knowledge that, however distant and lasting one's service, however abject one's duties or miserable one's life, God's presence at Baksar saw to it that there was a road back to one's peasant home.

I suggest that an unbroken tradition of peasant recruitment links the *zamīndāri* auxiliaries that served the Jaunpur sultans and Sher Shah, in the fifteenth and sixteenth centuries, with the Baksariyas serving the Mughal and the EIC in the seventeenth and eighteenth centuries. The field of action of these Baksariyas was, however,

26 Cunningham, *Report 1871–72*, 65.

27 Platts, *Dictionary*, 739. Grierson, 'Alha's Marriage', 211n.20, and *passim*. Rudal is the Bhojpuri equivalent of Udal. Cf. Shirreff, *Padmāvatī*, 109n.d.

more extensive than that of their sixteenth-century ancestors, the Purbiyas of Hindustan and Malwa. Already during the 1640s and 1650s almost all matchlockmen serving the Mughals in the Dekkan were Rajputs from Baksar.[28] Baksariyas were prominently mentioned among the besiegers of the Satara fort, which fell to Aurangzeb in 1700.[29] And in a *dastūr ul-ʿamal* written about 1690 'Baksariyahs and Bundelahs' seems to be an expression that sufficed to sum up the category of regular matchlockmen in the Mughal service.[30] Among the troops of the *sūbahdār* of Gujarat in 1730–31 were '4000 infantrymen consisting of musketeers from Buxar and Arabia'.[31] In the second decade of the eighteenth century the British East India Company employed them in Bengal.[32] The Ostend Company did the same and, in the 1740s and 1750s, they were, as the EIC's correspondence clearly shows, the most commonly found type of soldier in Bengal. Inevitably, Baksariyas served under Clive in 1757.[33]

Service conditions also changed to a certain extent. The Mughals advanced further on the road already shown by Sher Shah in turning the *jawāns* of Hindustan into fairly disciplined infantrymen. Regular shooting tests were held and the men were, according to their skill, placed into three classes and paid accordingly.[34] Soldiers were taken notice of as individuals and registered. Thus we know from the records that the Baksariya soldier Ganga Ram, the son of Khanna, a Chauhan Rajput and – probably because he was recruited there – registered as a resident of Baksar (*sākin baksar*), was 30 years of age on 24 September 1646, that he had blue eyes, several scars and three moles on his face and that his monthly pay was five rupees.[35] This is not to say that the Mughal infantry was composed of model units or that a military revolution comparable to that of seventeenth-century Europe was enacted in the imperial camps. Hindu soldiers, to be sure, were capable of creating trouble, especially over matters of pay,[36] and in the eighteenth century

28 Alavi, *Studies*, 30. 29 Samsam-ud-daula, *Maāṯẖir*, II, 937.
30 Quoted in Yule and Burnell, *Hobson-Jobson*, 136a. See also Irvine, *Army*, 168.
31 Ali Muhammad Khan, *Mirāt*, 468. 32 Wilson, *Early Annals*, 146, 279.
33 Boeva, 'Factory at Bankibazar', 59, 63. Hill, *Bengal*, I, 35, 41, 79, 111, 128, 257; II, 30, 35, 238, 331, 354, 366; III, 59. Saha, *Selections*, I, 7, 25, 68, 168n, 335, 357. H. N. Sinha, *Correspondence*, 79, 200, 364. Orme, *Military Transactions*, II sect. 2, 59, 61, 65, 271.
34 Yusuf Husain, *Selected Waqai*, 45, 46 (English); 64, 66 (Persian).
35 Yusuf Hasain, *Selected Documents*, 161. See also *ibid.*, 173, 217, 218, and Yusuf Husain, *Selected Waqai*, 52 (English); 78 (Persian).
36 Yusuf Husain, *Selected Waqai*, 45, 46 (English). See also Sangar, *Crime*, 225.

Mughal discipline was undoubtedly largely lost. We are even told that, in 1730–1, the 'soldiers of the Buxor regiment' plundered the houses of the well-to-do citizens of Ahmadabad in Gujarat.[37] But there can be no doubt about a degree of order among the Mughal contingents of matchlockmen during the heyday of empire that meant a departure from the ancient fighting tradition of the warband. This may be connected with another change that slowly made itself felt in the Bhojpuri and Awadh areas.

The Baksariya was a private soldier emancipated from *zamīndārī* patronage. The phenomenon of his emergence can probably be traced as far back as the demise of the Jaunpur sultanate and the scattering of its army of 'innumerable zamindars'. But towards the end of the sixteenth century the emancipation of the individual mercenary soldier went on at a quickened pace as a stable Mughal centre of power began largely to monopolise the demand for the Purbiya cream of Hindustani matchlockmen. This new development was complemented by a change occurring in the leadership of the Bhojpur and Awadh countryside where clans like the Bachgotis and the Ujjainiyas were subjected to severe pacification; gradually, though never completely, they were compelled to give up the large-scale employment of war-bands and forced to turn more exclusively to the management of their estates. Thus, though these changes were foreshadowed in the Purbiya episode of sixteenth-century Malwa, from now on a rather clear distinction can be made, at the level of management and brokerage, between *zamīndār* and *jamaʿdār*, between Ujjainiya and Baksariya, in other words between land control and military entrepreneurship.

This is not to suggest any sharp division between farming and *naukarī*. Estate management was unthinkable without the local employment by *zamīndārs* of bands of armed followers and, on the other hand, many 'men of Baksar' (*nafar baksariya, piyāda baksariya*) retained and cherished a connection with ancestral land or even acquired land towards the end of their careers. R. A. Alavi has noticed that the Baksariyas serving in the Dekkan during Shahjahan's reign appeared to be younger than other soldiers in the Mughal armies.[38] Here, one is reminded of Puran Mal's contingent of Purbiyas in Malwa in 1542, 'none of whom had attained the age of forty'.[39] After their army years, the Baksariyas as well as the Purbiyas traditionally returned to their region of origin or, as their

[37] Ali Muhammad Khan, *Mirāt*, 474.
[38] Alavi, *Studies*, 30.
[39] See chapter 3.

nineteenth-century successors would do, to the family farms they had left as young men of perhaps only sixteen years of age.[40] The enduring connection with rural society in the Bhojpur and Awadh regions would remain characteristic of the British East India Company's sepoys. This is not surprising, for, as we shall see, they represented a continuation of a tradition of peasant soldiering that lasted for at least four centuries, but was possibly much older than the period to which I have traced it back. The identities (Baksariya, Bundela, Rajput, Purbiya, Sepoy, etc.) around which this peasant-soldiers' tradition coalesced in different contexts and times, the conditions of clientship or employment, the discipline and method of recruitment of these men may have changed, but not their link with agrarian society, i.e. their peasant character, or their importance in the power game of the North Indian *ancien régime*.

To lessen the risks of crossing the line between these two levels of activity, some kind of brokerage was almost invariably called for. It appears that individual soldiers rarely applied directly to the commanders of, for instance, the Mughal armies for employment, but as a rule did so through some agency. And if, as suggested, the agency of landlords, whether Ujjainiya or otherwise, was on the decline during the seventeenth century, another kind of broker between army and would-be soldier became more prominent, namely the jemadars, who performed the task – well-known in the labour history of India – of jobbers. They must have been similar to the *muqaddam*s and *mirdah*s who organised and led the caravan soldiers mentioned in chapter 1. Though they too may have had some agrarian interest, the jemadars represent the service rather than the landed aspect of peasant society. There must always have been such men in the armies and war-gangs of India, as well as in the contingents of non-peasant origin. Among peasant troops, it is possible that many of these agents were at first members of the regional dominant clans of the recruiting areas, that they, in other words, issued at least partly from *zamīndārī* families. Thus one hears of a certain Dharnidhar Ujjainiya who, during a Mughal campaign in South Bihar in 1643, led a detachment of his own.[41] Though obscure as individuals, these jobber-commanders were taken into serious account by the Mughal nobles as is shown by an incident during the Mughal expedition against the Uzbeks in 1647.

40 Alavi, *Studies*, 30; as Subadar Sita Ram did (ch. 1, note 76) and as reported by Buchanan (see below).

41 Blochmann, 'Notes', 123.

During the march back across the Hindu Kush, thousands of soldiers died of cold in the snow and the available animals became too weak to carry the army's treasure. The imperial commander then 'ordered the treasure to be divided and assigned in numbered bags to the *jama'dārs*, who were asked to carry the bags on their horses'.[42] But normally, in this early period before Aurangzeb's reign, the jemadars remained a shadowy category of men. Just like the hindu *dīwāns* and petty bankers, who were their colleagues as subalterns of the imperial *mansabdārī* system, they would only emerge from anonymity with the gradual disintegration of the empire's elite structure in the eighteenth century.

Slowly, indeed, the jobber-officers gained in importance and assumed a more independent position in military matters. We hear that the officer put in charge of the newly conquered country of Kuch Bihar in 1661–2 was provided with two good jemadars who together commanded 1,400 horsemen and 2,000 musketeers.[43] From this time onwards, jemadars are occasionally mentioned in news reports and histories and, in a few decades' time, the frequency increases noticeably. The *Mirāt-i-Ahmadī*, a chronicle dealing with the history of Gujarat, teems with references to them from the year 1700 onwards and especially after 1730.[44] They could have as few as fifty men with them, or 1,000 or more.[45] The loyalty or disloyalty of the greater among them could materially affect the political fortunes of states, as the case of Golkonda illustrates. According to Khafi Khan, in 1673 the principal ministry of this sultanate was taken over by a Brahman called Madanna only after a number of jemadars were persuaded to change sides.[46] In the regional states of eighteenth-century North India, soon the jemadars' political prominence seems to have been the rule rather than the exception. Siraj ud-daula, the nawab of Bengal in 1756–7, had 20,000 Rajput musketeers in his service and depended crucially on his 'principal', 'considerable' or 'chief' jemadars,[47] whereas the famous outrage of the Black Hole was ascribed to the revenge of the 'lower' jemadars.[48] Clearly this time there was little left of the

42 Syed, *Aurangzeb*, 43. 43 *Ibid.*, 184.

44 Yusuf Husain, *Selected Waqai, 8.* Sangar, *Crime*, 106, 133, 209. Ali Muhammad Khan, *Mirāt*, 281, 287, 300, 315, 325, etc.

45 Ali Muhammad Khan, *Mirāt*, 281. See for a jemadar with 1,000 horse in 1720, Wilson and Firminger, *Early Annals*, 285.

46 Syed, *Aurangzeb*, 329–30.

47 Hill, *Bengal*, I, 216, 218, 220, 264, 265; II, 98, 358, 436. Jemadars are mentioned frequently in volume II.

48 *Ibid.*, I, 100, 111, 186; III, 134, 137, 138, 144, 145.

military leadership of the old Mughal nobility nor of direct recruitment by Mughal officials at Baksar. The jobber dominated the labour market for soldiers as never before and one is not surprised to hear that, in 1768, the commander of the British East India Company Army of Madras, in order to recruit his battalions, 'offered to such as could bring 50 recruits the rank of a jemadar in the service, the rank of havildar to such as brought 30, and to those that brought 20 the rank of a naig'.[49] Whether such small commanders themselves took the initiative to recruit their men in their home regions, is doubtful. In this respect, nineteenth-century practice, according to which men presented their brothers, nephews or friends to their commanding officers as recruits, is perhaps a more probable model to go by.

Some of these recruits would become jemadars themselves. Indeed, the rise of the jemadars as a category of fairly independent brokers not only signified their emancipation from *zamīndārī* and and *mansabdārī* control, it also represented the arrival of peasants like the Baksariyas in the centres of provincial power. The jobber-officers were often of recognisable peasant origin themselves. In Awadh (Oudh), after the battle of Baksar in 1764, Nawab Shuja ud-daula disbanded most of the 'itinerant Persian and Durrani Afghan units' his predecessors had been in the habit of hiring wholesale from Persia and Afghanistan. They were replaced by indigenous troops, mainly Rajputs and Brahmans. Under Asaf ud-daula, who succeeded Shuja in 1775, this was followed up, as has recently been shown, by the rise to influence of a group of newcomers 'who had been peasant soldiers only a few years before'. They were called, half-sarcastically, 'Tilanga Rajas' or 'trooper rajas' and described by a clearly more polished man as 'naked rustics, whose fathers and brothers were with their own hands guiding the plough ... Bhawani Singh, Moti Singh, Hulas Singh, Nawaz Singh and Maiku Singh'.[50] Elsewhere, 'buxerries', as the Baksariyas are called in the eighteenth-century English sources, became a conspicuous element in the regional economy. Many of them had settled in Bengal, very often doubtless after a successful career as soldiers or strongmen of *zamīndārs* and, as in Awadh, some achieved a position that allowed them to enter new fields of activity. A work on land revenue administration written in

49 Dodwell, *Sepoy Recruitment*, 21.
50 Barnett, *North India*, 75–83, 135, 136. See on the Awadh Telingas also Sleeman, *Journey*, 172, 195, 242, 254, 286.

Bengal about 1750 and quoted by Irfan Habib, shows that Baksariyas were powerful there as village moneylenders 'constantly taking compound interest' and thus ruining the Bengali peasants.[51] In South India, they were also to be found as in the Mughal period and, as late as 1766, the 'Buckserry' caste was recommended in the Military Regulations for the Madras Native Infantry as a fit reservoir for the recruitment of EIC sepoys.[52] But particularly in North India, on the eve of the establishment of British hegemony, the success of Bhojpur and Awadh mercenaries and jemadars had secured them political and economic power and prominence.

It is not surprising, therefore, that the armies of the EIC, destined to become the largest military employers of India, would turn to the tradition of soldiering the Baksariyas represented. Let us have a closer look at the relationship that developed between this European mercantile organisation and the category of peasant-soldiers, including their jobber-commanders, that we have traced through the ups and downs of medieval and 'early modern' North India.

The Purbiya inheritance in the colonial state

In 1684, the British in Bombay were allowed to raise two standing companies of Rajputs who could be commanded by their own officers and use their own weapons. It seems that only one company was raised then. Also it is not clear whether the men originated from Northern India. In 1739, it was said that the Bombay sepoys were 'formerly subjects and have relations and are intermarried with the inhabitants' of the Bombay neighbourhood.[53] But they may well have been of Northern origin as in 1747 the Council of Fort St David on the Coromandel Coast asked Bombay for 'the best Northern People ... as they are reported to be much better than ours, and not so liable to Desertion'.[54] The name of Purbiyas, familiar to us from an earlier phase in the history of Hindustani soldiering, was soon in general use in Bombay to denote these

51 Irfan Habib, *Usury*, 395. Cf. the moneylending sepoys of the EIC's garrison of Surakarta on the island of Java, *c.* 1815, Carey, 'Sepoy Conspiracy', 300.

52 W. J. Wilson, *Madras Army*, 225, 227.

53 *Bombay Gazetteer, XXVI 3*, 76–8, 87.

54 Yule and Burnell, *Hobson-Jobson*, 810a.

Northerners, thousands of whom would serve the company in Western India especially after 1818.[55]

In Madras, Rajputs were employed as early as 1664 to defend Fort St George and, from the earliest years of the Madras Army, people from outside the Presidency had been generally preferred as recruits to Madrasis. Rajputs and Hindustanis were sent for from Bombay and Bengal and Baksariyas, as we saw, had been considered fit for employment as late as 1766.[56] It is certain that the eight so-called Circar battalions of the Madras Army, broken up in 1785, whose language was Hindustani, were composed of men of Northern descent though it may have been generations since their families had settled in the South in search of service. However, unlike the Bombay army, the Madras Army would soon develop into a thoroughly Southern corps and an experiment, tried in the 1790s, of bringing sepoys directly from Bengal, would prove a failure.[57]

As for Bengal, the English at Hughly had Rajputs in their pay as early as 1682.[58] As noted above they employed Baksariyas in the second decade of the eighteenth century and continued to do so on a small scale until after Plassey. Of the 2,100 sepoys who helped Clive win the battle of Plassey in 1757, only 6–700 had been recruited in Bengal (which, at that time, included Bihar).[59] It has been said that the others, who had been brought from Madras, 'were all Talingas or Telougous born'.[60] The term Telinga, though, does not cover an Andhra ethnic identity. The commander of these men was Keshar Singh, a celebrated jemadar, and when they remitted money home to their families, a bill was drawn in favour of one Parbat Singh of Fort St David.[61] These names indicate rather a Rajput or Northern origin, which would be by no means surprising if one takes into account the recruiting practices current at Madras at the time. But though probably similar to Baksariyas and Bundelas in point of social origin and recruitment, their reintroduction into Bengal from Madras was a novelty and changed the military scene. The new infantryman, or, to use the new

55 Cadell, *Bombay Army*, 9, 29, 33, 161, 200, 304n. Mac Munn, *Indian Mutiny*, 220. See on Purbiya soldiers in Western India about 1780 *Bombay Gazetteer, XXVI* I, 425, 426. Forbes, *Oriental Memoirs*, III, 438, 439.

56 Love, *Vestiges*, I, 216. W. J. Wilson, *Madras Army*, 8.

57 Dodwell, *Sepoy Recruitment*, 34–7, 40.

58 Hedges, *Diary*, I, 33, 34.

59 Hill, *Bengal*, I, cxcvi, 412.

60 Yule and Burnell, *Hobson-Jobson*, 913a.

61 Hill, *Bengal*, I, cxlvi, 267; II, 214; III, 29, 33.

denominations, the Telinga or sepoy, was armed and clothed by the Company; he was furnished with firelocks rather than matchlocks, placed under European officers, and drilled and disciplined according to methods first tried out in the South in the decades preceding Plassey. Though in Bengal the name of Telinga would stick as an equivalent of sepoy – as a reminder of the fact that the new discipline was first tried out in the South – in the northwest the new type of soldier became commonly known again by the old name of Purbiya.[62] But the confused nomenclature, explainable in terms of the revolutionary character of the late eighteenth century, should not be allowed to obscure the fact that we are dealing with new incarnations of the same old soldiering tradition of Hindustan.

The first regular battalion of Bengal sepoys was raised at Calcutta as early as January 1757. From then onwards, the Bengal Army grew at a spectacular rate and a modern author has rightly drawn attention to the fact that the Directors in London seem hardly to have been aware of so momentous a 'military revolution' as the creation of this army must be considered to be. It was an autonomous development on the periphery of empire, to which only off-hand references can be found in the metropolitan Court's letters.[63] In 1781 there would be thirty-four battalions, henceforward called regiments, of about 1,000 men each. Most of these units had been raised in Bengal, some in Bihar – e.g. the third battalion, which was composed for the most part of men 'enlisted in the Bhojpur district' – or even as far up-country as Allahabad.[64] The Baksariyas, as we saw, had spread all over Bengal and many of them must willingly have submitted to the discipline of the new army. Until far into the nineteenth century, one finds mention of Baksar as the place of origin of Company recruits.[65] But the EIC soon stopped the recruitment of the old 'buxerry' matchlockmen under their own jemadars.[66] This, of course, was another radical break with the past. Though Indian officers in the Company's army would continue to play a role as far as the recruitment of fresh sepoys was concerned, they would henceforth rise from the ranks

62 Yule and Burnell, *Hobson-Jobson*, 365a, 724ab.
63 Barat, *Bengal Native Infantry*, 11, 12.
64 Cardew, *Sketch*, 5–34. See, for a list of battalions raised, also Williams, *Historical Account*, 6ff; Saha, *Selections*, 117.
65 Barat, *Bengal Native Infantry*, 119, 120.
66 H. N. Sinha, *Correspondence*, II, 79, 364.

mainly by seniority.[67] Clive's companion Keshar Singh had been one of the last representatives of the old tradition of leadership. Soon there was not a trace left in Bengal of the independent jobber-commander. Yet, even with these redoubtable men out of the way, the Company, whether it knew it or not, was never in total control of its new army.

Alarmed at what it considered a disproportion of numbers between European and 'native' infantry, the Calcutta authorities tried to lessen their dependence on sepoys. But there was great difficulty in procuring European recruits for the Company's army and the British predicament became even worse during the American war of independence. Meanwhile, the 'country powers' and the Indians in general progressed in the knowledge of the art of war according to the new techniques, whereas the importation of large quantities of modern small arms and military stores into India by the Marathas and a number of North Indian powers added to British apprehensions.[68] A further complication was the propensity to 'desertion' and 'mutiny' that some of the sepoy battalions evinced from time to time, though Indian rulers were also suffering from the traditional habit of the North Indian soldier to renegotiate the terms of his service. Thus the *nawāb* of Bengal complained in 1760 that 300 Telingas had fled from his service to that of the Birbhum raja.[69] One means of preventing 'cabals' in the Bengal army was to keep the battalions divided into three brigades, each with a European component. Clive recommended to have each battalion composed of an equal number of hindus and muslims and to encourage rivalry between them.[70]

During the early stage of the creation of the Bengal Army, 'Pathans, Rohillas, Jats, Rajputs and even Brahmans' were to be found in the new units: Bhojpuris, buxerries, or Avadhis by no means enjoyed a monopoly.[71] Clive's proposal, therefore, did not appear unrealistic. The question as to whether it was not expedient to have separate hindu and muslim battalions or to compose each unit of men out of both communities was long discussed in India. At last the latter mode seems to have been preferred; in 1789, Governor-General Cornwallis also agreed. By then, however, the

[67] See on the gradual curtailment of the Indian officers' position in the army e.g. Barat, *Bengal Native Infantry*, 37, 118, 182.

[68] Srinivasachari, *Correspondence*, 77, 96, 326, 450, 474.

[69] *Census Bengal 1901*, IV, pt 1, 437.

[70] N. K. Sinha, *Correspondence*, 100. Barat, *Bengal Native Infantry*, 27.

[71] Cardew, *Sketch*, 5.

course of events had rendered the dilemma largely irrelevant. The number of muslims necessary to complete the desired proportion of them in the units was reported to be absolutely unobtainable. Hindus from up-country 'having of late years become more partial to your Service', Cornwallis wrote to the Directors, they by then composed four-fifths of the Bengal Army. Also they were generally considered more acceptable as recruits. Nor did Cornwallis regret this development, though the prejudice of the hindus against sea embarkations and their fear of the climate and the bad water of the lower provinces of Bengal still had to be overcome. Many muslims, he reasoned, had left the Company's provinces, the Bengalis were unfit to be soldiers and many British officers had been able to acquire 'the confidence and consequently an ascendancy' over the Hindustani sepoy. Therefore, the British should resign themselves to the almost exclusive recruitment of soldiers from Bihar, Benares, and Awadh.[72]

In his expectation that the sepoys' reluctance to undertake sea voyages would disappear, Cornwallis was to be disappointed. The restriction as to the area of recruitment, however, proved irreversible and would long survive him. As early as 1780–1, a Frenchman living at Murshidabad in Bengal judged it characteristic that EIC sepoys who passed through the city with their regiment and quarrelled with some of the local people – over 'a hen and some roots' they had got hold of in a dark lane – should speak Bhojpuri.[73] These same men also said that they all considered themselves Raja Chait Singh of Benares' men and, indeed, the raja's removal from Benares, which was then impending, certainly paved the way for the Company to grow into the premier patron of the regional tradition of soldiering. Significantly, Chait Singh's fortress of Bijaigarh, probably built by Sher Shah some 70 km from both Chunar and Rohtas, was deemed 'a proper place for a nursery of *sepoy* recruits to be raised and distributed to the regiments'; it was in fact used as such until given up for financial reasons a few years later.[74] A centre like this soon became superfluous as the enlistment of fresh recruits became a self-operating process. The native officers of the regiment, no doubt well-connected and highly respected in the localities where they had left their families, brought along hopeful young men when returning from furlough. Sometimes they were told to do so or were

72 Prasad, *Correspondence*, 363, 364.
73 Ghulam Husain Khan, *Seir*, 8 (translator's preface).
74 Saletore, *Correspondence*, 310, 435, 436.

granted leave of absence to recruit men from their native villages. Only occasionally were recruiting parties sent out.[75] Thus, though regular jobbing was abolished, the market for military labour was left in the hands of Indian agency: like its medieval predecessors in India, as an employer of infantry the Company gained only partial and indirect control over recruitment, surely one of the most important aspects of modern army management. Here, the 'native' officer took over from the old jobber-commander.

By 1810, when Buchanan wrote his accounts of Bihar districts, Bhojpuri participation in military empire had become more prominent than ever before and Shahabad was, as of old, the centre of the market for military labour. The number of men absent from the district in the regular army was then stated to be 4,680 which was a much greater drain than from any of the districts Buchanan had surveyed so far, but even so he suspected the figure was 'very considerably' underrated. The Ujjainiya Raja of Bhojpur, still the man probably best informed about these things, assured him that from the northern half of the district alone 12,000 sepoys had joined the EIC's army. The poverty of the numerous gentry made them willing to enlist. A great many of these were married, their wives remaining at home, and they remitted to their villages 'as much money as pays the rent of a good farm, upon which their family lives in comfort'. The pattern, if compared to the old Baksariya tradition, looks familiar. Thousands of men were also privately employed rather than by the company, whether in the district or, more generally, outside it. Indeed Shahabad would continue to be the unchallenged centre of the EIC's recruitment of sepoys until the days of the Mutiny when the district would be one of the strongholds of the insurgents.[76]

The 'modern' doctrine of caste

Throughout this study, much attention has been paid to achieved identities, such as those of *naukar* and Rajput, that were connected with long-distance service and the self-definitions of soldiers. These identities, and others like them, took, in different places and periods, many forms and names according to changing social, economic, political, and religious events. Men were not restricted

75 Barat, *Bengal Native Infantry*, 126.

76 *Shahabad Gazetteer*, 29ff, 47. See for the great importance to the sepoys of the remittances of pay to their families Carey, 'Sepoy Conspiracy', 296, 297, 305, 311.

to only one of them and in the course of their lives found themselves activating other designations that gave expression to other roles in society. As we saw, the adoption of, for instance, the soldier's identity of Baksariya, which made sense in the North Indian military labour market, did not preclude a return to identities which made sense in village life. On the contrary, all these identities represented mutually implicated and, therefore, complementary levels of experience. No single identity covered all aspects of a man's life. There were tribal, ethnic and genealogical identities, a soldier's, a weaver's, and other occupational ones, whereas slavery, *jajmānī* relationships, pilgrimage centres, and sects also provided niches in society important enough to give birth to *loci* of security which people coalesced around and identified themselves with, sometimes forever, but more often with reference to only a temporary aspect of their lives' adventures. As no identity covered all fields of action or all spheres of life, it had to be complemented by others. Only the weak were debarred from the entrepreneurship that could produce the security of multiple identities. Perhaps further research could result in enumerating the main elements of some of the most common peasant strategies for risk-spreading and keeping one's fingers in many pies. It is almost certain that the analysis of such villagers' formulas would point out the essential part of, firstly, an agrarian, e.g. a *jajmānī*, identity, secondly a long-distance, monetised one, probably connected with *naukarī*, and, thirdly, a sectarian one. Together, such formulas of complementary part-time roles represent the contents of the peasant's survival kit, each element in itself providing only a limited security in a restricted domain and for a certain period of his life.

As these identities were chosen, not acquired by birth or 'ascribed', 'caste' is not the most important issue to be raised about the Baksariyas' or Purbiyas' identity, nor about medieval peasant society generally. Caste, of course, is the ascribed identity *par excellence* in Indian society, the endogamous group to which, inevitably, people are assigned by birth. In *ancien régime* India, caste may have dominated the lives of merchant families – *baniyās* – in towns and commodity markets, but peasant society was governed by different maxims. Whereas in a commercial context guild-like exclusiveness had a function to fulfil in guarding capital and a privileged access to markets, in agrarian society inclusiveness – e.g. in the form of *jajmānī* bondage or the exogamous connections of Rajput clans – facilitated the investment in relationships of patronage and alliance. Within the soldiering tradition we have traced through the centuries, the urge to break the constraints and risks of strictly agricultural pursuits is constantly discernible. In the case of the *naukar*, it is the labour, not the commodity market that he turns to.

In the fourteenth century, we still find the peasants-in-arms of the Purab region described as *zamīndārs*' levies: 'innumerable zamindars' is the standard expression used in the Persian sources. They were known by the clan names of their *jajmānī* patrons and as such they would, as a rule, continue to be labelled: Bachgoti, Ujjainiya, Bundela. Later, they served in Malwa far away from their agrarian base and fought under the name of Purbiya Rajputs, indicating geographical origin, rather than as Tomar, the Rajput clan name of some of their leaders. The ideal of Rajputhood, or martial *naukarī*, represented the desire for free vagabondage, emancipated from rural obligations. The opportunities offered by the Mughal conquest state, the emergence of the jobber-commander, reflecting a more open-structured military labour market, and of the Baksariya identity, denying – albeit temporarily and imperfectly – the old village identities, show that the fulfilment of this ideal was within the reach of many. The Baksariya is no longer one of an 'innumerable' host, but is literally numbered and registered as an individual. But then the ideal itself was emphatically realistic, unlike the dream of brahmanical renunciation, an essential element being the return home to the gentlefolk of one's village as an accomplished Rajput ascetic, ready to take up the burden of individual, i.e. detached, householdership and domesticity (*gārhasthya*). What we are witnessing is not a unilinear 'caste mobility' in which one identity is exchanged for another in a process of so-called Rajputisation or Brahminisation.[77] Often, what happened was that groups of people, in their continuous search for security, opened up for themselves additional domains of political, economic or religious power to which formerly they did not have access. As called for by the circumstances of the day, they proclaimed their presence in the several domains they participated in. The written sources of history, contemporary oral reference to these men, or British census reports, could not do justice to this multiplicity. They referred to them only by the identity that, in the relevant context, seemed to be most conspicuous and, therefore, the 'real' one. Whether any modern historian will ever, on the basis

[77] E.g. Sanyal, 'Social Mobility'.

of such sources, be capable of restoring to life the multifaceted and fluid character of *ancien régime* Indian social history, is doubtful.

Probably the oldest formula of multiple identities, used for centuries amongst the Purbiya peasantry, was the tribal-Rajput – or, perhaps, the tribal-Rajput-Saivite – one. In the Bhojpur district, it is traceable to the early fourteenth century, the period when the Ujjainiya Rajputs emerged as an identity distinct from that of the Chero tribe. As 'Rajputs' they ceased marrying their daughters to their former masters, the Chero chiefs. Perhaps marriage relationships became hypergamous, Chero brides still being accepted by the Ujjainiyas. Chero recruits now certainly went in the same direction. The followers of Gajpat Ujjainiya in 1574 are explicitly described as Cheros numbering 2,000, and, elsewhere, as Cheros and *pāyaks* (footsoldiers).[78] By then, the Cheros had largely lost their position as employers on the military labour market. It seems that this was Sher Shah's achievement. About 1540, this sultan had, on several occasions, sent his trusted general Khawas Khan against a certain Maharath (or Maharta) Chero and one chronicle mentions the defeat of this man as one of the three great works accomplished during his reign.[79] Another chronicler recorded that Sher Shah not only captured Maharath's 'wealth and huge treasures', but also 'his kith and kin'.[80] Sher Shah apparently was as much after Chero recruits as after the infidel's treasure. But to make sure that these tribals would first look to him for service opportunities, any would-be employer had again and again to prove his mettle whether as a sultan or as a Rajput chief. The Ujjainiyas of the seventeenth century found this increasingly difficult and Narayan Mal even depended on Delhi help to have his authority recognised amongst 'his' Cheros.[81]

Despite such heavy pressure, the Cheros always succeeded in keeping some options open. The achievement of a military identity, as we suggested above, did not amount to an immediate or even an eventually complete Rajputisation in the sense of a unilinear and permanent change in ritual status, a change of 'caste'. About 1812, the Cheros of the Shahabad district said that the Palamau raja, who also styled himself a Nagbansi Rajput, did belong to their commu-

78 Beveridge, *Nafāīs*, 237. Hodivala, *Studies*, 539.

79 Abbās, *Tārīkh*, 374, 377, 380, 382, 445, 449. Elliot and Dowson, *History*, IV, 380n.

80 Abbās, *Tārīkh*, 363n; the chronicle referred to is the *Tārīkh-i-Daudī*.

81 Hasan Askari, 'Bihar', 113n.

nity, and Cheros of high rank had marriage links with Rajputs and wore the sacred thread. Yet, other Cheros did not and had Brahman gurus and purohits.[82] A brahmanical or brahmanising identity, indeed, was often attractive and within reach; it was then part of another formula of identities in which concepts like vegetarianism and renunciatory purity fitted better than in a Rajput-centred one. The warlike Sakarwars, a peasant community in the Benares, Shahabad, and Bihar districts, illustrate the point: they partly became Bhumihar Brahmans and partly Rajputs, 'according as either title', to quote Francis Buchanan, 'was most in fashion when the different parts of the tribe adopted the doctrine of caste and rules of modern purity'.[83] Similarly, just north of the Ganges, in the Ghazipur district, the subdivisions of the Bhumihar Brahmans were often called by the name of one of the recognised Rajput *gotras* or clans, and in one case a Bhumihar and a Rajput tribe claimed descent from the same ancestor, each admitting that the pretensions of the other were well-founded.[84]

The peasant-soldier could ignore identities handed down to him, adopt new ones, or toy with them for a lifetime. The Bhumihars, i.e. 'military Brahmans', of the Ghazipur district in the nineteenth century, though commonly called Rai, took the affix of Singh to their name when enlisting in the army or leaving the district, no doubt taking up the old nomenclature when that made more sense in changing circumstances.[85] Identities, like sets of tools, each instrument in turn being activated as the angle of approach to the job called for its special skill, were plural; they did not stick to a man as in the 'system' of caste. Modern administrators, as well as historians, cannot help thinking in terms of single community membership and one-dimensional identities. But about 1810, Buchanan wrote that Bhumihars, just like Rajputs, were 'not scrupulous in admitting into their number whatever tribes adopted their manners'.[86] And in 1834, it was detected that a number of sepoys enlisted in the 59th regiment as Rajputs, were 'in fact' Brahmans.[87] Eric Stokes has with penetrating insight written that British officers 'had recourse to an instinctive belief in the finity of

82 Buchanan, *Journal*, 81. 83 Buchanan, *Shahabad*, 186, 187.

84 Oldham, *Ghazeepoor*, I, 43.

85 See for this process of Chero Rajputisation (some became Chauhans) e.g. *Palamau Gazetteer*, 61, 62. Buchanan, *Shahabad*, 190, 209. Oldham, *Ghazeepoor*, I, 43.

86 Buchanan, *Shahabad*, 153, 154.

87 Barat, *Bengal Native Infantry*, 123.

ethnological types, a secular variant in its way of the doctrine of original sin and original virtue'.[88]

It is true, however, that with respect to the Bengal Native Infantry of the early nineteenth century, such an essentialist view of identities begins to be justified by sociological fact. In the Bengal Army taken as a whole, in 1842, of a total of 67,000 hindus, there were 28,000 registered as Rajputs and 25,000 as Brahmans including Bhumihars. It is not wrong, therefore, as has generally been done, to characterise the Bengal Army as 'high caste',[89] though it would be better to speak about Rajput-Bhumihar and Brahman predominance. But this had not always been so. It has been said that the sepoys who fought for Clive had been chiefly low caste and that the army changed composition because the recruiting officers, over a series of years, confined their choice to the tallest, handsomest, and cleanest looking men.[90] The real reason appears to be that the Indian officers, permitted from at least as early as the 1770s to bring new recruits, showed an increasing preference to enlist their own kin and 'this led to the Bengal sepoy army being doubly unusual in that it was predominantly high caste Hindu in composition and was restricted as to the area of recruitment'.[91]

This phenomenon can, it seems, only be explained as the successful endeavour of dominant groups in the Bhojpur and Awadh region to reserve to themselves what quickly became the most important redistributive institution of the new British empire in India, to wit the Bengal Army. This seems also to have been the view of Buchanan who wrote about the Kurmi peasants of the Shahabad district that 'the great number of idle gentry had in a great measure thrust them out' of armed employment.[92] An inevitable ritual complement of this closed shop social strategy was a tendency towards brahminical exclusiveness, in other words, towards the doctrine of caste. The new monomania for the privileges of employment soon took on religious overtones and stands in sharp contrast to the old survival strategies characterised by multiple layers of identity of Cheros, Bhumihars and 'spurious' Rajputs, and by the open attitude towards adoption and recruitment that

[88] Stokes, *The Peasant Armed*, 123.

[89] Barat, *Bengal Native Infantry*, 121, 123. The 'high caste' view of the sepoy army has become generally, but uncritically, accepted; see for a recent example Carey, 'Sepoy Conspiracy', 295, and Hibbert, *Great Mutiny*, 47.

[90] M. P. Singh, *Indian Army*, 157. Chattopadhyaya, *Sepoy Mutiny*, 72. See on the fighting traditions of the lower classes, above pp. 28, 117ff.

[91] Barat, *Bengal Native Infantry*, 49, 118ff.

[92] Buchanan, *Shahabad*, 198.

had been typical of centuries of peasant soldiering. The Bhojpuri and Avadhi soldier-elite, securely ensconced in the new empire, now adopted the 'modern' – to use Buchanan's epithet – ideology of caste. It justified their closed shop practices. The East India Company's recruiting policy, constituted as it was, could do little else but follow this trend. It is probable that, as early as the 1780s, closed shop tendencies were supported by EIC measures like that exempting hindu sepoys from the pilgrim taxes levied at Gaya, Puri and Allahabad.[93] But the British Government gradually went much further than this and, by 1818, had given its official sanction to the elite groups taking over. They would stick to this policy until the Mutiny. As late as 1855, the printed General Regulations of the Bengal Army required that special care be taken to exclude all men of inferior caste such as Telis, Gadariyas, Lodhas, Kahars, Malis, Kachhis and others.[94]

This was a radical change. But, then, the old world was fast disappearing. The explanation is to be found in the East India Company's conquest that had drastically shaken Hindustan. Perhaps for the first time in Indian history, the British suppressed what had been most characteristic of North Indian peasant society: the workings of its military labour market. During a long series of campaigns, the most spectacular of which was the Pindari war of 1817–19, the Company largely achieved the demilitarisation, if not of the Indian countryside, then certainly of politics at the regional level. It meant the disestablishment of much that had been basic to peasant society, especially to those segments of it specialised as servicemen. For centuries, the demand for their military labour had allowed them to secure and bring home part of the proceeds or loot of the unabating all-India power game. Now, the creation of the East India Company's empire, commanding unprecedented resources and investing heavily in pacification, radically reduced the employment opportunities for the military labour force of India. In the 1830s, a common maxim in North India was '*Company ke amal men kuchh rozgār nahin hai*', i.e. 'There is no employment in the Company's dominion'.[95] In the princely states things remained as they had been for a while. As late as 1850, Sleeman, while travelling through the region of the present-day Unao and Rae Bareli districts of the then kingdom of Awadh, found there

93 Saletore, *Correspondence*, 507. Barat, *Bengal Native Infantry*, 43, 150.
94 Bute, *Private Journal*, II, 324. Chattopadhyaya, *Sepoy Mutiny*, 72.
95 Sleeman, *Rambles*, 166.

were at least 50,000 men there 'armed to fight against each other, or their government and its officers' in a space where, under the Company's rule, not 1,000 men of the same class would be in arms.[96] By then, British North India was almost totally demilitarised and the opportunities for military employment had dwindled. Competition for service had become acute and, in the old areas of recruitment, the groups best placed for regional dominance and for their share in the appointment of officers in the new imperial army were in a position to edge out those less fortunate men who had been brothers-in-arms in a former dispensation. Already in the 1780s, in Company territory, competition for scarce jobs must have increased greatly. The result inevitably was that the lower classes were hardest hit by the pacificatory policy of the Europeans and that hierarchy and brahminisation were given a boost. The sepoy army became a high caste preserve.

These changes appear to have been typical of the Bengal Army and did not, or only to a much lesser degree, affect the Bombay Army, though the latter was largely recruited from the same area as the former. A high caste man, who had felt compelled to resign from the Bengal Army because his caste feelings had been injured, found that in Bombay he could allow his behaviour to be ruled by different maxims, saying: '*Hindustān zāt kī ghairat, Bombay palṭan kī ghairat*', i.e. 'In Hindustan it is jealousy of caste, in Bombay jealousy of regiment'.[97] Because he also made the comparison with Bombay, we may, of the many authors who have commented on the caste feelings that made the Bengal Army into a kind of complex caste *sabhā*, select Brigadier-General John Jacob. Among the serious faults of the Bengal Army, he wrote in 1851, was 'the most pernicious practice of attending to the caste of native soldiers, thereby frequently excluding from our ranks the best material for soldiers, and enlisting the very worst'.

The effect of enlisting men of a certain caste or creed, to the exclusion of others, in the Indian army, is to subject that army to the control, not of the Government and of the Articles of War, but to that of Brahmins and Goseins, Moollas and Fakeers. By this system a man is not to be chosen on account of his fitness to be a soldier, his willingness and strength, docility and courage, but because he is a twice-born worshipper of Vishnoo.

Jacob had known a Bengal commanding officer express his regret at being compelled to discharge an excellent sepoy, because the other

[96] Sleeman, *Journey*, 170. [97] Cadell, *Bombay Army*, 161

men had discovered him to be of inferior caste and had demanded his dismissal. This, he commented, amounted to open mutiny, but it was the normal state of affairs in the Bengal Army. That an altogether different set of attitudes was possible, was shown in the army of Bombay,

> wherein hundreds and thousands of men from Hindoostan, from the same villages, of the same caste, and even of the same families, – brothers of the same fathers and mothers – as the fine gentlemen of the Bengal army, are seen in the ranks, shoulder to shoulder – nay even sleeping in the same tent – with the Maratha, the Dher, and the Purwaree [i.e. the Mahar], without scruple or thought of objection. The one prides himself on being a Hindoo, the other on being a soldier.

Put otherwise, it was the difference between the 'modern' doctrine of caste and the ancient tradition of *naukarī* or achieved warrior status, between brahmanical fashion and the old Rajput or armed peasant values, represented so well by the Purbiya identity. According to Jacob, the Bombay sepoy was well aware of this opposition. A Brahman of the Bombay Army, when asked by a Bengal officer to comment on the case of a Mahar who had risen to be *sūbahdār* by his own merit, commented: 'What do I care; is he not the soldier of the state?'[98] In this respect, indeed, the old North Indian tradition of service suited the modern state better than the 'modern' emphasis on exclusiveness.

So, whereas the Bombay Army for a while kept intact some of the ancient characteristics of North Indian soldiering and preserved the non-caste features that were associated with it for so long, in Hindustan, Rajput and Brahman officers were in a position to transform the Bengal Army into a high caste preserve. This can largely be explained by the drastic reduction of military employment resulting from the imposition of the Company's peace on a region that had, for centuries, almost monopolised military recruitment in North India. However, the Mutiny of the Bengal sepoys in 1857 still showed that two crucial features of the old service tradition survived when the old Purbiya gentry closed its shop. Firstly, until the end, the sociological link between soldiering and agrarian society was preserved and the sepoy would continue to remit a large part, even as much as three-quarters, of his pay to his family for its maintenance.[99] Secondly – a feature that was lost in

[98] Jacob, *Views*, 103, 108–10, 119.
[99] Barat, *Bengal Native Infantry*, 177. Kaye, *Sepoy War*, 334.

Bombay – the peasant-soldier's insistence on what was his birthright, i.e. to negotiate his own alliances or, in other words, to choose his employers himself would be wildly reasserted in 1857. This the European state could not tolerate.

After the Mutiny, the colonial administration in disgust dropped Hindustan as a recruitment area, emphatically dissociating themselves from a tradition that had been the very centre of their empire during the first century of its existence. For the Bhojpuri gentry and peasantry these changes were a severe loss, though opportunities for armed employment or migratory service did not cease altogether. There were alternatives, at least for some period of time. Even at the beginning of the twentieth century, 'every Bengal zamindar keeps a posse of these men [i.e. Purbiyas], euphemistically termed *darwāns*, to keep his tenants in order. Calcutta . . . is full of them.'[100] A recent study has analysed the mobility of the peasants of the area as seasonal agricultural labourers.[101] Thousands also emigrated to the British and Dutch colonies overseas and these movements must be seen as a continuation of the old military migratory patterns associated with the Bhojpur country for so long. Yet, 1857 was a real watershed and there can be little doubt that its demographic and economic effects on the Bhojpur region and its labour market must have been profound and negative. Any assessment of the deepening poverty in Bihar during the last hundred years will have to take into account the *longue durée* features of the region's employment history.[102]

The tradition of soldiering we have tried to trace from the fifteenth to the nineteenth centuries, was indeed characterised by great demographic and 'folk' continuity. The agrarian economy of the Purab area – because of the complementary income earned by its *jawāns* – as well as its identity as a region owed much to this long-standing involvement in military entrepreneurship. Though the underlying characteristics of this tradition were constant, the several faces it showed in the course of about four centuries, and its surprising adaptability to the changing circumstances of the military labour market, mark the main phases of North Indian history. After the collapse of the Jaunpur sultanate late in the fifteenth century had reduced the opportunities of the peasants of Hindustan to find employment as warriors in the northern plains, they migrated as so-called Purbiyas in small adventuring groups into

100 Buchanan, *Shahabad*, 50, 51. 101 Yang, 'Peasants', 37–58.

102 See for a study of present-day violence: Mukherjee and Yadav, *Bhojpur*.

Malwa and, beyond, to Gujarat. Next, these men manifested themselves as Ujjainiyas, a name that drew attention to the success of one clan of *zamīndārs*-cum-*jamaʿdārs*, who, encouraged by Sher Shah, took large numbers of these men in their pay and employed them near home as well as, for instance, in Bengal. Then, as the Ujjainiya warlords yielded to Mughal pressure and lost their monopolistic control over Bhojpuri infantry-recruits, a largely new category of broker emerged. Whereas for the old commanders and warlords a stake in regional land control had been an essential part of their entrepreneurial strategy – expressed in the basically dynastic and genealogical designation of Ujjainiyas – the new jemadar looked to the *mansabdārs* of the empire for service and, fittingly, derived his name and identity from the supra-regional recruitment and pilgrimage centre of Baksar on the Ganges. The name of sepoy, representing the last avatar of the series, aptly expresses the relative discipline and uniformity that the East India Company succeeded in introducing in the late eighteenth- and early nineteenth-century representatives of this warrior tradition.

Every change of label, though always with a new accent, also bore witness to the unabated martial vigour of the agrarian society of Eastern Hindustan, the region that again and again succeeded in renegotiating their terms of service in a way that secured a continuation of their agrarian-cum-service way of life. Their alliances and conditions of service may have been overhauled every so often, but this seeming whimsicality served only one purpose: to keep intact a regional culture that was military, migratory, that made sense economically, and that was accessible to all men to whom the Rajput identity appealed. The history of the British Indian sepoy, culminating in the wars and mutinies of 1857–9, would show how hard it was to break the heroic thread of *naukarī* in North Indian social history. It was broken only when the market for military labour ceased to be a sellers' market. As long as military service was a commodity in demand, the peasant soldier of North India could choose his own employers, the relationship with whom was much in the nature of a terminable contract. Since the fifteenth century, some categories of Bhojpuri and, to a lesser extent, Avadhi clans had practically monopolised brokerage between employers and recruits; they were the jemadars and, later, the majority of the EIC's Indian officers. The Shahabad Rajputs may have been helped by the marcher character of their homeland and by their access to tribal labour, but that advantage explains only their initial success. That the gentry and peasantry of the area managed to hold on to the profits of first-class service throughout centuries of tremendous political change, is witness to their organisational qualities and to the extent to which the tradition of martial service had become integrated in the regional culture of the Purab region. Only in the nineteenth century, when they came under increasing economic pressure, would the gentry close shop and reserve recruitment for their own kith and kin.

The reputation of the Bhojpuri man as a fighter was carried far into the twentieth century. In Bihar even today there is a proverb which says:

> The people of Bhagalpur are prone to run away,
> The Kahalgaon people are cheats,
> In Patna people are swindlers;
> These three are notorious enough.
> If a Bhojpuri comes to hear of them,
> He will break the heads of all three.

And after World War II a special type of Bhojpuri drama known as *Videśiya*, i.e. foreigner, became popular – the subject being the suffering of the wife, the *virahinī*, on account of her separation from her husband who has gone far away from home for his work. The author is one Bhikhari Thakur of Chhapra. Pirated editions of these plays were put out and, about 1960, except for Tulsi Das' *Rāmcaritmānas*, no books were read more widely by the common people of the region.[103]

[103] Tiwari, *Bhojpuri*, xxiii, xxvi.

EPILOGUE

Historians of the Indian subcontinent may well be at a loss what to make of concepts like 'Asiatic mode of production', 'oriental despotism', India's 'other-worldliness' or 'inner conflict'. Although such labels obviously cannot do justice to the highly complex and dynamic societies of South Asia, simply to reject them does not solve the problem posed by the undoubtedly singular and unique nature of Indian history. What concepts fit the observed reality of India's past better than those rather essentialist models? The answer seems to be twofold. On the one hand, concepts such as nationalism, bureaucracy, and the labour market, which bring Indian history within the compass of world history – where it belongs – should always be used warily, i.e. without the connotations uncritically derived from other parts of the world. In other words, though of universal validity, their relative importance in the configuration of Indian society and civilisation may be different from its importance elsewhere, just as the linkages between the elements of the structure may be different in India. On the other hand, specific concepts like *dharma*, *fitna*, *jajmānī*, or *jauhar*, which may evoke the semantic fields in which Indians deal with particular social and cultural problems, though indispensable, can never be used as 'theories', which in themselves pretend to any explanatory value. Their place in the evolving configuration of Indian culture has to be defined. This study has been an attempt to combine concepts taken from both the universal and the specifically Indian categories and to weld them into an image that does justice to the flux as well as the facts of history. In themselves neither the term 'military labour market' in the title nor others like 'state formation', 'shifting alliances', 'survival strategies', etc., nor Indian concepts, used equally profusely, like '*naukar*', 'Rajput' or 'sepoy' contribute much to the analysis of Indian historical material, unless it is made clear how they relate to each other, i.e. in which configuration they are supposed to become operative.

In the post-orientalist age, Indian history has learned not to venture a formulation of ultimate, irreducible elements which govern South Asian realities. But in the present context it may be useful to try and name some of the factors which make the Indian agro-historical configuration unique. They include – in random order, because none of them is autonomous or stands 'at the beginning', but all are interlinked and help to define each other – the demographic factor of the sheer numbers of Indian people, the unpredictable nature of India's monsoon climate and, as a result, of its harvests, the occupational multiplicity and armed mobility of its peasants as they grope for security in the face of local harvest failure and all-India political flux, and the inability of states to collect resources that suffice to bind or demilitarise a significant proportion of India's huge peasant population. From the anthropological point of view there is a bewildering richness and flux of forms and codes. There is the security often found in a group solidarity which makes sense economically, but is also psychologically wholesome to an 'inner world' preserved, as Sudhir Kakar has shown, from one century to another by continuously reproduced patterns of marriage and infant socialisation.[1] But there is also the contrapuntal urge to assert individuality in an ascetic effort which provides a rallying point of charismatic authority as well as of political power in a society in which most of the participants are constantly rearticulating their circle (*maṇḍala*) of conflict and alliances.

It is against the background of such a configuration of features that the issue of manpower assumes its specifically Indian significance. As we saw, linked to it in the Indian context is the issue of hoarded treasure which enables its owner, sometimes without actually distributing it and merely on the basis of creditworthiness, to play a role in the military labour market, i.e. in politics – as the Hindi proverb puts it, 'if a man has treasure buried, his forehead shines'.[2] But as no single employer could provide to the full the security or wages the innumerable peasantry were in search of, this background also explains why Indian peasant-sepoys, whether in the service of the Mughal or the British East India Company, did not easily resign themselves to having only one master. Their need

[1] Kakar, *Inner World*.
[2] '*Gāḍā hai bhaṁdāra, barata hai lilāra*', quoted by Shirreff, *Padmāvatī*, 234n.

to keep several options open not only formed their 'mutinous' character, it also explains why ascribed identities, whether caste, ethnic, or genealogical, were much less important in North Indian history than traditional anthropological observation has suggested.

The long parade of peasant identities this study represents, reminds one of the evolution of the Sikh community as described by McLeod: a centuries-long series of changes and reassertions of cohesion, crystallisations of new institutions and lapses back into old ones.[3] The difference is only that my approach was not to trace the history of a single community which, in the course of its evolution, entered the military labour market in full force, but to place the market for peasant soldiers itself at the centre of my enquiry. It was the same tradition, I found, that inspired the Purbiya, Ujjainiya, Baksariya, Sepoy, etc. identities. Indeed in this continuity an evolution was discernible from subregional *zamīndārī* – perhaps *jajmānī* – service to a labour market that covered several of the major regions of India.[4] But the basic features of the configuration did not change. It is doubtful whether 'an all-India military culture' emerged only in the eighteenth century.[5] For muslim soldiers (Afghans, Habshi, Turki slaves) the all-India character of the military labour market appears to have been achieved much earlier and for Hindustani soldiers it was at least as old as the Mughal empire. At the regional level, however, a military culture was an even older feature of Indian agro-history. Armed peasant resistance to energetic imperial attempts to establish the sultans' authority was as fierce in the fourteenth century as it was in Akbar's and Jahangir's time. Ibn Battuta's description of Muhammad Tughluq's (1324–51) reign and the reported half a million dead amongst the population as a result of Muhammad Shah Bahmani's (1358–73) campaigns, do not present stories that are very different from those mentioned at the beginning of this study for the early Mughal period.[6] And Ashoka's Orissa killings and deportations in the third century BC may well have been a very similar affair, a manifestation of the same abiding features of the Indian polity.

3 McLeod, *Evolution*.

4 I am referring to the three or four major zones or regions as defined in Kulke and Rothermund, *A History*, 11–14, 113.

5 As suggested by Bayley, 'Prehistory', 181, 183–4. I also find it difficult to agree with Lorenzen who suggests an increasing militarisation of North Indian society from the sixteenth century onwards, Lorenzen, 'Warrior Ascetics', 68ff.

6 Ibn Battuta, *Travels*, 215ff. Kulke and Rothermund, *A History*, 182.

Indeed, in this respect as in others, there is striking continuity in Indian history. The structural features discussed here clearly inform Kautiliya's *Arthaśāstra* which teaches that the 'power of might' consists of 'the power of the treasury and army'.[7] 'Territory and manpower' were also crucial to the seventh-century king Harsha. But no king really achieved a monopoly of treasure, manpower and territory. Harsha, during his frequent tours of the empire, always burnt his camp on his departure, presumably to prevent it from becoming the locus of a local warlord or *sāmanta*'s claim to royal authority. His preeminence depended on the 'peace and alliances' he was able to realise, in other words, on maintaining himself as the centre of a circle of states (*rājāmaṇḍala*) as described by Kautiliya, the foremost political scientist of pre-modern India whose *Arthaśāstra* beautifully analyses the constraints put on politics by the configuration of ancient and medieval Indian society.[8]

As we have suggested, the terms *naukar* and Rajput should be interpreted with these broad characteristics of the Indian polity in mind, as the identities of roaming gentlemen-at-arms. *Naukar* was originally a Mongolian word meaning retainer, comrade, a soldier in the service of a Mongolian clan he did not belong to by birth, a free warrior. In the latter sense it was still used in Turkish in nineteenth-century Khiva and Bokhara. In Persian it was used at least since the thirteenth century.[9] In India too there was pride in this calling. When Sultan Bahlul Lodi died, in 1488, there was opposition to his son Sikandar succeeding him because his mother was a goldsmith's daughter. The impasse only ended when Khan Khanan Farmuli said: 'I am Padshah Sikandar's *naukar* and nobody else's.'[10] Soon, the word *naukarī*, replacing the term *ūlaga* used earlier, became familiar in peasant society to denote long-distance soldiering. In this context, the honourable calling of *naukarī* acquired, in addition, strong ascetic overtones. The enactment of the duties of the warrior, with the attached notions of dharmic kshatriya-hood, called for studied self-control. Those who took up this role, easily identified with, even became Rajputs, comrades of a just and deserving king. It is indeed not surprising that in a Braj song attributed to Tulsidas, the sixteenth-century poet, who must

[7] Kangle, *Arthaśāstra*, 6.2.33.

[8] Devahuti, *Harsha*, 106, 175, 187, 201; on the *maṇḍala*, x, 155–9, 265.

[9] Doerfer, *Elemente*, I, 521–6. See also Minorsky, 'A Civil and Military Review', Németh, 'Wanderungen', and Inalcik, *The Khan and the Tribal Aristocracy*.

[10] Siddiqi, *Some Aspects*, 27, 28.

still have been familiar with the old Rajput fighting tradition, Hanuman, Lord Rama's faithful ascetic warrior, should have been praised as a Rajput: '*Pavana ko pūta rajapūta rūro*'.[11] We have described a number of *jauhars*, terminal crises in which Rajput-ascetics, acting out what in the last analysis their role in life was all about, performed their own death scenes in what the *Mahābhārata* calls a battle sacrifice (*raṇayajña*).[12] We have shown that this tradition of soldiering eventually led to the British company's Bengal army and largely moulded the character of the Indian sepoy.

Confrontation and alliance, battle and marriage, were the essence of *maṇḍala* politics. *The Lay of Alha*, quoted earlier, was a clear example of this. In Jaisi's *Padmāvatī* also, when the bridegroom approaches the palace of his beloved, it is explained to the bride that, first 'some kind of fight' will have to be fought for her sake. The battle scene is indeed of a kind with the marriage that it secures. When at last Padmavati and Ratansen fall into each other's arms, there is 'a battle like that between Ravan and Rama: the couch was crushed and broken in the battle of love. He took Lanka . . .'.[13] Yet, in the life of the individual who participates in the power game, asceticism and eroticism have, to allow them their complementary functions, to be kept apart.[14] It is the Rajput's self-mortification in battle that makes possible the marriage alliances of his patron, just as the king's largesse to his austere *naukars* enables them in the end to return home and take up the altogether different duties of householdership and domesticity. *Artha* and *kāma* remain distinct but complementary; together they keep a man's life in dharmic balance.

As is shown in folklore and written literature alike, these codes were a substantial part of peasant consciousness. However, in medieval and early modern times their specific manifestations were various and evolved in course of time. At this level of the multiplicity of options and identities, we have tried to do justice to the changing semantics and contexts of terms like Rajput, Baksariya, etc. which mark the evolution of the market for long-distance and military labour in Hindustan. What is constant in all this flux, is firstly, the complementarity of domesticity and austere service far

11 'Pavan's son is a great Rajput', *Hanumān Bāhuka* as quoted in Candra Śobha, *Tulasī, Sūra*. See also Tulasī Dāsa, *Tulasī Graṁthāvalī*, 207.

12 Hiltebeitel, *Ritual of Battle*, 318.

13 Shirreff, *Padmāvatī*, 126, 194–5. Jayasi, *Padamāvatī*, 198, 318.

14 See on this theme O'Flaherty, *Śiva*.

afield and, secondly, the kind of complementarity spoken of by Pocock and Dumont when they launched their *Contributions to Indian Sociology*: 'In the final analysis traditional India did not recognize the individual as he appears in our modern theory of social life. One frequently finds it illuminating to substitute for the idea of an individual agent that of an agent formed by a pair of individuals: a pair of allies or of brothers-in-law, or in turn the pair constituted by a superior and an inferior.' I agree: marriage alliances and patron–client relationships were very much at the centre of the world I have described. But to me they did not appear to be encompassed, as in Dumont and Pocock's view of Indian civilisation, by 'the two fundamental factors of kinship and caste'.[15] On the contrary, the omnipresence of cognatic kinship and caste in North India seems to me to be a relatively new phenomenon that only became dominant in the early Mughal and British periods respectively. Historically speaking, the alliance and the open status group, whether war-band or religious sect, dominated medieval and early modern Indian history in a way descent and caste did not. This is not to say that the latter were absent. They may even have been important, especially in urban and commercial centres, but they moved to the centre only as a result of relatively late closed-shop strategies, for instance, to name the two cases familiar to the reader of this book, when many, especially Western, Rajput families turned to the Mughal court during Akbar's reign and sharpened old cognatic notions into an acute genealogical awareness, and, secondly, when the gentry of central Hindustan, towards the end of the eighteenth century, sought to exclude other members of the peasantry from the Bengal Native Infantry by adopting the 'modern' ideology of caste.

To sum up, the polarity of alliance and asceticism is one of the central normative forms of organisation found in North India during the period studied and, it seems, much earlier. On the forces of asceticism and eroticism in Śaiva mythology, Wendy Doniger has written that on the cosmic level 'each force must be allowed to develop to its extreme, and then a balance is sought by the rechannelling or transformation of any force which is out of control; in this way, the universe pulses from extreme to extreme

[15] Pocock and Dumont, 'For a Sociology', 18, 19. Veena Das has correctly remarked that relationships that matter do not necessarily assume the form of pairs of binary relations such as king and braham, or renunciation and householdership, *Structure and Cognition*, 7.

like a pendulum'. On the psychological level, Sudhir Kakar has drawn attention to the pervading theme of the erotic alliance in Indian childhood where the child's 'differentiation of himself from his mother ... is structurally weaker and comes chronologically later than in the West', whereas later in life 'the individual functions as a member of a group rather than on his own'. This characteristic can help to explain the great value set on asceticism, precisely because of the difficulties of the separation of the individual from his 'primordial' ties. The themes, first of the departure from home and from the mother who once gave her milk to her son, and then of his return home to his wife to start a new life as a householder, have been shown in this study to be as real in medieval Indian history as they were crucial to Kakar from a late twentieth-century psychological point of view.[16]

The austere wanderer was not a *saṁnyāsī* or renouncer, because at the proper time his accumulated ascetic power was to be used in the world, whether in battle or in fathering his children after his return home. Indeed, the dialogue between *saṁnyāsa* and domesticity around which so much of Indian civilisation revolves is reflected in the life of both the ascetic and the householder.[17] This dialogue is very much part of the Indian historical experience. That is why a concern with history can contribute to an increasing understanding of the structural categories of Indian society, for the latter, as Veena Das has written, 'are continuously redefined and manipulated in different social contexts'.[18]

Anthropology, History, or Indology do not claim an exclusive right to the pursuit of these questions. It is hoped that this study, undertaken at the confluence of these disciplines, has contributed something to the concerns they share.

[16] O'Flaherty, *Śiva*, 317. Kakar, *Inner World*, 104, 107; see p. 147 for the theme of the mother's milk (cf. the song of Gopi Chand discussed in chapter 3).

[17] Pocock and Dumont, 'For a Sociology', 17. The complementary alternation between the roles of householder and wanderer, suggested by Heesterman for a pre- 'axial age' India, remains of uninterrupted importance throughout ancient and medieval North Indian history, Heesterman, 'Householder and Wanderer', 267; see also T. N. Madan, *Non-Renunciation*.

[18] Veena Das, *Structure and Cognition*, 140.

BIBLIOGRAPHY

Abbās Khān Sarwānī. *Tārīkh-i-Śēr Śāhī*, Trans. B. P. Ambashthya, Patna 1974.

The Tārīkh-i-Sher Shāhī (Persian text and English translation) ed. S. M. Imamuddin, 2 vols., Dacca 1964.

Abu-l Fazl. *The Akbarnāma of Abu-l Fazl (Bibliotheca Indica)*, trans. H. Beveridge, 3 vols., Calcutta 1897–1921; vols. I and 2, repr. Delhi 1972.

Abū'l Fazl 'Allāmī. *The Ā'īn-i Akbarī*, trans. H. Blochmann and H. S. Jarrett, 2nd rev. edn by D. C. Phillott and Jadunath Sarkar, 3 vols., 1927–49, repr. New Delhi 1977–8.

Ahmad Alavi, Rafi. *Studies in the History of Medieval Deccan*, Delhi 1977.

Ali Muhammad Khan. *Mirāt-i-Ahmadī: A Persian History of Gujarat (Gaekwad's Oriental Series, 146)* trans. M. F. Lokhandwala, Baroda 1965.

Ambashthya, Brahmadeva Prasad. 'The Accounts of the Ujjainiyas in Bihar', *JBRS* 47 (1961), 420–40.

Archer, W. G. 'Seasonal Songs of Patna District', *MI* 22 (1942), 245–50.

The Vertical Man: A Study in Primitive Indian Sculpture, London 1947.

Askari, Syed Hasan. 'Bihar in the Time of Aurangzeb', *JBRS* 32 (1946), 155–81.

Askari, Hasan. 'The Ujjainiā Ancestors of Babu Kuar Singh', *JBRS* 41 (1955), 106–31.

Athar Ali, M. *The Mughal Nobility under Aurangzeb*, 2nd edn Bombay 1970.

The Apparatus of Empire: Awards of Ranks, Offices and Titles to the Mughal Nobility (1574–1658), Delhi 1985.

Bābur. *Bābur-Nāma of Zahiru'd-dīn Muḥammad Bābur Pādshāh Ghāzī*, trans. A. S. Beveridge, 1922, repr. (2 vols. in 1) New Delhi 1970.

Al-Badāoni, 'Abdu-l-Qādir ibn-i-Mulūk Shāh. *Muntakhabu-t-Tawārīkh*, vol. I, trans. G. S. A. Ranking, Calcutta 1898; vol. II, trans. W. H. Lowe, Calcutta 1924.

Barat, Amiya. *The Bengal Native Infantry, Its Organisation and Discipline, 1796–1852*, Calcutta 1962.

Barnett, Richard B. *North India between Empires: Awadh, the Mughals and the British, 1720–1801*, Berkeley 1980.

Barros, João de. and Diogo de Couto. *Da Asia*, 24 vols., Lisbon 1777–80.

Bayley, Edward Clive. (trans.) *The Local Muhammadan Dynasties: Gujarat*, 1886, 2nd edn Nagendra Singh, Delhi 1970.

Bayly, C. A. *Rulers, Townsmen and Bazaars*, Cambridge 1983.

'The Prehistory of "Communalism"? Religious Conflict in India, 1700–1860', *MAS* XIX (1985), 177–203.

Bernier, F. *Voyages*, 2 vols., Amsterdam 1699.

Travels in the Mogul Empire A.D. 1656–1668, trans. A. Constable, 2nd edn V. A. Smith, London 1914.

Best, C. C. *Briefe über Ost-Indien. . .*, Leipzig 1807.

Beveridge, H. 'The Nafāīsu-l-Maāṣir', *JASB*, N.S. 1 (1905), 236–7.

'Some Account of Silhadī, otherwise Salāhu d-Dīn (Saladin), a Rajput Renegade. . .', *AR* 7 (1915), 383–97.

Bhadra, Gautam. 'Two Frontier Uprisings in Mughal India' in Ranajit Guha (ed.), *Subaltern Studies II*, Delhi 1983, 43–59.

Bhimsen's 'Tarikh-i-Dilkasha and Nuskha-i-Dilkasha' in V. G. Khobrekar (ed.), *Sir Jadunath Sarkar Birth Centenary Commemoration Volume: English Translation of Tarikh-i-Dilkasha*, Bombay 1972.

Blochmann, H. 'Notes from Muhammadan Historians on Chutiā Nāgpūr, Pacheṭ and Palāmau', *JASB* 40 (1871) pt. 1, 111–29.

Boeva, Luc. 'The Factory of Bankibazar in Bengal', *Bengal Past and Present* 99 (January – June 1980), 57–63.

Bombay Gazetteer, vol. XXVI pt. 1, Town and Island of Bombay, History, Bombay 1893.

Bombay Gazetteer, vol. XXVI pt. 3, Town and Island of Bombay, Administration, Bombay 1894.

Bosworth, C. E. *The Ghaznavids: Their Empire in Afghanistan and Eastern Iran 994–1040*, Edinburgh 1963.

Brett-James, Antony. *Wellington at War 1794–1815: A Selection of his Wartime Letters*, London 1961.

Buchanan, F. *Journal of Francis Buchanan, Kept During the Survey of the District of Shahabad in 1812–1813*, ed. C.E.A.W. Oldham, Patna 1926.

An Account of the District of Shahabad in 1809–10, Patna 1934.

An Account of the District of Bhagalpur in 1810–11, Patna 1939.

An Account of the Districts of Bihar and Patna in 1811–1812, 2 vols., Patna n.d.

Budhwar [Zaidi], Sunita. 'The Qayamkhani Shaikhzada Family of Fatehpur-Jhunjunu', *Proceedings 39th Indian History Congress*, Hyderabad 1978, vol. 1, 412–25.

Budike, Fred, and Bim Mungra. *Creolen en Hindostanen*, 1986.

Burnes, Alexander (ed. and introduction by James Lunt). *Travels into Bokhara together with a Narrative of a Voyage on the Indus*, 3 vols., Karachi repr. 1973.

Bute, The Marchioness of (ed.) *The Private Journal of the Marquess of Hastings*, 2 vols., London 1858.

Cadell, Patrick. *History of the Bombay Army*, London 1938.

Candra Śobha, Sāvitrī. *Tulasī, Sūra evaṁ Dādū meṁ Samāja aura Saṁskṛti*, New Delhi 1976.

Cardew, F. G. *A Sketch of the Services of the Bengal Native Army to the Year 1895*, Calcutta 1903.

Carey, P. B. R. 'The Sepoy Conspiracy of 1815 in Java', *BTLV* 133 (1977), 294–322.

Castanheda, Fernão Lopes de. *História do descobrimento e conquista da India pelos portuguêses*, 4 vols., Coimbra 1924–33.

Census of the Madras Presidency 1871, vol. I (Report) and *vol. II (Supplementary Tables)*, Madras 1874.

Imperial Census of 1881, Madras vol. IV, Madras 1883.

Census of India 1891, vol. XIII, XIV and XV (Madras), Madras 1893.

Census of India 1901, vol. VI (The Lower Provinces of Bengal and their Feudatories), pt. I (Report), Calcutta 1902.

Census of India 1901, vol. VI-A pt. II (The Imperial Tables), Calcutta 1902.

Census of India 1901, vol. XV pt. I and *vol. XV-A pt. II (Madras)*, Madras 1902.

Census of India 1921, vol. XIII (Madras), pt. I (Report) and *pt. II (Tables)*, Madras 1922.

Census of India 1921, vol. XV (Punjab and Delhi), pt. I (Report), Lahore 1923.

Chand Bardāī. *The Prithirāja Rāsau*, trans. by A. F. R. Hoernle (Bibliotheca Indica), pt. 2, fasc. 1, Calcutta 1881.

Chattopadhyaya, Haraprasad. *The Sepoy Mutiny, 1857: A Social Study and Analysis*, Calcutta 1957.

Chekhovich, O. D. *Samarkandskie Dokumenti, XV–XVI vv*, Moscow 1974.

Chijs, J. A van der, J. E. Heeres, H. T. Colenbrander (eds.). *Dagh-Register gehouden int Casteel Batavia. . .*, 31 vols., Batavia–The Hague 1887–1931.

Cohn, Bernard S. 'Anthropology and History in the 1980s', *JIntH* 12 (1981–82), 227–52.

An Anthropologist among the Historians and Other Essays, Delhi 1987.

Coolhaas, W. Ph. (ed.) *Generale Missiven van Gouverneurs-Generaal en Raden aan Heren XVII der Verenigde Oostindische Compagnie*, 8 vols., The Hague 1960–85.

Couto, Diogo do. *O soldado prático*, ed. M. Rodrigues Lapa, Lisbon 1954.

Cox, Arthur F. and Harold A. Stuart, *North Arcot (Madras District Manuals, vol. I)*, Madras 1895.

Crooke, W. *The Tribes and Castes of the North Western India*, 4 vols., repr. Delhi 1974 [Original title: *The Tribes and Castes of the North Western Provinces and Oudh*].

Cunningham, Alexander. *Report for the Year 1871–72 (Archaeological Survey of India, III)*, Calcutta 1873.

Report of a Tour in the Central Provinces and Lower Gangetic Doab in 1881–82 (Archaeological Survey of India, XVII), Calcutta 1884.

Dames, Mansel Longworth. (trans.) *The Book of Duarte Barbosa (Hakluyt Society)*, vol. 1, London 1918.

Das Gupta, Ashin. *Indian Merchants and the Decline of Surat ca. 1700–1750*, Wiesbaden 1979.

Datia State Gazetteer (The Central India State Gazetteer Series) by C. E. Luard and Lala Chhote Lal, Lucknow 1907.

Datta, K. K. *Biography of Kunwar Singh and Amar Singh*, Patna 1957.

Day, Upendra Nath. *Medieval Malwa: A Political and Cultural History, 1401–1562*, Delhi 1965.

Devahuti, D. *Harsha: A Political Study*, Delhi 1983.

Digby, Simon. 'Dreams and Reminiscences of Dattu Sarvani, a Sixteenth Century Indo-Afghan Soldier', *IESHR* 2 (1965), 52–80, 178–94.

War-Horse and Elephant in the Delhi Sultanate: A Study of Military Supplies, Oxford 1971.

Dodwell, H. *Sepoy Recruitment in the Old Madras Army*, Calcutta 1922.

(ed.) *The Diary of Ananda Ranga Pillai, vol. IV*, Madras 1916.

Doerfer, Gerhard. *Türkische und Mongolische Elemente im Neupersischen*, 4 vols., Wiesbaden 1963–75.

Donzel, E. van. *Foreign Relations of Ethiopia, 1642–1700: Documents Relating to the Journeys of Khodja Murād*, Istanbul–Leiden 1979.

Dow, Alexander. *The History of Hindostan*, 3 vols.; repr. New Delhi 1973.

Dubois, J. A. *Moeurs, institutions et cérémonies des peuples de l'Inde*, 2 vols., Paris 1825.

Hindu Manners, Customs and Ceremonies, trans. by K. Beauchamp, 3rd edn, Oxford 1924.

Elliot, H. M. *Memoirs on the History, Folk-lore and Distribution of the Races of the North Western Provinces of India*, revised edn John Beames, London 1859; repr. Osnabrück 1976 (2 parts in 1 vol.).

Elliot, H. M. and J. Dowson (eds.), *The History of India as told by its own Historians: The Muhammadan Period*, 8 vols., London 1867–77.

Elwin, Verrier. *Folk Songs of Chhattisgarh*, Madras 1946.

Fawcett, Charles (ed.) *The English Factories in India, vol. II (N.S.) (The Eastern Coast and Bengal) 1670–1677*, Oxford 1952.

Ferishta, Mahomed Kasim. *History of the Rise of the Mahomedan Power in India, till the year A.D. 1612*, trans. John Briggs, 4 vols., London 1829.

Forbes, James. *Oriental Memoirs. . . Written during Seventeen Years Residence in India*, 4 vols., London 1813.

Foster, William (ed.) *The English Factories in India 1634–1636*, Oxford 1911.

Early Travels in India, 1583–1619, London 1921.

Fox, Richard G. *Kin, Clan, Raja, and Rule: State–Hinterland Relations in Preindustrial India*, Berkeley 1971.

Fraser, Hugh. 'Folklore from Eastern Gorakhpur', *JASB* 52 (1883) pt. 1, 1–32.

Fuchs, Stephen. *The Aboriginal Tribes of India*, Delhi 1973.

Gazetteers: *see under individual place names*.

Geleynssen de Jongh, W. *De Remonstrantie van W. Geleynssen de Jongh (Linschoten-Vereeniging, 31)*, The Hague 1929.

Ghulam Husain Khan, Saiyid. *Seir Mutaqherin*, trans. Nota Manus, 4 vols., Calcutta 1789; repr. Lahore 1975.

Grant Duff, James. *History of the Mahrattas*, ed. J. P. Guha, 2 vols., New Delhi 1971.

Grierson, George A. 'The Song of Manik Chandra', *JASB* 49 (1878) pt. 1, 135–238.

'The Song of Bijai Mal', *JASB* 53 (1884) pt. 1 (Special Number), 94–150.

'Some Bihārī Folk-Songs', *JRAS* 16 (1884), 196–246.

'The Song of Alha's Marriage: A Bhojpuri Epic', *IA* 14 (1885), 209–27.

'Two versions of the Song of Gopī Chand', *JASB* 54 (1885) pt. 1, 35–55.

'Selected Specimens of the Bihārī language, pt. II: The Bhojpuri Dialect, The Gīt Nāīkā Banijar'wā', *ZDMG* 43 (1889), 468–524.

Linguistic Survey of India, 11 vols., Calcutta 1903–28.

Growse, F. S. *Mathurā: A District Memoir*, 2nd edn, no place of publication, 1880.

'Notes on the Fatehpur District', *JASB* 54 (1885) pt. 1, 145–62.

Guha, Atul Chandra. *A Brief Sketch of the Land Systems of Bengal and Behar*, Calcutta 1915.

Gupta, Bhagwan Das. *Life and Times of Maharaja Chhatrasal Bundela*, New Delhi 1980.

Gwalior State Gazetteer (The Central India State Gazetteer Series) by C. E. Luard and Dwārka Nāth Sheopuri, 4 parts, Calcutta 1908–9.

Habib, Irfan. *The Agrarian System of Mughal India (1557–1707)*, Bombay 1963.

'Usury in Medieval India', *CSSH* 6 (1963–4), 393–419.

'Forms of Class Struggle in Mughal India', *Papers on Medieval Indian History, Indian History Congress, Bombay 1980*, published by the Centre of Advanced Study, Department of History, Aligarh Muslim University, 1980.

Habib, Mohammad, and Khaliq Ahmad Nizami (eds.) *A Comprehensive History of India, vol. V, The Delhi Sultanat (A.D. 1206–1526)*, Delhi 1970.

Haig, W. and R. Burn (eds.) *The Cambridge History of India, vol. IV, The Mughul Period*, Cambridge 1937.

Halim, A. 'The Foundation of the Saiyad Dynasty. . .' *JIH* 31 (1953), 199–212, *JIH* 32 (1954), 157–69, *JIH* 33 (1955), 31–40.

Hameeduddin. 'The Lodis' in R. C. Majumdar (ed.), *The Delhi Sultanate (The History and Culture of the Indian People, VI)*, Bombay 1960, 139–54.
Hedges, William. *The Diary of William Hedges Esq. during his Agency in Bengal. . . (1681–1687), (Hakluyt Society)*, 3 vols., ed. R. Barlow, London 1887–9.
Heesterman, J. C. *The Inner Conflict of Tradition*, Chicago and London 1985.
'Householder and Wanderer', *CIS* (n.s.) 15 (1981), 251–71.
'The King's Order', *CIS* (n.s.) 20 (1986), 1–13.
Hibbert, Christopher. *The Great Mutiny: India 1857*, London 1978.
Hill, S. C. (ed.) *Bengal in 1756–1757 (Indian Records Series)*, 3 vols.; repr. of the 1905 edn, New York 1968.
Hiltebeitel, Alf. *The Ritual of Battle: Krishna in the Mahābhārata*, Ithaca and London 1976.
Hivale, Samrao. *The Pradhans of the Upper Narbada Valley*, Bombay 1946.
Hodivala, S. H. *Studies in Indo-Muslim History: A Critical Commentary on Elliot and Dowson's History of India as told by its own Historians*, Bombay 1939.
Ibn Battuta. *Ibn Battuta, Travels in Asia and Africa, 1325–1354*, trans. by H. A. R. Gibb, London 1929.
The Imperial Gazetteer of India, new edn, 25 vols., Oxford 1907–9.
Inalcik, Halil. 'The Khan and the Tribal Aristocracy: The Crimean Khanate under Sahib Giray I', *Harvard Ukrainian Studies* 3/4 (1979–80) pt. 1, 445–66.
Irvine, W. *The Army of the Indian Moghuls*, London 1903.
Jacob, John. *The Views and Opinions of Brigadier-General John Jacob, C. B.*, ed. Lewis Pelly, London 1858.
Jahangir. *Memoirs of the Emperor Jahangueir written by himself*, trans. David Price (Oriental Translation Committee), London 1829; republished Calcutta 1904.
The Tūzuk-i-Jahāngīrī or Memoirs of Jahāngīr, trans. and ed. A. Rogers and H. Beveridge, 2 vols., London 1909–14.
Jan Kavi. *Kayam-Khan-Raso*, Jaipur 1953.
Jāyasī, Malik Muḥammad. *Padamavat*, ed. Vāsudeva Śaraṇa Agravāla, Chirgaon (Jhansi) 1961.
Jhansi: A Gazetteer (District Gazetteers of the United Provinces), vol. XXIV by D. L. Drake-Brockman, Allahabad 1911.
Jogendra Nāth Rae, Bābū. 'Baiswāṛī Folk Songs', *JASB* 53 (1884) pt. 1, 232–59.
Joshi, Rita. *The Afghan Nobility and the Mughals (1526–1707)*, New Delhi 1985.
Kakar, Sudhir. *The Inner World: A Psycho-analytic Study of Childhood and Society in India*, 2nd edn, Delhi 1981.

Kalichbeg Fredunbeg, Mirza (trans.) *The Chachnamah, An Ancient History of Sind*; repr. Delhi 1979.

Kangle, R. P. The *Kauṭilīya Arthaśāstra, Pt II An English Translation*, Bombay 1963.

Kaye, J. W. *A History of the Sepoy War in India, 1857–1858*, 3 vols., London 1870–6.

Keśavadāsa. 'Kavipriyā' in Viśvanāthaprasāda Miśra (ed.), *Keśava-Graṁthāvalī*, vol. 1, Allahabad 1954.

Khan, Hussain. *Sher Shah Sur Ustad-i-Badshahan alias Sher Shah Suri*, Lahore–Rawalpindi–Karachi 1987.

Khan, Iqtidar Alam. *The Political Biography of a Mughal Noble: Mun'im Khan Khan-i Khanan, 1497–1575*, New Delhi 1973.

Khan, Iqtidar Alam. 'The Tazkirat ul-Muluk by Rafi'uddin Ibrahim Shirazi as a Source on the History of Akbar's Reign', *SH* 2 (1980) 2, 41–55.

Kulke, Hermann, and Dietmar Rothermund. *A History of India*, London and Sydney 1986.

De La Flotte. *Essais Historiques sur l'Inde, précédés d'un Journal de Voyages. . .*, Paris 1769.

Lal, K. S. *Twilight of the Sultanate*, Bombay 1963.

Larus, Joel. *Culture and Political-Military Behavior: The Hindus in Pre-Modern India*, Calcutta 1979.

Long, J. *see under* M. P. Saha (ed.)

Lorenzen, David N. 'Warrior Ascetics in Indian History', *JAOS* 98 (1978), 61–75.

Love, Henry Davison. *Vestiges of Old Madras, 1640–1800*, 3 vols., 1913; repr. New York 1968.

Lyall, Alfred C. *Asiatic Studies: Religious and Social*, London 1882.

McEvedy, Colin, and Richard Jones. *Atlas of World Population History*, London 1978.

McLeod, W. H. *The Evolution of the Sikh Community: Five Essays*, Oxford 1976.

Mac Munn, George. *The Indian Mutiny in Perspective*, London 1931.

Madan, T. N. *Non-Renunciation: Themes and Interpretations of Hindu Culture*, Delhi 1987.

Majumdar, A. K. 'Mālwa' in R. C. Majumdar *et al.* (eds.) *The Delhi Sultanate (The History and Culture of the Indian People, VI)*, Bombay 1960, 173–86.

Majumdar, R. C., *et al.* (eds.) *The Delhi Sultanate (The History and Culture of the Indian People, VI)*, Bombay 1960.

Manucci, Niccolao. *Storia do Mogor or Mogul India 1653–1708*, trans. W. Irvine, 4 vols., London 1907–8.

Mendonca, Francis A. (trans.) *Chronica Geral dos Sucessos do Reyno de Gusarte a Qm. Chamao Cambaya* (*General Chronicle of the events in the kingdom of Gujarat which is called Cambay*), Baroda (M. S. University) 1981.

Minhaj-ud-Din. *Tabakāt-i-Nāsiri by Minhāj-ud-Dīn*, trans. H. G. Raverty, London 1881.

Minorsky, V. 'A Civil and Military Review in Fārs in 881/1476', *Bulletin of the School of Oriental and African Studies* 10 (1940–2), 141–78.

Mirzapur: A Gazetteer (District Gazetteers of the United Provinces, vol. XXVII) by D. L. Drake-Brockman, Allahabad 1911.

Father Monserrate. *The Commentary of Father Monserrate, S. J., on his Journey to the Court of Akbar*, eds. T. S. Hoyland and S. N. Banerjee, London 1922.

Moreland, W. H. *The Agrarian System of Moslem India*, Cambridge 1929.

Mukherjee, Kalyan, and Rajendra Singh Yadav. *Bhojpur, Naxalism in the Plains of Bihar*, New Delhi 1980.

Mukhia, Harbans. *Historians and Historiography during the Reign of Akbar*, New Delhi 1976.

Mundy, Peter. *The Travels of Peter Mundy in Europe and Asia, 1608–1667*, ed. R. C. Temple, 5 vols., London 1914–24.

Muzaffarnagar: A Gazetteer (District Gazetteers of the United Provinces, vol. III) by H. R. Nevill, Allahabad 1920.

Naqvi, Hameeda Khatoon. *Urbanisation and Urban Centres under the Great Mughals, 1556–1707*, Simla 1971.

Nathan, Mirza. *Bahāristān-i-Ghaybī*, trans. M. I. Borah, 2 vols., Gauhati 1936.

Neamet Ullah. *History of the Afghans*, trans. Bernard Dorn, 1829–36; repr. London–Santiago de Compostela 1965.

Németh, J. 'Wanderungen des mongolischen Wortes *Nökür* "Genosse" ', *Acta Orientalia* (Budapest) 3 (1953), 1–23.

Niamatullah. *Niamatullah's History of the Afghans, pt. 1 (Lodi Period)*, trans. Nirodbhusan Roy, Santiniketan 1958.

Nightingale, Pamela. *Trade and Empire in Western India 1784–1806*, Cambridge 1970.

Nizami, A. H. 'Biramdeo Baghela Muqaddam of Gahora', *JIH* 32 (1954), 145–6.

Nizamuddin Ahmad. *The Ṭabaqāt-i-Akbarī of Khājah Niẓāmuddīn Aḥmad (Bibliotheca Indica)*, Persian text ed. Brajindranath De, 3 vols., Calcutta 1913–35; trans. Brajindranath De, 3 vols., Calcutta 1927–39.

Nurul Hasan, S. 'Revenue Administration of the Jagir of Sahsaram by Farid (Sher Shah)', *Proceedings Indian History Congress Sect. II* (Medieval India), 26 (1964), 102–7.

'Three Studies of Zamindari System' in K. A. Nizami (ed.), *Medieval India: A Miscellany I*, London 1969.

O'Flaherty, Wendy Doniger. *Śiva: The Erotic Ascetic*, Oxford 1981.

O'Hanlon, Rosalind. 'Maratha History as Polemic: Low Caste Ideology and Political Debate in late Nineteenth-century Western India', *MAS* 17 (1983), 1–33.

Oldham, Wilton. *Historical and Statistical Memoir of the Ghazeepoor District, pt. I*, Allahabad 1870.

Orchha State Gazetteer (The Central India State Gazetteer Series) by C. E. Luard and Shri Ram Nait, Lucknow 1907.

Orme, Robert. *A History of the Military Transactions of the British Nation in Indostan*, 3 vols., London 1803.

Palamau (Bihar and Orissa District Gazetteers) by L. S. S. O'Malley, Patna 1926.

Panna State Gazetteer (The Central India State Gazetteer Series) by C. E. Luard and Shambu Dayal, Lucknow 1907.

Patwardhan, R. P. (ed.) *Fort William–India House Correspondence (Public Series), vol. VII (1773–1776)*, Delhi 1971.

Pelsaert, Francisco. *De Geschriften van Francisco Pelsaert over Mughal Indië, 1627: Kroniek en Remonstrantie (Linschoten-Vereeniging, 81)*, ed. D. H. A. Kolff and H. W. van Santen, The Hague 1979.

Pipes, Daniel. *Slave Soldiers and Islam: The Genesis of a Military System*, New Haven and London 1981.

Platts, J. T. *A Dictionary of Urdū, Classical Hindī and English*, London 1911.

Pocock, D. F. and L. Dumont. 'For a Sociology of India', *CIS* I (1957), 7–22.

Pogson, W. R. *A History of the Boondelas*, Calcutta 1828.

Pradhan, M. C. *The Political System of the Jats of Northern India*, London–Bombay 1966.

Prasad, Bisheshwar (ed.) *Fort William–India House Correspondence (Military Series), vol. XIX (1787–1791)*, Delhi 1975.

Prinsep, Henry T. *History of the Political and Military Transactions in India during the Administration of the Marquess of Hastings, 1813–1823*, 2 vols., London 1825.

Qanungo, Kalikaranjan. *Sher Shah and his Times: An Old Story Retold. . .*, Bombay 1965.

Rana, R. P. 'Agrarian Revolts in Northern India during the Late 17th and Early 18th Century', *IESHR* 18 (1981), 287–326.

Rawson, P. S. *The Indian Sword*, London 1968.

Raychaudhuri, Tapan, and Irfan Habib (eds.) *The Cambridge Economic History of India, vol. I: c. 1200–c. 1750*, Cambridge 1982.

Rewah State Gazetteer (The Central India State Gazetteer Series) by C. E. Luard and Janki Prasad, Lucknow 1907.

Riazul Islam (ed.) *A Calendar of Documents on Indo-Persian Relations (1500–1750), vol. I*, Tehran–Karachi 1979.

Rieu, Charles. *Catalogue of the Persian Manuscripts in the British Museum*, 3 vols., London 1879–83.

Risley, Herbert. *The People of India*, 2nd edn by W. Crooke, Calcutta 1915.

Rizvi, S. A. A. *Religious and Intellectual History of the Muslims in Akbar's Reign*, New Delhi 1975.

Robertson, E. P. *Glossary of Gujaratee Revenue and Official Terms*, Bombay 1865.
Roçu, Arion. 'Les *Marman* et les arts martiaux indiens', *Journal Asiatique* 269 (1981), 417–51.
Rowe, William L. 'The New Cauhāns: A Caste Mobility Movement in North India' in James Silverberg (ed.), *Social Mobility in the Caste System in India (CSSH, Suppl. 3)*, The Hague–Paris 1968, 66–77.
Roy, Nirodbhusan. 'New Light on Sher Shah's Early Career', *JASL* 18 (1952), 53–62.
Roy, N. B. 'Anecdotes of Sher Shah (from the manuscript of Tarikh-i-Daudi)', *Islamic Culture* 32 (1958), 250–61.
Roy, N. B. 'Some Interesting Anecdotes of Sher Shah from the Rare Persian ms. of Tazkirat-ul-Mulk', *JASL* 20 (1954), 219–26.
Russell, R. V. and Hīra Lāl. *The Tribes and Castes of the Central Provinces of India*, 4 vols., London 1916.
Saeed, Mian Muhammad. *The Sharqi Sultanate of Jaunpur*, Karachi 1972.
Saha, M. P. (ed.) *Selections from Unpublished Records of Government for the Years 1748 to 1767 inclusive by the Revd. J. Long*, Calcutta 1973.
Saletore, B. A. (ed.) *Fort William–India House Correspondence (Public Series), vol. IX (1782–1785)*, Delhi 1959.
Nawwāb Ṣamṣām-ud-daula Shāh Nawāz Khān and his son 'Abdul Ḥayy, *The Maāthir-ul-Umarā (Bibliotheca Indica)*, trans. H. Beveridge and Baini Prashad, 3 vols., Calcutta 1911–64.
Sangar, S. P. *Crime and Punishment in Mughal India*, Delhi–Jullundur 1967.
Sanyal, Hitesranjan. 'Social Mobility in Bengal: Its Sources and Constraints', *IHR* 2 (1975), 68–96.
Sarkar, Jadunath. *History of Aurangzib*, 5 vols., Calcutta 1924–30.
Fall of the Mughal Empire, 4 vols., Calcutta 1932–50.
Sarkar, Jagdish Narayan. (trans.) *The Military Despatches of a Seventeenth Century Indian General. . .*, Calcutta 1969.
Shahabad (Bihar and Orissa District Gazetteers) by L. S. S. O'Malley and J. F. W. James, Patna 1924.
Sharar, Abdul Halim. *Lucknow: The Last Phase of an Oriental Culture*, trans. and ed. E. S. Harcourt and Fakhir Hussain, London 1975.
Sherring, M. A. *Hindu Tribes and Castes as Represented in Benares*, Calcutta 1872.
Shirreff, A. G. [and G. A. Grierson] (trans.) *Padmāvatī of Malik Muhammad Jaisi (Bibliotheca Indica)*, Calcutta 1944.
Shulman, David. 'On South Indian Bandits and Kings', *IESHR* 17 (1980), 283–306.
Siddiqi, Iqtidar Husain. 'Rise of the Afghan Nobility under the Lodi Sultans (1451–1526 A.D.)', *MIQ* 4 (1961), 114–36.
Some Aspects of Afghan Despotism in India, Aligarh 1969.
History of Sher Shah Sur, Aligarh 1971.
Mughal Relations with the Indian Ruling Elite, New Delhi 1983.

Siddiqi, N. A. *Land Revenue Administration under the Mughals (1700–1750)*, Bombay 1970.
Silberrad, C. A. (ed.) 'A Contribution to the History of Western Bundelkhand [by Bijhe Bahadur Mazbut Singh]', *JASB* 71 (1902) pt. 1, 99–135.
Sinder, Leon. *Caste Instability in Moghul India*, Seoul International Culture Research Centre, Chung-ang University 1964.
Singh, Madan Paul. *Indian Army under the East India Company*, New Delhi 1976.
Singh, Śrī Nārāyaṇ, and G. A. Grierson. 'The Battle of Kanarpī Ghāṭ', *JASB* 54 (1885) pt. 1, 16–35.
Sinha, C. R. P. 'Buxar in Archaeological Perspective', *JBRS* 49 (1963), 107–10.
Sinha, H. N. (ed.) *Fort William–India House Correspondence (Public Series), vol. II (1757–1759)*, Delhi 1957.
Sinha, N. K. (ed.) *Fort William–India House Correspondence (Public Series), vol. V (1767–1769)*, Delhi 1949.
Sinha, Ram Narain. *Bihar Tenantry (1783–1833)*, Bombay 1968.
Sircar, D. C. *The Guhilas of Kiṣkindhā*, Calcutta 1965.
Rām, Sītā. *From Sepoy to Subadar: Being the Life and Adventures of a Native Officer of the Bengal Army Written and Related by Himself*, trans. Lt.-Col. Norgate and ed. Lt.-Col. D. C. Phillott, Calcutta 1911.
Skelton, Robert, *et. al. The Indian Heritage: Court Life and Arts under Mughal Rule*, Exhibition Catalogue, Victoria & Albert Museum 1982.
Sleeman, W. H. 'History of the Gurha Mundala Rājas', *JASB* 6 (1837) pt. 2, 621–44 (part 1).
Rambles and Recollections of an Indian Official, ed. Vincent A. Smith, 1915; repr. Karachi 1973.
Sleeman in Oudh, an Abridgement of W. H. Sleeman's A Journey through the Kingdom of Oude in 1849–50, ed. P. D. Reeves, Cambridge 1971.
Smith, John D. *The Vīsaḷadevarāsa: A Restoration of the Text*, Cambridge 1976.
Smith, Vincent A. 'Popular Songs of the Hamīpur District in Bundelkhand, N.W.P.', *JASB* 44 (1875) pt. 1, 389–92.
Smith, W. C. 'Lower-class Uprisings in the Mughal Empire', *Islamic Culture* 20 (1946), 21–40.
Spear, Percival. *A History of India, vol. 2*, Harmondsworth 1965.
Srinivasachari, C. S. (ed.) *Fort William–India House Correspondence (Public Series), vol. IV 1764–1766*, Delhi 1962.
Stokes, Eric. *The Peasant Armed: The Indian Rebellion of 1857*, ed. C. A. Bayly, Oxford 1986.
Streusand, Douglas E. 'The Formation of the Mughal Empire, 1556–1582', unpublished PhD thesis, University of Chicago 1987.
Syed, Anees Jahan. *Aurangzeb in Muntakhab-al Lubab [by Khafi Khan]*, Bombay–New Delhi 1977.

Tavernier, Jean-Baptiste. *Travels in India*, trans. by V. Ball; 2nd edn by W. Crooke, 2 vols., London 1925.

Thomas, E. *The Chronicles of the Pathan Kings of Delhi*, 1871; repr. Delhi 1967.

Thurston, Edgar. *Castes and Tribes of Southern India*, 7 vols., 1909; repr. Delhi 1975.

Tikkiwal, Harish Chandra. *Jaipur and the later Mughals (1707–1803 A.D.): A Study in Political Relations*, Jaipur 1974.

Tiwari, Udai Narain. *The Origin and Development of Bhojpuri (The Asiatic Society Monograph Series)*, Calcutta 1960.

Tod, James. *Annals and Antiquities of Rajasthan, or the Central and Western Rajput States of India, 1829–32*, ed. W. Crooke, 3 vols., London 1920.

Tulasī Dāsa. *Tulasī Graṁthāvalī, vol. 2 (Nāgarī Pracāriṇī Graṁthamālā, 32)*, eds. Rāmacaṁdra *et al.*, Kāśī 2031 Vi [Indian calendar].

Ulughkhani. *An Arabic History of Gujarat: Zafar ul-Wālih bi Muzaffar wa Alih, by 'Abdallah Muhammad. . .Ulughkhānī*, ed. E. Denison Ross, 3 vols., London 1910–28.

Zafar ul Wālih bi Muzaffar wa Ālihi by Abdullāh Muhammad. . .al-Ulughkhāni Hājji ad-Dabir, trans. M. F. Lokhandwala, 2 vols., Baroda 1970–4.

Unao: A Gazetteer (District Gazetteers of the United Provinces, vol. XXXVIII) by H. R. Nevill, Lucknow 1923.

Valentijn, F. *Oud en Nieuw Oost-Indiën. . .*, 5 parts in 8 vols., Dordrecht–Amsterdam 1724–6.

Varady, Robert Gabriel. 'North Indian Banjaras: Their Evolution as Transporters', *SA*, N.S. 1 (1979), 1–18.

Vaudeville, Charlotte. *Les Duhā de Ḍhola-Mārū, une ancienne ballade du Rājasthān (Publications de l'Institut Français d'Indologie, 21)*, Pondichéry 1962.

Bārahmāsā: Les Chansons des Douze Mois dans les littératures Indo-Aryennes, Pondichéry 1965.

Veena Das. *Structure and Cognition: Aspects of Hindu Caste and Ritual*, 2nd edn, Delhi 1982.

Wadley, Susan Snow. *Shakti: Power in the Conceptual Structure of Karimpur Religion*, The University of Chicago, Department of Anthropology, 1975.

Washbrook, David. Review of Richard G. Fox's *Kin, Clan, Raja, and Rule* in *MAS* 6 (1972), 360–4.

Waterfield, William and George A. Grierson. *The Lay of Alha: A Saga of Rajput Chivalry as sung by Minstrels of Northern India*, Oxford 1923.

Williams, J. *An Historical Account of the Rise and Progress of the Bengal Native Infantry, 1757–1796*, London 1817; repr. London 1970.

Wilson, C. R. (ed.) *The Early Annals of the English in Bengal, vol. II pt. I (1711–1717)*, London 1900.

Wilson, C. R. and W. K. Firminger (eds.) *The Early Annals of the English in Bengal, vol. III (1718–1722)*, Calcutta 1917.

Wilson, H. H. *The History of British India VIII*, London 1848.

Wilson, W. J. *History of the Madras Army*, Madras 1882.

Wink, A. *Land and Sovereignty in India: Agrarian Society and Politics under the eighteenth-century Maratha svārajya*, Cambridge 1986.

Woods, John E. *The Aqquyunlu: Clan, Confederation, Empire: A study in 15th/9th century Turko-Iranian politics (Bibliotheca Islamica)*, Minneapolis and Chicago 1976.

Yang, Anand A. 'Peasants on the Move, A Study of Internal Migration in India', *JIntH* 10 (1979–80), 37–58.

Yule, H. and A. C. Burnell, *Hobson-Jobson, a Glossary of Colloquial Anglo-Indian Words and Phrases. . .*, new edn. by W. Crooke, London 1903.

[Yusuf Husain Khan (ed.)] *Selected Documents of Shāh Jahān's Reign*, Daftar-i-Dīwānī Hyderabad–Deccan 1950.

Yusuf Husain. *Selected Waqai of the Deccan (1660–1671 A.D.)*, Hyderabad [Dekkan] 1953.

Zaidi, S. Inayat Ali. 'Ordinary Kachawaha Troopers Serving the Mughul Empire', *SH* 2 (1980), 57–68.

Ziegler, Norman P. 'The Seventeenth Century Chronicles of Mārvāṛa: A Study in the Evolution and use of Oral Traditions in Western India', *HA* 3 (1976), 127–53.

'Marvari Historical Chronicles: Sources for the Social and Cultural History of Rajasthan', *IESHR* 13 (1976), 219–50.

'Some Notes on Rajput Loyalties during the Mughal Period' in J. F. Richards (ed.), *Kingship and Authority in South Asia*, Madison (Wisconsin) 1978, 215–51.

INDEX

Note: Words and names like Hindustan, Mughal, Rajput, etc., which occur on almost every other page in the text, have been omitted from the index.

Ingram Content Group UK Ltd.
Milton Keynes UK
UKHW011933230723
425649UK00001B/7